CONTEMPORARY ECONOMIC ISSUES
Volume 1: Regional Experience and System Reform

This is IEA conference volume no. 121

CONTEMPORARY ECONOMIC ISSUES

Congress Editor: Michael Bruno

International Economic Association
Series Standing Order ISBN 0–333–71242–0
(*outside North America only*)

You can receive future titles in this series as they are published by placing a standing order. Please contact your bookseller or, in case of difficulty, write to us at the address below with your name and address, the title of the series and the ISBN quoted above.

Customer Services Department, Macmillan Distribution Ltd
Houndmills, Basingstoke, Hampshire RG21 6XS, England

Contemporary Economic Issues

Proceedings of the Eleventh World Congress of the International Economic Association, Tunis

Congress Editor: Michael Bruno

Volume 1 REGIONAL EXPERIENCE AND SYSTEM REFORM

Edited by

Justin Yifu Lin

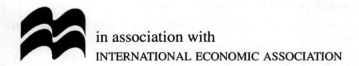

in association with
INTERNATIONAL ECONOMIC ASSOCIATION

First published in Great Britain 1998 by
MACMILLAN PRESS LTD
Houndmills, Basingstoke, Hampshire RG21 6XS and London
Companies and representatives throughout the world

A catalogue record for this book is available from the British Library.

ISBN 0–333–69805–3

 First published in the United States of America 1998 by
ST. MARTIN'S PRESS, INC.,
Scholarly and Reference Division,
175 Fifth Avenue, New York, N.Y. 10010

ISBN 0–312–21506–1 (vol. 1)

Library of Congress Cataloging-in-Publication Data
International Economic Association. World Congress (11th : 1995 :
Tunis, Tunisia)
Contemporary economic issues / congress editor Michael Bruno.
p.   cm. — (IEA conference volume ; 121, 122, 123, 125)
Includes bibliographical references and index.
Contents: — v. 1. Regional experience and system reform / edited by
Justin Yifu Lin — v. 2. Labour, food and poverty / edited by Yair
Mundlak — v. 3. Trade, payments and debt / edited by Daniel Cohen
— v. 5. Macroeconomics and finance / edited by Holger Wolf.
ISBN 0–312–21506–1 (cloth : v. 1) — ISBN 0–312–17744–5 (cloth :
v. 2). — ISBN 0–312–17760–7 (cloth : v. 3). — ISBN 0–312–17759–3
(cloth : v. 5)
1. Economics—Congresses.   2. Economic policy—Congresses.
3. Finance—Congresses.   I. Bruno, Michael.   II. Mundlak, Yair,
1927–   .   III. Cohen, Daniel, 1953–   .   IV. Wolf, Holger C.
V. Title.   VI. Series: I.E.A. conference volume ; no. 122, etc.
HB21.I65 1995
330—dc21   95–4526
                                                                CIP

UNESCO Subvention 1994 –95/SHS/IDS/41

This book is printed on paper suitable for recycling and made from fully managed and
sustained forest sources.

10   9   8   7   6   5   4   3   2   1
07   06   05   04   03   02   01   00   99   98

Printed and bound in Great Britain by
Antony Rowe Ltd, Chippenham, Wiltshire

Contents

The International Economic Association

A non-profit organization with purely scientific aims, the International Economic Association (IEA) was founded in 1950. It is a federation of some sixty national economic association in all parts of the world. Its basic purpose is the development of economics as an intellectual discipline, recognizing a diversity of problems, systems and values in the world and taking note of methodological diversities.

The IEA has, since its creation, sought to fulfil that purpose by promoting mutual understanding among economists through the organization of scientific meetings and common research programmes, and by means of publications on problems of fundamental as well as of current importance. Deriving from its long concern to assure professional contacts between East and West and North and South, the IEA pays special attention to issues of economies in systemic transition and in the course of development. During its nearly fifty years of existence, it has organized more than a hundred round-table conferences for specialists on topics ranging from fundamental theories to methods and tools of analysis and major problems of the present-day world. Participation in round tables is at the invitation of a specialist programme committee, but eleven triennial World Congresses have regularly attracted the participation of individual economists from all over the world.

The Association is governed by a Council, composed of representatives of all member associations, and by a fifteen-member Executive Committee which is elected by the Council. The Executive Committee (1995–98) at the time of the Tunis Congress was:

President:	Professor Jacques Drèze, Belgium
Vice-President:	Professor Anne Krueger, USA
Treasurer:	Professor Erich Streissler, Austria
Past President:	Professor Michael Bruno, Israel (deceased 26 December 1996)
Other members:	Professor Anthony B. Atkinson, UK
	Professor Vittorio Corbo (Chile)
	Professor Karel Dyba, Czech Republic
	Professor Jean-Michael Grandmont, France

Sir Austin Robinson was an active Adviser on the publication of IEA Conference proceedings from 1954 until his final short illness in 1993.

The Association has also been fortunate in having secured many outstanding economists to serve as President:

Gottfried Haberler (1950–53), Howard S. Ellis (1953–56), Erik Lindahl (1956–59), E. A. G. Robinson (1959–62), Ugo Papi (1962–65), Paul A. Samuelson (1965–68). Erik Lundberg (1968–71), Fritz Machlup (1971–74), Edmund Malinvaud (1974–77), Shigeto Tsuru (1977–80), Victor L. Urquidi (1980–83), Kenneth J. Arrow (1983–86), Amartya Sen (1986–89), Anthony B. Atkinson (1989–1992) and Michael Bruno (1992–95).

The activities of the Association are mainly funded from the subscriptions of members and grants from a number of organizations, including continuing support from UNESCO, through the International Social Science Council.

Preface

Michael Bruno

The World Congress of the International Economic Association held in Tunis in December 1995 was the eleventh in a series that started in Rome in 1956, with the most recent one being held in Moscow in 1992. This Congress was marked by being the first to take place in Africa and the Middle East. This was reflected in having special sessions devoted to the Economic Development of Sub-Saharan Africa, Maghreb Economies and the Economics of the Middle East Peace Process, besides a wide array of topics in contemporary economics of development, trade, economic growth and general economic theory. Quoting from the opening speech by the President of Tunisia, His Excellency Zine El Abidine Ben Ali:

> Tunisia is very proud that your Association is holding its eleventh congress – the first such event to take place in Africa and the Middle East – on our soil. This will give you a good opportunity to concentrate your attention on the most recent developments in economics and their role in strengthening development, as can be seen from the items on your agenda. The situation now prevailing in many countries, particularly those on our African continent, more than confirms the necessity of giving such issues an essential place in contemporary economic thinking.

Tunisia's impressive recent development effort, marking both a vigorous growth rate, low inflation, marked improvement in its social indicators, greater openness to international trade, as well as its ample cultural and historical treasures, made it a particularly interesting host country for our Association. It was a very lively Congress, with many high quality sessions, interspersed with several cultural and other events which introduced the broadly international group of attendees to the host country's institutions and culture.

The Congress programme consisted of four plenary sessions (those by Professor Edmond Malinvaud, Professor Robert Putnam, the Austin Robinson Memorial lecture delivered by Professor Assar Lindbeck, as well as the Presidential Address). It had three panel sessions (chaired by Professors U. Reinhardt, A. Tornell and S. Fischer), and 41 regular sessions. In these there were 43 invited papers and 278 contributed papers. The Congress was attended by about 700 participants coming from 68 different countries.

The full list of the Programme Committee is as follows:

Bina Agarwal, University of Delhi, India
Kenneth Arrow, Stanford University, USA
Anthony Atkinson, Oxford University, UK
David Audretsch, Wissenschaftszentrum Berlin, Germany
Richard Baldwin, University of Wisconsin, USA
Kaushik Basu, Delhi School of Economics, India
David Begg, Birkbeck College, London, UK
François Bourguinon, DELTA, Paris, France
Daniel Cohen, CEPREMAP, Paris, France
Vittorio Corbo, Catholic University of Chile, Santiago, Chile
Partha Dasgupta, University of Cambridge, UK
Peter Diamond, MIT, Cambridge, Mass, USA
Juan Dolado, CEMFI, Madrid, Spain
Bernard Dumas, Groupe-Hautes Etudes Commerciales, Jouy-en-Josas, France
Ibrahim Elbadawi, African Economic Research Consortium, Nairobi, Kenya
Riccardo Faini, University of Brescia, Italy
Stanley Fischer, The World Bank, Washington, USA
Nancy Folbre, University of Massachusetts, USA
Alberto Giovannini, Department of the Treasury, Rome, Italy
Vittorio Grilli, Department of the Treasury, Rome, Italy
Oliver Hart, Harvard University, USA
Sergiu Hart, Hebrew University of Jerusalem, Israel
Elhanan Helpman, Tel Aviv University, Israel
Wontack Hong, Seoul National University, Korea
Susan Horton, University of Toronto, Canada
Peter Howitt, Université des Sciences Sociales, Toulouse, France
Ponciano Intal, Philippine Institute for Development Studies, Manila, Philippines
Takatoshi Ito, NBER, Cambridge, Mass, USA
Ravi Kanbur, The World Bank, Washington, USA
Heinz Kurz, University of Graz, Austria
Jean-Jacques Laffont, Université des Sciences Sociales, Toulouse, France
Donald Lessard, MIT, Cambridge, Mass, USA
Justin Yifu Lin, China Centre for Economic Research, Beijing, China

Millard Long, The World Bank, Budapest, Hungary
Karl-Göran Müller, Stockholm School of Economics, Sweden
John Moore, London School of Economics, UK
Yair Mundlak, University of Chicago, USA
Mustapha Kamel Nabli, University of Tunis, Tunisia
Benno Ndulu, African Economic Research Consortium, Nairobi, Kenya
Takashi Negishi, Aoyama Gakuin University, Tokyo, Japan
Siddiq Osmani, University of Ulster, Coleraine, UK
Kirit Parikh, Indira Gandhi Institute of Development Research, Bombay,
    India
Richard Portes, CEPR, London, UK
Martin Ravaillon, The World Bank, Washington, USA
Sergio Rebelo, University of Rochester, USA
Uwe Reinhardt, Princeton University, USA
Dani Rodrik, Columbia University, New York, USA
Agnar Sandmo, Norwegian School of Economics, Bergen, Norway
Murat Sertel, Boğaziçi University, Istanbul, Turkey
Dennis Snower, Birkbeck College, London, UK
Jan Svejnar, CERGE, Charles University, Prague, Czech Republic
Peter Swan, University of New South Wales, Kensington NSW, Australia
Peter Temin, MIT, Cambridge, Mass, USA
Jacques Thisse, Ecole Nationale des Ponts et Chaussées, Paris, France
Aaron Tornell, Harvard University, Cambridge, Mass., USA
Hirofumi Uzawa, Japan Development Bank, Tokyo, Japan
Oliver Williamson, University of California at Berkeley, Cal., USA
Charles Wyplosz, INSEAD, Fontainebleau, France
Shahid Yusuf, The World Bank, Washington, USA
Stefano Zamagni, University of Bologna, Italy
Klaus Zimmerman, University of Munich, Germany

The proceedings of the Congress are being published in five volumes
under the general title *Contemporary Economic Issues*:

Vol. 1: *Regional Experiences and System Reform* edited by Justin Yifu Lin
Vol. 2: *Labour, Food and Poverty* edited by Yair Mundlak
Vol. 3: *Trade, Payments and Debt* edited by Daniel Cohen
Vol. 4: *Economic Behaviour and Design* edited by Murat Sertel
Vol. 5: *Macroeconomics and Finance* edited by Holger C. Wolf

I would like to record our gratitude to our Tunisian hosts who made this
a highly successful conference. Besides thanking our illustrious host, His

Excellency President Zine El Abidine Ben Ali, I would like to thank the local Organizing Committee, and first and foremost its Chairman, Mustapha Kamel Nabli, who bore the brunt of the responsibility for the logistics and successful implementation of the Congress. He was helped by Mongi Safra (Vice-Chairman), Mongi Azabou (Executive Secretary), Salah Maoui (Minister of Tourism), Salah Baccari (Minister of Culture) and the able Tunisian staff assisting them in their task.

I would like to thank Francis Ghilès (Volume 1), Michael Kaser (Volume 2), John Butler (Volume 3), Maureen Hadfield (Volume 4) and Lesley Cook (Volume 5) for taking charge of the editorial preparation of these volumes. I am as always grateful to Michael Kaser, the General Editor of these series. Finally, I would like to record my thanks to Jean-Paul Fitoussi, the Secretary General of the International Economic Association, not only for initiating the Congress in Tunis, but for his constant support with the preparations along the way.

List of Contributors

Hisham Awartani	An-Najah National University and Center for Palestinian Research and Studies, Nablus, PNA
Fang Cai	Population Institute, Chinese Academy of Social Sciences, Beijing, China
Vittorio Corbo	Pontificia Universidad Católica de Chile, Santiago, Chile
Marek Dąbrowski	Center for Social and Economic Research, Warsaw, Poland
John S. Flemming	Wadham College, Oxford, UK
Ashok Guha	Jawaharlal Nehru University, New Delhi, India
Wontack Hong	Seoul University, Korea
Takatoshi Ito	Hitotsubashi University, Tokyo, Japan
Ephraim Kleiman	Hebrew University of Jerusalem, Israel
Justin Yifu Lin	Hong Kong University of Science and Technology, Hong Kong
Christian Morrisson	University of Paris–Sorbonne, France
Hassouna Moussa	Hosei University, Japan
John Page	The World Bank, Washington, DC, USA
Béchir Talbi	University of Tunis, Tunisia
John Underwood	The World Bank, Washington, DC, USA

List of Abbreviations

ASEAN	Association of South-East Asian Nations
BCT	Central Bank of Tunisia
BTO	Build, transfer and operate
CACOM	Central American Common Market
CARICOM	Caribbean Community
CEE	Central and Eastern Europe
CEPAL	UN Economic Commission for Latin America and the Caribbean
CIS	Commonwealth of Independent States
CMEA	Council for Mutual Economic Assistance
CORA	Agrarian Reform Corporation (Chile)
CORFO	Development Corporation (Chile)
CPI	consumer price index
DC	developed country
DFI	direct foreign investment
DOP	Declaration of Principles (Gaza Strip)
EBRD	European Bank for Reconstruction and Development
ECLAC	(UN) Economic Commission for Latin America and the Caribbean
ENAP	Petroleum National Company (Chile)
FCC	formerly communist country
FDI	foreign direct investment
FSU	former Soviet Union
FTA	free trade agreement
GATT	General Agreement on Tariffs and Trade
GDP	gross domestic product
GNP	gross national product
HIODS	heavy industry-oriented development strategy
IDB	International Development Bank
IEQ	Institut d'Economie Quantitative
IMF	International Monetary Fund
IS	import substitution
ISI	import-substituting industrialization
KOTRA	Korea Trade Promotion Corporation
LDC	less-developed country
MENA	Middle East and North Africa

MITI	Ministry of International Trade (Japan)
NAFTA	North American Free Trade Agreement
NIC	newly industrializing country
NIE	newly industrializing economy
OECD	Organization for Economic Cooperation and Development
PNA	Palestinian National Authority
QR	quantitative restriction
R&D	research & development
SEZ	Special Economic Zone (China)
SOE	state-owned enterprise
TFP	total factor productivity
TVE	township-and-village enterprise (China)
UGTT	Union Général Tunisienne du Travail
UNICEF	United Nations Children's Fund
WTO	World Trade Organization

Introduction

Justin Yifu Lin

The twelve chapters in this volume deal with the experiences of economic development in different countries since the Second World War and the experiences of system reform and economic integration in various countries in the last decade. I shall briefly highlight the main arguments in each chapter.

After the industrial revolution in the eighteenth century, countries in the world can be divided into two groups. The first group is the developed countries (DCs). Their economies are characterized by high *per capita* income, industrialization, and extensive use of capital-intensive technology. The second group is less-developed countries (LDCs) which are poor, agrarian, and use predominantly traditional technology in their production. The wealth of DCs is based on their advanced industries and technologies. Therefore, how to industrialize the economy and catch up with the DCs have interested not only political leaders in the LDCs but also many intellectuals in the world since the nineteenth century. However, only a small number of countries in East Asia have succeeded in their modernization attempts. Many studies have recently reviewed the successful experiences of East Asian newly-industrializing economies (NIEs) and the failures of countries in other parts of the world. The five chapters in Part I are a welcome addition to the literature.

Chapter 1, by Wontack Hong, 'The Catching-up: Lessons of East Asian Development', attempts to identify the most conspicuous common factors that have contributed to the successful development of East Asian NIEs. For more than three decades, the 'Four Little Dragons' of East Asia – Korea, Taiwan, Hong Kong and Singapore – grew by 10 per cent per annum on average. Japan also grew at a similar rate during the period between 1952 and the first oil shock of 1973. The new NIEs – Thailand, Malaysia, Indonesia and China – have recently begun to reveal similar high growth performances. It is an interesting question why out of more than 150 LDCs in the world, only a handful of economies in the East Asia had commenced the process of catching-up. In his chapter, Hong argues that for an economy to achieve sustained high growth, it has to institutionalize a system that can maximize the energy and effort of each individual member of the society, channel the individual energy into economic activities that are most productive for the society as a whole, maintain an autogenous dynamism and minimize the unnecessary frictions among the members of the society. In Hong's view, the economic success of the East Asian NIEs in the past 30 years can be attributed to their governments' ability to adopt policies that promote export-oriented growth, because such policies reduce the rent-seeking opportunities and, at the same time, maximize the rates of return on productive activities in these economies and hence maximize their motivation to save, work effort, enterprising spirit and innovative activities.

Chapter 2, by Takatoshi Ito, 'Japanese Economic Development: Idiosyncratic or Universal?', also attempts to provide an explanation for the extraordinary growth in East Asian NIEs, but from a different angle. Japan is the first country outside the western hemisphere to become industrialized. Its success has been regarded as a 'miracle'. Early works on how Japan succeeded in achieving rapid economic growth emphasized idiosyncratic cultural and economic institutions of Japanese society. It was implied that Japan's success could not be duplicated elsewhere. The view of Japan as an idiosyncratic miracle lost ground in the 1980s, for two reasons: First, many economic institutions in Japan can actually be explained with regular economic tools with generalized assumptions; and second, other East Asian economies sustained a period of high economic growth, reminiscent of Japan's miracle some decades earlier. In addition to the export-oriented growth, as identified by Hong, Ito finds that one interesting feature of East Asian economic development is the industrial sequencing, or the 'flying geese' pattern. These countries have upgraded their industries in an orderly fashion. First, the textile industry flourishes, then light machinery industry follows, and heavy industries – such as steel, shipbuilding, transportation vehicle industries, and various chemical industries – have to wait until the textile and light machinery industries find success in the world market. Ito argues that the industrial policies in Japan and other East Asian NIEs are helpful because their policies aim to promote export and industrial sequencing.

In the last decade or so, South Asian economies also achieved a uniformly rapid growth, next only to the miracle economies of East Asia. Chapter 3, by Ashok Guha, 'Factor Endowments and Policies in South Asian Growth', to provide an analysis of this area's growth performance. Guha shows that factor endowment, specifically the abundance of labour, has been the basis of South Asian growth. Based on a modified Rybczynski theorem, Guha proposes that the relative labour-abundant economies would have relatively lower prices of labour-intensive goods under autarchy. They would in consequence have lower wages but higher rates of profit. A high rate of profits induces a high propensity to save and invest. Low wages encourage labour-intensive techniques in each industry while lower prices of labour-intensive goods induce consumer substitution in their favour. Both factors reduce the capital-labour ratio. A higher propensity to save and invest and a lower capital–labour ratio both accelerate growth. Opening up the economy may induce a Stolper–Samuelson effect, raising wages and eroding profits. However, if labour supply is highly elastic, what ensues is less a Stolper–Samuelson process than an Arthur Lewis process: wages hardly rise, rates of profit are sustained and the expansion of the labour-intensive export sector rapidly increases employment. For regions like South Asia and China, it is perhaps the latter model that is more relevant.

Among the South Asian countries, India achieved the high growth rate in 1970–93 with about twice the saving ratio of Pakistan and three times that of Bangladesh. The main reason is because the Pakistani and Bangladesh economies have far more labour-intensive structures than the Indian. In 1988, the heavier industries contributed 65.3 per cent of value added by manufacturing in India. The same groups accounted for just 38 per cent in Pakistan and 32.6 per cent in Bangladesh. Thus capital output ratios were substantially higher in India. Therefore, in addition to the factor endowments, infrastructure, political stability, and so on, the choice of technologies and industrial structures that are consistent with the endowment structure of the economy is also an important factor determining an economy's growth performance.

The last two chapters in Part I, by Christian Morrisson and Béchir Talbi and by Hassouna Moussa, review Tunisia's economic development in the post-independence period. The Tunisian authorities carried out very varied policies between 1956 and 1995, ranging from a liberal economy to collectivization with central planning. However, Chapters 4 and 5 both show that the Tunisian economy has achieved a respectable average growth rate during the last three decades. In the period, the country has managed to increase the population's living standard by 160 per cent, greatly slowed population growth, eliminated extreme poverty, created a large middle class, and reduced inequality. Tunisia now ranks among the middle-income countries. Morrisson and Talbi argue that this achievement is mainly explained by a continuity of two elements of public finance – a high level of public investment in infrastructure and education – whatever the economic strategy being followed. However, the performance was associated with an investment GDP ratio similar to that observed in the NICs of Asia who achieved significantly higher growth. Moussa's study finds that the disparity in growth rates cannot be explained by a difference in the availability of resources nor to a difference in monetary policy. Moussa argues that the disparity arises mainly from lack of coordination of international trade, domestic trade and industrial policies. The Tunisian market is small, yet regulations, from price control to tariffs and quotas, were pervasive. These regulations stifle competition and promote monopoly. Morrisson and Talbi attribute the extensive government intervention to the excessive political weight of interest groups until 1987 that slowed the reforms which would have increased the economy's efficiency and thus stimulated growth in the interest of the whole population.

Part II contains five chapters on system reforms. The transition to the market economy in formal socialist countries may be the most important political and economic event in the world history of the last decade of the twentieth century. The results of the transition are very different. Eastern Europe as a whole saw a GDP decline and has experienced a small recovery since 1993, while China has sustained a rapid growth since the reforms started in 1979. The first two chapters in Part II review the experiences of Eastern Europe and the Former Soviet Union's transition and the third and fourth chapters on China's experiences. The last chapter in Part II provides an overview of Latin American reforms with a focus on Chilean experiences. Latin American countries have also engaged in economic reform, although their changes are not as massive as in the socialist countries. Nevertheless, some of their lessons may be relevant to the transition in Eastern Europe and in China.

Chapter 6, by Marek Dąbrowski, 'Strategies of Transition: A Political Economy Approach' deals mainly with the problems of how quickly and radically the new market rules and their individual components should be adopted in the formerly communist countries and what factors determine the optimal speed. Arguments in favour of rapid transition concern three areas: (1) the requirements of some important components of the transition process (e.g. macroeonomic stabilization cannot be carried out gradually); (2) no effective coordination mechanisms exist for the half-way stage between plan and market; (3) the so-called period of 'extraordinary politics' after the collapse of communism – limited patience of society, danger of rebuilding pressure groups, credibility issues and other political economy considerations. The advantages of gradual reform concern two areas: first, gradual changes make accommodation to the new rules of game and institutions easier; and slower restructuring of SOEs can, to some extent, dilute political resistance against change, as too large a number of bankruptcies in a relatively short period of time and too high a level of open unemployment are probably not acceptable politically, even for the most popular government. D'browski's study finds, generally speaking, that empirical experience in Eastern Europe and the Former Soviet Union in 1989–94 shows that a faster and comprehensive economic reform gives more chances to minimize the economic, social and political costs of this process and avoid chronic macroeconomic mismanagement.

Chapter 7 by J. S. Flemming, 'Welfare in Economic Transition', focuses on the welfare consequences of transition in Eastern Europe and the Former Soviet Union. Under communism, the transition economies were recorded as delivering greater equality, better education, literacy and health than other economies with comparable levels of *per capita* income. The data surveyed by Flemming suggests that there is a serious welfare problem in the transition. Eastern Europe as a whole saw a sharp GDP decline: There is little reason to doubt that the region has experienced a setback to output larger than that experienced in the Great Depression of the 1930s. Unemployment, traditionally reported as negligible throughout the region, has risen everywhere, poverty and extreme poverty have risen significantly; income distribution has deteriorated unprecedentedly. Flemming urges for more coherent and radical reform programmes to reintegrate the 'grey economy', and transfer social provision from enterprises to government. However, he cautions against a bigger and better social safety net to compensate any 'victims' of transition.

China started systemic reforms much earlier than Eastern Europe and the Former Soviet Union and obtained a remarkable output growth. Chapter 8 by Justin Yifu Lin, 'What Can We Learn From China's Economic Reform?' analyzes how China achieved this performance and what lessons can be drawn from China's reforms. Lin argues that the economic problems in China before the reforms were the low incentives and the misallocation of resources among sectors, which were the results of pursuing a capital-intensive heavy industry-oriented development strategy in a capital-scarce economy. China's gradual approach to reforms first created a new stream of resources by improving material incentives and then allowed the newly created stream of resources to be allocated to the sectors which were suppressed under the original development strategy. Because the production of the 'existing stock' of resources is not disrupted and the new 'stream' of resource is allocated to the more productive sectors, the national economy enjoys a continuous growth in the reform process. Because low incentives and the suppression of non-priority sectors are common features for all economies adopting the heavy industry-oriented development strategy, Lin argues that China's approach to reform has a general implication for other economies which adopted a similar development strategy with a similar endowment structure.

Chapter 9, by Fang Cai, 'The Roles of Chinese Economists in the Economic Reform', discusses the roles of economists. Cai's chapter shows that before the economic reform, the main function of Chinese economists was to use Marxist ideology to defend the government's policies. They rarely played any important role in policy decision-making. When serious policy mistakes caused severe setbacks in the Chinese economy, it was the political leaders themselves who corrected their own mistakes. As such, the role of economists was very limited. China started the transition without a blueprint designed by economists, which was very different from the reforms in Eastern Europe and the Former Soviet Union. However, as the ideological constraint was lessened when the transition to the market was increasingly accepted by the government as the goal of China's reform, Chinese economists started to play a bigger role. They not only criticized the traditional planning system and advocated a market system, but they also provided alternative reform programmes to the government. The change in this role can be attributed to the increasing sophistication of economists' research and the political leaders' demand for policy advice in a more complicated market economy.

The final chapter in Part II, Chapter 10 by Vittorio Corbo, 'Economic Reform in Latin America: The Decade of Hope', provides an overview of Latin America's reform experience, especially that of Chile. Latin American countries for many decades pursued an import-substitution strategy. To a lesser degree, the problems caused by that strategy are similar to those of the heavy industry-oriented development strategy in the socialist economy. After the second oil crisis, the countries in Latin America had one by one to adjust their policies, as they could no longer continue to finance the large current account deficits of the pre-crisis period. There also emerged a consensus on policy reforms. The new model emphasizes macroeconomic stability, integration with the world economy, deregulation and competitive market structures, and a government sector responsible for putting in place the institutions and infrastructure necessary for the functioning of a market economy. Chile was the first country in Latin America to start the reform, and the reforms undertaken in other countries in the region have drawn on Chile's rich experience. Chile's approach to the reform of the social security system is especially innovative and relevant to the reforms in Eastern Europe and China.

Part III contains two chapters on the effects of economic integration. In Chapter 11, 'Growth, the Maghreb and the European Union' John Page and John Underwood assess the impact on Tunisia and Morocco of the Free Trade Agreements with the European Union. Trade experts have traditionally viewed regional integration schemes as offering few benefits compared with universal trade liberalization. The costs of diversion of trade away from least-cost suppliers may outweigh the potential gains of trade creation among members of the agreement, and even when net trade creation effects are positive, the estimated welfare gains from partial liberalization are frequently small. Nevertheless, efforts to create regional trading blocs proceed world-wide. The potential dynamic benefits of integration agreements – that is, the possibility of increased investment flows and the positive impact of integration agreements on productivity and technological change – are usually put forward as the rationale for their existence. Page and Underwood's study finds that, while the integration with the European Union offers Morocco and Tunisia an important opportunity to accelerate growth and raise incomes toward Southern European levels, substantial benefits will not accrue to either country automatically. To realize the potential gains, both countries need to accelerate the liberalization of trade, improve decisively the investment climate, and adopt policies to accelerate the rate of productivity change.

In the final chapter, Chapter 12, Hisham Awartani and Ephraim Kleiman look at the impact of economic integration among the six countries participating in the Arab–Israeli peace process. They find that the tendency for these groups of countries to trade among themselves is very weak. However, it is not the state of hostilities between most of them and Israel that has hindered intra-regional trade because the trade among the Arab members of these groups is also small. The low level of inter-regional trade cannot be attributed to poor trade policies either, because of the relatively high tendency to trade with a country outside the group, Turkey. Awartani and Kleiman conclude that these six countries do not constitute a 'natural' trading bloc and, consequently, the scope for expanding trade among these six countries arising from the peace process is rather limited. But because of proximity of location, the Israel–Jordan–Palestinian territories have the potential of developing considerable border-type trade and various sorts of joint ventures.

Part I
Regional Experience

1 The Catching-up: Lessons of East Asian Development

Wontack Hong
SEOUL UNIVERSITY, KOREA

1 INTRODUCTION

For more than three decades, the export-oriented East-Asian NICs, or the so-called 'NICs 4' – i.e. Korea, Taiwan, Hong Kong and Singapore – grew by nearly 10 per cent per annum on average. Japan also grew at a similar rate during the period between the regaining of her independence in 1952 and the first oil shock of 1973, far exceeding the so-called 'post-Meiji long-run trend rate' of 4 per cent, eventually becoming a full-fledged advanced-country by the 1980s. The new NICs – i.e. Thailand, Malaysia, Indonesia and China – have recently begun to reveal similar high growth performance. These East Asian economies are often regarded as unique because they have combined rapid, sustained growth with a relatively equal distribution of income. Be it the result of extraordinary resource mobilization or technological catch-up (i.e. inputs-driven or efficiency-driven à la Krugman, 1994), the very natural questions are how out of more than 150 underdeveloped countries, the catching-up process commenced in these handful of countries and growth dynamism been maintained in these economies over such a long period of time.

Every nation consists of minds that may be regarded as a set of specific action-bound instincts trained by experience and learning, but triggered by outside stimuli. These human instincts may have been designed by natural selection to respond in specific fashion to various challenges and motivations. The differences in growth performances among countries may then be the result of different environmental triggers or motivations acting on the same genetic nature.

The *outward-looking export-orientation* of the East Asian NICs may well have acted as a specific kind of environmental trigger on the genetic nature of the people in these countries. The policy-cum-institutional approaches adopted by these NICs, however, have ranged from the so-called *positive-non-intervention* in Hong Kong to Korea's aggressive intervention in market mechanisms. One may therefore have to delve into the most conspicuous

3

similarities as well as differences among the East Asian NICs in order to see whether any kind of generalization on their catching-up process is possible (See also World Bank, 1993, and Ito and Krueger, 1995).

Taiwan after the arrival of the Chiang Kai-shek government in 1949, and Korea after the Korean War (1950–3) both depended heavily on US grant-in aid. Anticipating a rapid decline in US aid, however, these two densely populated and resource-poor countries had launched long-term development plans by the late 1950s and the early 1960s, respectively, and eventually moved towards an export-oriented growth path (see Hong, 1993). Hong Kong was from 1843 until June 1997 ruled by a British-appointed governor and colonial bureaucracy. The communist take-over of Mainland China in 1949 brought a massive influx of people, increasing Hong Kong's population from 0.6 million in 1945 to 2.4 million in 1950. At the same time the UN's embargo on China during the Korean War crippled Hong Kong's traditional entrepôt trade. Singapore had flourished as an entrepôt ever since Raffles had obtained British control over Singapore harbour in 1819. While its entrepôt growth had been inhibited by the rising economic nationalism and direct trading in Southeast Asia, the aborted Federation of Malaysia (1963–5) banished any illusion of a Chinese-dominated Singapore to create a Malay hinterland for an import-substitution-oriented growth. Draconian measures introduced in 1967–8 *à la* Lee Kuan Yew, however, initiated Singapore's DFI-led export-oriented growth.

A country's capability to start catching up seems to depend on a social history that is particular to itself. Therefore, our object is not to investigate *why* but rather to investigate *how* the catching-up process is initiated and growth dynamism maintained.[1] We contend that the export-oriented growth strategy enabled the East Asian NICs to start the catching-up process and that export-oriented growth based on price-quality competition in international markets enhanced what Kindleberger (1962) calls the 'capacity to transform', and hence enabled them to maintain growth dynamism. Export-orientation and the associated openness of an economy is what really enhances a country's receptivity to changing environmental circumstances.[2]

2 EXPORT-ORIENTED GROWTH

Beginning with Hong Kong, and soon followed by Taiwan and then Korea and then by Singapore, the NICs 4 have been pursuing export-oriented growth under the vigorous leadership of highly centralized, obviously non-democratic, and yet fairly efficient governments that have espoused economic growth as their principal objective and been able to elicit popular consent. Political stability plus weak labour union activities in these countries have lengthened time horizons of entrepreneurs and made investment in export manufacturing a feasible alternative to commerce or import-substitution activities. Not only in non-interventionist Hong Kong but also in highly interventionist Korea, the government has recognized the primacy of market mechanism while the government–business relationship has stimulated and guided the energies of private enterprise towards export-oriented activities with universal export incentives.

Singapore's regime, for example, is often characterized as having puritanical Confucian paternalism, and yet the government policy has rather been non-ideological and even somewhat non-theoretical. As Mason (1980, p. 261) says of Korea, government policy, with varying intensity and coverage, has been highly pragmatic in the sense that the government has been quick to intervene with the market mechanism whenever it believes the market is not working properly. Furthermore, although non-discretionary manipulation of incentives is regarded as a theoretically superior form of market intervention, government policy has shown no hesitation in devising very particular means to achieve its objective. In Singapore nearly 500 government-owned companies and statutory boards are directly involved in manufacturing and service activities, presumably on a no-subsidy profit-making basis. One can, however, observe more frequent use of sector-specific discretionary manipulation in Korea than in Singapore or in Taiwan whose implementation procedures have been more akin to non-discretionary manipulation. Of course the trend over time is toward greater liberalization and deregulation in all these NICs that is more congenial to the functioning of a competitive market economy. All these NICs are now searching for a more sustainable mode of conflict resolution that can replace their traditional non-democratic polity.

3 EXPORT-ORIENTED PRODUCTION

The effort to expand exports and reap the gains from trade can stimulate savings and investment activities, enhancing the mobilization of material and entrepreneurial resources, and also can stimulate the technical process (i.e. international technological catch-up and domestic spillovers). The greatly enhanced profit opportunities in export activities can further motivate people to establish and expand other activities and hence communicate progress to the rest of the economy. The character of export production activities may, however, influence the type of resulting external dynamics effects. According to Kindleberger (1962, p. 199), the labour-intensive activities of producing milk, butter and cheese in Denmark, New Zealand, Switzerland, the Netherlands or Wisconsin require peasants who have the capacity to encourage transformation, while land-intensive meat production (raising cattle on the range instead of fattening stock in feeder lots) flourishes with a feudal type of society that does not enhance training effect or encourage rapid progress, as in Argentina or Texas.

The labour-intensive manufacturing activities in the East Asian NICs required an energetic group of entrepreneurs who had the capacity to stimulate transformation. The mode of production (such as the Japanese-style business-group-cum-small-subcontractors) may, however, differ significantly in importing new technologies, in spreading growth, in nurturing entrepreneurship, and in the effects on income distribution, household savings, tax system and the social system in general. One might further argue that the big-business-oriented export expansion in Korea (or Singapore) is less conducive for sustained growth in the long run than the small-business-oriented export expansion in Taiwan (and Hong Kong) because the former represents not only the concentration in large-scale industry with standard processes and labour-saving machinery involving less technical change or high-grade specialized labour but also a mono-polization of entrepreneurship, while the latter represents a more extensive participation of entrepreneurial talents in the society as well as a large upward social mobility (cf. Kindleberger, 1962, p. 202).

4 HONG KONG'S APPROACH

The essence of Hong Kong's non-interventionist approach has been, first, to maintain macroeconomic stability – i.e., keeping inflation low, real interest rates positive and exchange rates stable so as to encourage people to save and to encourage far-sighted entrepreneurs; second, to actively invest in human capital in order to supply the economy with a well educated labour force capable of acquiring new skills and of adapting to changing demands; and, third, providing an adequate physical infrastructure.

The Hong Kong government stayed away from picking winners or devising subsidies to promote strategic industries, assuming that business-men normally know what they are doing. The Hong Kong government did, however, try to ensure that manufacturers knew what product standards had to be complied in their export markets and that the technical capability existed locally to enable them to meet these standards. It tried to allocate available industrial estates to the land-saving, high-value-added manufacturing firms that could introduce advanced technologies. The Industry Department served as a 'One Stop Unit' – i.e. a single point of contact for the prospective investors – because government officers can liaise more effectively with the different departments which have to be consulted before a company can be set up, and hence substantially reduce red tape.

The Hong Kong government, with the exception of land allocation policies that substantially influence the costs of business, took no specific measures to shape its development into a specifically desired pattern, and hence Hong Kong's industrial growth may be regarded to have been primarily the result of a natural market process. Hong Kong greatly enjoyed the flexibility that the market economy could provide for a free enterprise system (see Lin and Mok, 1985).

5   OTHER APPROACHES

In promoting export manufacturing and industries with high growth potential or in supporting selected firms, the principal instruments of intervention adopted in Korea, Taiwan and Japan have been subsidized credit rationing (a practice termed 'financial repression'), preferential tax treatment for investment (without generating large fiscal deficits), protectionist import restrictions (combined with relatively free imports of low-cost intermediate and capital goods), maintenance of a unified but somewhat undervalued exchange rate, socialization of risk and vigorous administrative support (so-called 'paternalistic administrative guidance', see Tsuru, 1994, p. 83). The government has amplified the market profit signal by exaggerating the rates of return on export activities.

In a country with an advanced financial sector, a profitable project with a long gestation period may be financed either by issuing stocks and bonds or by bank lending at market rates, almost regardless of the magnitude of funds involved. In Korea, Taiwan, Japan, and even in Singapore, however, the governments have attempted to overcome country's financial backwardness by means of direct or indirect credit rationing, although such an approach delayed the development of the financial sector. Due to the scarcity of information, the government believed that the price of long-term funds would be too high if it were determined by the competitive market, and hence regulated the banking system to encourage it to finance large amounts of fixed long-term capital investment at subsidized rates, using short-term bank funds. Banks have been supported by deposit rate control and central bank credits (see Teranishi, 1994, p. 43).

In order to channel the energy and effort of a country into designated productive activities, the governments of East Asian NICs (except Hong Kong) created a system of non-market contest-based competition that provides clear-cut rules to elicit broad participation (such as using non-traditional export performance as a yardstick), competitive discipline and substantial rewards (such as preferential access to credit and foreign exchange, quasi-rent due to import restrictions, or capacity licensing as a tool of entry restriction) (see World Bank, 1993, pp. 93–102).

Kaname Akamatsu (1961) called the sequence of importation – domestic production – exportation the 'flying geese pattern' of industrial development. Shinohara (1982, p. 13) added the phase of 'overseas investment' following exportation that was introduced in Vernon's (1966) product cycle theory. Japan commenced the era of high growth (just like the other East Asian NICs) with a large body of disguised unemployment that had substantially weakened the bargaining position of labour (see Tsuru, 1994, pp. 68–9). Komiya (1992) views the period 1955–73 in Japan as the time of the 'easterly wind' of industrial structure policy overwhelming the 'westerly wind' of free trade and market mechanisms.[3] According to Shinohara, the pre-1972 industrial policy of MITI was to 'develop self-contained modern industries within its borders and to strengthen their international competitive position across the board'. The pre-1972 Japanese exchange rate of 360 yen to a dollar installed by Joseph Dodge in 1949 had very much undervalued the yen in terms of purchasing power parity after the late 1950s, and hence was extremely favourable for the export promotion of Japanese industries. Shinohara contends that the undervalued yen enabled most of Japan's major industries to participate in the export boom by the beginning of the 1970s, and 'as a result, a large number of modern industries became export-oriented, and the growth rate of Japanese exports has become among the highest in the world'.[4] In other words, Japan's pre-1972 exchange rate policy (in addition to the traditional government instruments of market intervention) quickened the shift of entire Japanese industries from domestic market-oriented production to export-oriented production, enabled them to take advantage of the virtually infinite effective demand of international markets, and hence made the geese 'fly faster'.

Shinohara (1982) anticipated the phase of rapid expansion in Japanese DFI (direct foreign investment) in response to growing hostilities against Japanese exports in industrial nations, and also in response to the pressure on Japan to undertake structural adjustment (i.e. the internationalization of Japan's industrial structure based on horizontal division of labour) in face of the emerging NICs. According to Shinohara, the Japanese DFI in NICs caused the so-called 'negative boomerang effect' causing Japan to relinquish its traditional third-country export markets of labour-intensive goods to NICs on the one hand, but also caused the 'positive boomerang effect' of expanding Japanese exports of high value-added intermediate and capital goods to those NICs. Japanese DFI in cheap-labour countries was also expected to cause a 'negative boomerang effect' of *reverse imports* (of simple labour-intensive manufactures) into Japanese domestic markets. All these effects, however, are expected to quicken the structural transformation of Japanese industries and hence enhance the overall efficiency of the Japanese economy.

6 DIFFERENT AVENUES

The policy-makers of Singapore believed that transforming domestic (entrepôt) commercial entrepreneurs into export-oriented manufacturing or servicing entrepreneurs would be too slow and uncertain a process, and hence decided to attract export-oriented DFI in a massive scale by providing various pecuniary incentives and physical infrastructures (including low-cost industrial estates and public housing for workers), enforcing labour discipline (based on house unions and enterprise paternalism), offering permanent residentship to foreign investors, maintaining price stability and supplying educated and vocationally trained low-wage workers (see Chia, 1985). Other East Asian NICs, however, depended mainly on native entrepreneurship (and, in the case of Korea) also on massive foreign borrowings. The New NICs – i.e. Thailand, Malaysia and Indonesia – seem to be depend more on DFI than on native entrepreneurship.

Policy-makers in the East Asian NICs have, consciously or unconsciously, relied upon the price mechanism. Unlike their contemporary communist comrades, they did not deny the primacy of market operation. However, while those in other NICs 4 have shown considerable respect for the power of market forces, the Koreans have more frequently shown disdain and ignorance of the competitive market mechanism, as revealed in preferential treatment in credit rationing and tax concessions bestowed on selected firms and industries. The Taiwan government actively facilitated the establishment of new enterprises by greatly lowering the entry barriers against those with potential entrepreneurial talents. It established a large number of industrial parks and districts to provide infrastructure facilities, and office-space-cum-factory-sites on a low-rental basis. Unlike in Korea, there have been no policies in Taiwan to encourage the growth of big conglomerates. A large number of workers in Taiwan have used their jobs to accumulate enough savings to start their own enterprises, and small innovative companies headed by dynamic Chinese with experience abroad have created a new niche in the world market (see Gold, 1986, p. 104). In both Korea and Taiwan, the banking sector has, directly or indirectly, been operated by the government. In Taiwan, however, there has been no concentration of heavily subsidized credit rationing in favour of a small number of selected business groups. The Taiwan government has been ideologically against the excessive concentration of economic powers in the hands of a few *guanxiqiye*-related enterprise groups that are owned and controlled by big families (see Fields, 1995, pp. 63–92). Bank interest rates have been positive in real terms and been maintained closer to the equilibrium rate that, together with price stability, helped to enhance household savings in formal financial institutions, reducing dependence on foreign borrowing, encouraging labour-intensive methods of production and restraining the rate at which the size of the individual enterprise grows (Scitovsky, 1985). According to Kuo and Fei (1985), although the real interest rates of bank loans in Taiwan during 1952–70 were high, they were far exceeded by the still higher rates of profit.

According to Suzuki (1980, p. 56), the weighted average deposit interest rates in postwar Japan were regulated to around 4 per cent (the variable cost per unit of deposit-raising activity was less than 1 per cent) and the effective bank lending rate (including the compensatory deposit or the burden of collateral) amounted around 9 per cent while, according to Murakami (1982), the 'equilibrium lending rate' was probably much higher than 9 per cent. In order to reap the spreads, the banks engaged in fierce competition for deposits of households and self-employed businessmen by expanding the number of branches and intensifying non-price competition. This facilitated the persistence of indirect financing in firm sectors. Japanese firms depended heavily on external borrowing, though there appeared a substantial increase in equity financing in 1987–90 (see Teranishi, 1992). The issuing terms of bonds were regulated to be on par with the 'controlled nominal bank lending rate', and hence new issues were usually purchased by banks as another form of bank lending, resulting in an extremely underdeveloped secondary bond market. Japanese firms, on the other hand, did not rely on stock financing and hence their dividends on stocks were quite low. Alternative financial assets substitutable for bank deposits were therefore closed to the Japanese households who nevertheless kept saving in the form of bank deposits in spite of the low rates of return.[5] Japanese households, as well as those in other East Asian NICs, rarely enjoyed the benefit of consumer loans.

In Japan, the Ministry of Finance allowed generous licensing of branches to *sogo* (mutual) *banks* and *sinkin* (credit union) *banks*, making financial institutions more convenient to small savers and also facilitating assessment of the creditworthiness of small and medium-sized firms.

In Korea and Taiwan, the estimated share of the borrowing from informal financial market in total business loans varied from 10 per cent to 40 per cent. In both countries the informal credit market, in its wide variety of creative forms and instruments, has been most important to small and medium-sized firms. The Taiwan government, however, has facilitated the operation of the market by more actively implementing the Law of Negotiable Instruments since 1965, which gave the holder of a postdated (anywhere from 10 days up to a year later) cheque the right to invoke the sanction of criminal law and up to 3 years' imprisonment against anyone who wrote a bad cheque. Though the criminal sanctions were dropped in 1987, the extensive use of postdated cheques in Taiwan enabled small and medium-sized enterprises with checking accounts to obtain credits more readily without collateral (see Fields, 1995, pp. 162–8).

The rapid increase in national savings in Singapore owes much to the mandatory savings mechanism, i.e. the compulsory personal savings through the Central Provident Fund that was introduced in 1965. The rates of contribution from workers and employers steadily increased over the years to reach 22 per cent of salary contributed by employees and 23 per cent contributed by employers in 1982 (see Chia, 1985).

In Japan, *Zaibatsu* developed into a system of highly centralized family control (through holding companies) employing non-family managers, and then re-emerged as modern *Keiretsu* – firms clustering around core city banks that maintained some policy coordination. Business groups maintain a high degree of interdependence in terms of mutual stock holdings, and group (main) banks tend to give priority in financing fellow companies as a shareholder or as a member of a *Keiretsu*. Each parent company maintains a great number of affiliated firms in a vertical hierarchy through stock ownership. Considering the extensive network of subcontracting, there must have been a strong orientation toward buyer's monopoly (monopsony) that makes small enterprise subcontractors prone to the exploitation by the parent company. According to Shinohara (1982, pp. 37–9), 'the flexible structure of business groups provides a cushion ... and Japan's success was achieved by harnessing the economy to a dynamic combination of flexibility and rigidity'.

In Korea, the promotion of gigantic octopus-like conglomerates, in spite of the danger of resource waste arising from their rigid bureaucratic method of management, was supposedly based on economies of scale as opposed to economies of specialization. As a reward for undertaking investment in projects promoted by the government, the conglomerates enjoyed subsidized credit rationing, been rescued when projects went wrong, and been able to expect bad debts to be taken over by the government (government-operated banks) when bankruptcy occurred. The extensive socialization of risks made the investment activities of conglomerates almost risk-free and enabled them to adopt highly aggressive investment activities.

7   BEHAVIOURAL COMPLIANCE

Mason *et al.* (1980, p. 265) describe the implementation procedure in Korea in the following fashion: '[If] a firm does not respond as expected to particular incentives [it] may find that its tax returns are subject to careful examination, or that its application for bank credits is studiously ignored, or that its outstanding bank loans are not renewed.' The Korean government relied on non-institutionalized command devices to secure compliance – i.e. various pressures were brought upon an enterprise's behaviour in order to ensure compliance. Selective criminal prosecution of tax evasion, and selective control of bank credit and access to foreign borrowings for highly leveraged Koreans firms were sufficient behavioural compliance mechanisms.

According to Murakami (1982), the crux of the administrative regulations and guidance in postwar Japan was the building of a consensus for voluntary compliance in industrial investments, formulation of recession cartels, regulating new entries using technology import licences, influencing bank loan allocations or rationing Bank of Japan credit. Since the system was based on broadly phrased regulatory statutes, the consensus for voluntary compliance was essential for effective enforcement, and such consensus, in turn, required some measure of 'fairness' among firms and industries. Within this quasi-legal framework, each firm was given sufficient freedom so that 'compartmentalized' or 'managed competition' by bureaucrats was maintained in every industry.

8   POLICIES TO FACILITATE EQUITY AND GROWTH

A trade-off relationship between equity and growth is commonly postulated: a welfare state as a mode of conflict resolution is likely to inhibit growth. Extreme inequality, however, may well lead to social unrest and aggravate militant trade unionism. There may, however, be policies which can enhance both equity and growth. An income supplement for the low-paid such as subsidized low-cost housing (as well as education and medical service) in Hong Kong and Singapore may be a much better way to help the poor than a minimum wage, because such a policy can also substantially reduce the wage cost of entrepreneurs and hence promote not only equity, but also growth.

According to Scitovsky (1985), the high-interest policy in Taiwan contributed to egalitarian income distribution because the typical lender was a small saver and the typical borrower was the large corporation so that high interest rates favoured the lower-income saver and limited the profits of business enterprise. This in turn restrained the rate at which the size of the individual enterprise could grow and hence facilitated small business-oriented growth, avoiding an excessive concentration of productive power.

9   CONCLUDING REMARKS

The enormous potential in human energy and intelligence can be nullified by institutionalizing a system that represses such latent energies, or a system (or legal regime) that let one energy offset another, or channels energies into the least productive activities. Therefore, for an economy to achieve sustained high growth, it may have to institutionalize a system that can, first, maximize the energy and effort of each individual member of the society, second, minimize the rate of return on rent-seeking and other non-productive activities and channel individual energies into economic activities that are most productive for the society as a whole, third, maintain an autogenous (self-generated) dynamism and, fourth, minimize the unnecessary frictions among members of the society.[6] This may be achieved by greatly strengthening the motivation of workers and entrepreneurs by maximizing the potential rates of return on their work, investment and enterprise, so as to harness all the latent energies in the society.

The World Bank (1993) attributes the extraordinary growth of the East Asian NICs essentially to macroeconomic stability, high levels of household and corporate savings, market-friendly policies (keeping price distortions within reasonable bounds), some selective 'reward-distributing', 'contest-based' interventions addressed to failures in the market coupled with a fair system of monitoring economic performance (such as credit rationing based on competitive export performance), and universal primary and secondary education. They also note that the institutional context within which policies are implemented is important to their success. We contend, by contrast, that the economic success of the East Asian NICs during the past 30 years has been due to the government's ability: (1) to identify the most productive form of economic activities for the nation's economy – i.e. international specialization in, say, labour-intensive manufacturing taking advantage of the virtually infinite effective demand in the world market; (2) to institutionalize an export-promotion system that maximized the energy and effort of each individual member of society, and channeled those energies into the most productive and most dynamic activities – i.e. export activities; (3) to maintain the autonomous dynamism of the new system by exposing people to incessant price-quality competition on the international market; and (4) to suppress possible social friction by using naked force and also by preventing excessive inequalities in income distribution.

The export-oriented growth of the East Asian NICs maximized the rates of return on productive activities in these countries and hence maximized their motivation to save, work effort, enterprising spirit and innovative activities.[7]

Notes

1.   Kindleberger (1962, pp. 224–6) observes that in face of the fall in wheat price after 1875, the British dismantled its agricultural sector, driving a quarter of a million agricultural workers into urban slums, while the French preserved the highly labour-intensive family farm by raising the tariff on wheat in the name of social stability and social values. In face of changing market conditions, the British pursued adaptation for economic efficiency while in France the traditional specialization in agriculture led to fossilization, involving an external diseconomy. Britain, however, unlike Denmark, the Netherlands or New Zealand, lost a chance to readapt its agriculture at a later stage in favour of dairy products, thus taking advantage of free trade. The question then arises: why is a society, at certain point in time, capable of absorbing short-term social instability which the transitional process may inflict and hence avoiding the worse results in the long run while others resist change and block economic adaptation? This, however, is the kind of question we do not address in this chapter.

2.   Such a proposition may also be empirically verifiable in the near future. Japanese or Korean agriculture, as presently organized, is a serious drag on each country's rapid economic growth. Will the regime of open economy that has been imposed upon Korea and Japan because of their export-orientation indeed induce their agricultural sector to transform, under the impending threat of import competition, into a larger-scale capital-cum-technology-

intensive bio-engineering sector, further accelerating the growth rate of these countries?

3. As Kwon (1994) states, from the very beginning, economic development in Japan was an integral part of nation building: 'Having perceived the urgency and need to catch up the West, and lacking experienced capitalists, the Meiji government itself assumed the role of industrialist by constructing and managing modern factories.'

4. The undervalued domestic currency had also discouraged importation of foreign products and hence enhanced the competitive edge of Japanese manufactures in domestic markets. This aspect was not elaborated by Shinohara.

5. Postal savings, which are mostly time deposits by small and rural savers, amounted to nearly one-quarter of total bank deposits in 1975. They were channeled to the Trust Fund Bureau of the Ministry of Finance and utilized according to the budgetary plan of the Treasury Investment and Loan Authority that financed infrastructure and declining industries (see Tsuru, 1994, p. 109).

6. Baumol (1990) contends that the productive contribution of the society's entrepreneurial activities varies because of their allocation between productive activities such as innovation and unproductive activities such as rent-seeking or organized crime, and also contends that this allocation is heavily influenced by the relative pay-offs (profits) society offers to such activities. Baumol believes that government policy can influence the allocation of entrepreneurship more effectively than it can influence its supply.

7. Export production activities have mostly depended on imported new technologies and imported intermediate and capital goods whose prices mostly reflect their rates of return in advanced countries that are very much below their actual rates of return in these East Asian NICs. This is one of the important sources of high rates of profits and – with consistent underestimation of their expected rates of return – enormous capital gains.

References

Akamatsu, Kaname (1961) 'A Theory of Unbalanced Growth in the World Economy', *Weltwirtschaftliches Archiv*, Heft 2.

Baumol, William J. (1990) 'Entrepreneurship: Productive, Unproductive, and Destructive', *Journal of Political Economy*, vol. 98, no. 5, pt 1, pp. 893–921.

Chia, Siow Yue (1985) 'The Role of Foreign Trade and Investment in the Development of Singapore', in Galenson (1985, pp. 259–97).

Fields, Karl J. (1995) *Enterprise and the State in Korea and Taiwan* (Ithaca: Cornell University Press).

Galenson, Walter (ed.) (1985) *Foreign Trade and Investment: Economic Development in the Newly Industrializing Asian Countries* (Madison: University of Wisconsin Press).

Gold, Thomas B. (1986) *State and Society in the Taiwan Miracle* (Armonk: M. E. Sharpe).

Hong, Wontack (1990) 'Export-Oriented Growth of Korea: A Possible Path to Advanced Economy', *International Economic Journal*, vol. 4, no. 2 (Summer).

—— (1993) 'Trade and Development: The Experience of Korea and Taiwan', in G. Hansson (ed.), *Trade, Growth and Development: The Role of Politics and Institutions* (London: Routledge).

—— (1994) 'Trade and Growth: The Role of Trade in the Catch-Up Process', in *Trade and Growth: A Korean Perspective* (Seoul: Kudara International), pp. 3–24.

Huff, W. G. (1987) 'Patterns in the Economic Development of Singapore', *Journal of Developing Areas*, vol. 21 (April), pp. 305–26.

Ito, Takatoshi and Krueger, Anne O. (eds) (1995) *Growth Theories in Light of the East Asian Experience*, Chicago: NBER and University of Chicago Press.

Kindleberger, Charles P. (1962) *Foreign Trade and the National Economy* (New Haven: Yale University Press).

Komiya, Ryutaro (1992) 'Three Stages of Japan's Industrial Policy after the World War II', *MITI/RI Discussion Paper*, no. 92-DF-13 (March).

Krugman, Paul (1994) 'The Myth of Asia's Miracle', *Foreign Affairs*, vol. 73, no. 6 (November/December), pp. 62–78.

Kuo, Shirley W. Y. and John C. H. Fei (1985) 'Causes and Roles of Export Expansion in the Republic of China', in Galenson (1985), pp. 45–84.

Kwon, Jene (1994) 'The East Asia Challenge to Neoclassical Orthodoxy', *World Development*, vol. 22, no. 4, pp. 635–44.

Lin, Tzong-biau and Victor Mok (1985) 'Trade, Foreign Investment and Development in Hong Kong' in Galenson (1985), pp. 219–56.

Mason, Edward S., *et al.* (1980) *The Economic and Social Modernization of the Republic of Korea* (Cambridge, Mass., Council on East Asian Studies, Harvard University).

Morishima, Michio (1982) *Why Has Japan 'Succeeded'? Western Technology and the Japanese Ethos* (Cambridge: Cambridge University Press).

Murakami, Yasusuke (1982) 'Toward a Socioinstitutional Explanation of Japan's Economic Performance', in Yamamura (1982) pp. 3–46.

Pang, Eng Fong (1982) 'The Distinctive Features of Two City-States' Development: Hong Kong and Singapore, *In Search of an East Asian Development Model, 1982*, pp. 220–37.

Scitovsky, Tibor (1985) 'Economic Development in Taiwan and South Korea: 1965–81', *Food Research Institute Studies*, vol. X, no. 3.

Shinohara, Miyohei (1982) *Industrial Growth, Trade and Dynamic Patterns in the Japanese Economy* (Tokyo: University of Tokyo Press).

Suzuki, Yoshio (1980) *Money and Banking in Contemporary Japan* (New Haven: Yale University Press).

Teranishi, Juro (1992) 'Financial System Reform after the War', in Yutaka Kosai and Juro Terinashi (eds), *Economic Reform and Stabilization Policy in Postwar Japan* (London: Macmillan).

—— (1994) 'Japan: Development and Structural Change of the Financial System', in Y. C. Park and H. T. Patrick (eds), *The Financial Development of Japan, Korea and Taiwan* (New York: Oxford University Press).

Tsuru, S. (1994) *Japan's Capitalism: Creative Defeat and Beyond* (London: Cambridge University Press, 1994).

Vernon, Raymond (1966) 'International Investment and International Trade in the Product Cycle', *Quarterly Journal of Economics* (May).

World Bank (1993) *The East Asian Miracle: Economic Growth and Public Policy* (New York: Oxford University Press).

Yamamura, Kozo (1982) *Policy and Trade Issues of the Japanese Economy* (Tokyo: University of Tokyo Press).

2 Japanese Economic Development: Idiosyncratic or Universal?*

Takatoshi Ito

INTERNATIONAL MONETARY FUND, WASHINGTON,
USA, AND INSTITUTE OF ECONOMIC RESEARCH,
HITOTSUBASHI UNIVERSITY, TOKYO, JAPAN

1 INTRODUCTION

Japanese economic development has been regarded as a 'miracle' or an 'outlier', which requires an explanation based on something other than mainstream economics. Both non-economic factors, such as culture, religion, and social tradition and economic factors, such as lifetime employment and industrial policy, were discussed as unique, exogenous elements that explained the economic success of Japan. It was implied that those factors were so unique that it could not be repeated elsewhere. However, the view of Japan as an idiosyncratic miracle waned in the 1980s, for two reasons: mainstream economics became more sophisticated so that what were regarded as inexplicable economic institutions in Japan came to be explained with regular economic tools with generalized assumptions, while other East Asian economies, with economic institutions and policies similar to those of Japan, sustained a period of high economic growth, reminiscent of Japan's 'miracle' some decades earlier, appearing to show that Japanese economic development could be replicated. This chapter reviews these two strands of thought: what appears unique in Japanese economic development, from the 1950s to the 1980s, in fact makes economic sense and is replicable by other developing economies given the right initial conditions. The role of industrial policy is examined closely.

An extensive literature on how Japan succeeded in achieving economic growth in the 1950s and 1960s can be divided into two groups of contributions: One emphasized the idiosyncratic features of Japanese economy and society (e.g. Morishima, 1982), and the other the principles common to any other industrial economies (e.g. Ito, 1993). Independently, many papers have recently been written on East Asian economies which grew

18

rapidly in the 1980s. Many papers and books (i.e. World Bank, 1993) analyzed common and unique features of the Asian newly industrialized economies (NIEs) (namely Korea, Taiwan, Hong Kong and Singapore) and other fast-growing economies, such as China, Malaysia, Thailand and Indonesia. This chapter, draws on these contributions in the literature.[1]

The rest of this chapter is organized as follows. The next section reviews stylized facts on Japanese and Asian economic development. The following section offers views on industrial policy, especially export promotion, described by the World Bank (1993) as a key for successful growth. The next section attempts to extract common features among the NIEs experiences, mainly in the 1980s, and then analyzes seven keys (basic preconditions) and four deep principles, It offers the view that there is a successful economic system which could be a substitute for or supplement to the competitive, spot market mechanism. The next section reviews the Japanese economic development and industrial policy in the 1950s and 1960s. The last section gives some closing remarks and topics for further study.

2 JAPANESE EXPERIENCE OF ECONOMIC DEVELOPMENT AND INDUSTRIAL POLICY

Traditional Breed of Flying Geese

A salient feature of Japanese economic development was a constant upgrading of industries, a development from simple, light industries to heavy, chemical industries, to high-tech industries. Different industries, in formation, took off from import substitution to export promotion. The way gross imports and gross exports change for a particular industry or commodity shows the pattern of an inverse 'V' (with 'value' on the vertical axis and 'time' on the horizontal axis). The next industry (or commodity) repeats the pattern. This is loosely called the 'flying geese' pattern of economic development (see Akamatsu, 1961).[2]

The 'flying geese' pattern is the stylized fact of economic development, but it implies at least two propositions that are interesting and testable. First, the pattern asserts the existence of standard patterns (or stages) of economic development, from simple, light industries to sophisticated, heavy industries. It had been known that when several conditions are met, particular industries flourish, and economic development (in manufacturing sectors) takes off, and this aspect is called the start of modern economic growth, as defined by Kuznets (1959).[3] What the 'flying geese' suggests is the pattern after the initiation of economic growth, when different industries take charge of production and export growth. Comparative advantage is not given to an economy, but it endogenously changes as the economy develops.

The second implication of the 'flying geese' is the role of exports and foreign direct investment (FDI). The pattern states that one product (or industry) for a country goes from imports to domestic production, to exports. The next step from exports to FDI is called the 'product cycle hypothesis' (see Vernon, 1966). The 'flying geese' hypothesis combined with the product cycle hypothesis completes the life cycle of a particular industry in the economy.

Three reasons explain this industrial sequencing. First, capital is limited in developing countries, so that high-tech industries with a large initial investment (sunk costs) cannot be tolerated. However, this can be surmountable if the country invites in foreign capital. Second, many industries with advanced technology need upstream industries which supply parts and technology. Japanese automobile industries are famous in their close relationships with parts suppliers. They have to be consulted years in advance for new products. The design in process necessitates a long-term relationship between the high-tech manufacturing industries and suppliers. Without nearby upstream industries, reliable in quality and delivery time, the industry may not succeed, but this can be surmountable if neighbouring countries have these upstream industries, and parts can be shipped immediately. Third, the most important factor in industrial sequencing is human capital accumulation. The workforce as well as managerial talents have to be trained in new kinds of industry. Experience in less complicated industries usually gives good experience for the next stage of industrialization.

In fact, Malaysia and Singapore seem to have shortcut some of these stages by inviting in foreign capital and already possessing a highly educated work force.

New Breed of 'Flying Geese'

More recently, the 'flying geese' pattern has been applied to the phenomenon of a group of neighbouring countries (in this case, Asia) climbing up the ladder of economic development in order. One country is a leader, with the most sophisticated high-tech industries and provides machines and technologies to other neighbouring countries. As the leader country moves on to a higher stage of development, some simpler industries in that country lose comparative advantage, most often due to higher wages. The void is filled by the second-tier countries, which leaves yet other industries to the third-tier countries. For a particular industry, a major producer and exporter in the region shifts from the leader country to second-tier countries, and then to third-tier countries, as time goes by. For a particular country, industrial and trade structures change constantly from light, to heavy and chemical, to high-tech industries (the traditional 'flying geese' pattern). And the process is underpinned by extensive trade and investment relationships.

Table 2.1 summarizes experiences in the 'flying geese' pattern, both traditional and more recent. Decades of major growth in production and exports for various industries are identified for Japan and the four 'tigers' – Korea, Taiwan, Hong Kong and Singapore. The 'four tigers' follow roughly, but not exactly, the path that Japan took some years ago. Each nation started with light industries, and then moved to more sophisticated ones.

Japan started its industrialization, or 'modern economic growth' in the Kuznets sense, just before 1900. Its success in the textile and food industries was followed by machinery, metal, chemical, and wood products in

Table 2.1   Flying geese pattern (sequencing of star industries)

	Japan	Korea	Taiwan	Hong Kong	Singapore
Textile	1900–30 1950s		1960s 1970s	Early 1950s (dominant)	Early 1960s 1970s
Clothing, apparel	1950s		1960s 1970s	1950s–1960s	
Toys, watches footwear	1950s		1960s 1970s	1960s–70s	
Refining		(promo) early 1960s			
Steel	1950s–1960s	(promo) late 1960s– early 1970s			
Chemicals	1960s–1970s	Late 1960s Early 1970s	1970s		
Shipbuilding	1960s–1970s	1970s			
Electronics	1970s	Late 1970s 1980s	1980s		1970s
Automobile	1970s–1980s	1980s			
Computers, semiconductors	1980s	Late 1980s			
Banking and finance				Late 1970s 1980s	1980s

Source: Japan, Korea, Taiwan: author's elaboration; Hong Kong, Singapore: Young (1992); the table is reproduced from Ito (1994).

the interwar period.[4] Although the Second World War devastated Japan, the pattern continued. After a brief period of strong exports in textiles in the late 1940s and 1950s, the industrial structure shifted to 'heavy' industries – steel, petrochemicals, shipbuilding and automobiles.

Korea carried out infant industry protection for cement, fertilizers and petroleum refining in the early 1960s; steel and petrochemicals in the late 1960s and early 1970s; shipbuilding, other chemicals, capital goods, and durable consumer items in the mid to late 1970s; and electronics and other components in the 1980s.[5] Import controls kept domestic markets captive of domestic makers, while exports were encouraged.

Singapore also accelerated modernizing industries. Using inward FDI, Singapore successfully combined foreign capital and local labour. In 1978, Singapore launched a programme to promote high-technology industries.

However, too rapid growth is risky. Workers may not be trained for higher skilled jobs, and the learning of technology may not occur fast enough to earn profits. Young (1992) contends that Singapore pursued up-grading too fast. A new industry was promoted before an old industry had started to enjoy benefits (extra production) from learning. This explains how Singapore invested heavily, in comparison to Hong Kong, but that returns to capital remained low.[6] However, this aspect, if true, may not be 'damaging' to Singapore for two reasons. First, growth even just with factor accumulation is better than no growth. Technological progress may be realized at the end of sequence, even if not during it. Second, Singapore has invited foreign investors to build factories, more so than other countries; low return to capital may not be a concern from the Singaporean point of view, at least in the short run. Wage increases do not seem to lag behind other countries.

Japan and East Asia: Similarities and Differences

Experiences in rapid growth in East Asian countries offer important evidence for industrial policies. Korea, Taiwan, Hong Kong and Singapore, often grouped as newly industrialized economies (NIEs) achieved very high economic growth rates after the beginning of the 1980s. Thailand, Malaysia and Indonesia followed a similar pattern of industrialization in the second half of the 1980s.

Until the 1980s, Japan was the only country among non-European countries that had succeeded in industrialization. Any discussion of Japan's success could not have been credibly associated with replicability. However, as more countries successfully industrialized, the importance of industrial policies was considered to be more universal than simply

Japan's 'unique' experience. In the inductive method of analyzing industrial policy, it is important to have more countries in the sample of 'successful' countries.

At first glance, NIEs share obvious common traits. They are poor in natural resources and densely populated. The NIEs are culturally similar – all in the Confucian tradition. The population is highly educated and the saving rate is high. Exports provide a necessary boost for the economy. Except for Hong Kong, the government has intervened in the market to help industrialization. Many people have made the observation that Korea is a second Japan, or that NIEs are emulating Japan's industrial policy. Close examination, however, reveals the experiences of the NIEs and those of Japan to be somewhat different, and NIEs differ among themselves in some important aspects. Korea's industrial structure is dominated by large industrial conglomerates, while Taiwan has retained small-scale businesses. The Korean industry group, known as a '*chaebol*', is similar to the Japanese '*Keiretsu*'. Japan did not rely on foreign capital for its investment, while Korea borrowed from abroad. In fact, Korea borrowed so much that it was one of the most indebted countries in the beginning of the 1980s, but had successfully reduced the debt through rapid growth and exports by the end of the 1980s. Financial institutions in Taiwan are government-owned, while Korean financial institutions are private and strongly connected to large companies in the *chaebol*.

3   INDUSTRIAL POLICY[7]

Definition

If the above description of the economic development pattern is accepted as universal, then there seems to be scope for a government role in economic development. First, preparing conditions for take-off, especially those with public goods, seems to be an obvious task where the government can help. Also the dynamic change in industrial structure may be helped by subsidies, tax breaks, and tariff protection. Government intervention in order to change resource allocation in favour of particular industries is called 'industrial policy'. This is a rather broad definition, but it is often claimed that the most striking aspect of the economic development of the Japanese and other East Asian economies is its development of manufacturing industries and high-tech industries through industrial policy.

Industrial policy includes policies concerning picking winners and helping losers through taxes, subsidies and subsidized loans, promoting exports, protecting domestic markets from imports, setting the exchange rate from sectoral viewpoints and managing labour markets. The government has many ways to intervene in market activities. The mere existence of government, or activities financed by tax revenues, is an intervention from the viewpoint of classical economists. The extreme laissez-faire advocate would like to limit the government's role to national security and maintaining police and legal systems. However, in reality, various governments give preferences to particular industries at the cost of taxpayers, in discrimination against other industries, or with the sacrifice of consumers' surpluses. Industrial policies may take forms of quantitative measures and/or price incentives, or just 'coordination' of information-sharing and research activities. Quantitative measures include not only preferential allocation of capital (credit rationing) and raw materials (or foreign currencies toward their purchase) to a preferred industry, but encouragement of mergers, control of entry and exit to and from the industry, control of expansion of facilities, and a quota (or tariff) on competing imports. These quantitative measures are more controversial.

Price incentives may be given in the form of subsidies for production, purchase guarantees, export subsidies, subsidized (low interest rate) loans, and an accelerated depreciation schedule. Subsidies are often financed by government expenditures. They can be given through commercial banks' lending; however, a common strategy in Japan and Korea was to establish government long-term banks and finance industry-specific long-term loans.

It should be noted that this policy is almost always aimed at nurturing (or phasing out) an industry, not a particular firm. The industry is usually composed of several firms and the firms compete among themselves. This aspect makes Japanese industrial policy distinct from a command economy policy of having one nationalized monopoly. Japanese industrial policy still keeps 'managed competition' among firms, although the industry as a whole is preferentially treated. When the industry is judged to be on the structural decline, or crowded with firms of too small a scale for efficient production size, the government suggests mergers of firms, or an orderly exit. Treating a 'sunset industry' with care is an important part of Japanese industrial policy.

Theoretically, industrial policy can be justified as rectifying market failures. It is easier to justify the role of government in projects involving producing public goods and services and others with large externalities, such as infrastructure investment in telecommunication, transportation, and others. To justify industrial policy beyond infrastructure becomes more controversial, but some work has been done (see, for example, Itoh *et al.*, 1991, for rigorous theoretical arguments). Recent literature on endogenous growth which emphasizes increasing returns also gives a possible rationale for industrial policy. One strand of the literature emphasizes 'endogenous' technological change. Technological progress can be explained as a function of past output, capital formation or human capital accumulation – more output will enhance learning-by-doing. In this kind of framework, subsidies to research and development, possibly funded by long-term bonds, can yield higher output in the future exceeding the market interest rate, so that it is socially desirable in the long run.[8] Another strand of the literature emphasizes the simultaneous development of several industries at a critical stage of economic development.[9] According to this theory, it is important to orchestrate and convince several industries to take aggressive investment projects at the same time. Markets alone may not produce such a coordination. However, new growth theory is not fully consistent with the empirical observations described in the preceding section of this chapter (see also Ito, 1994).

Export Promotion: Why Does it Work?

As emphasized above, one of the salient features of Japanese economic development was a constant upgrading of industries from simple light to heavy chemical to high-tech. Each industry which became an engine for economic growth was achieved through success in the world market. Successful exports are identified as a key for Asian economies in the World Bank study (1993).

The Japanese experience in export promotion is well known. A similar pattern is observed in East Asia: Korea, Taiwan and Singapore were successful in promoting industries in their export-promotion policy.[10] In Korea, 13 items were targeted for exports in 1965: silk, cotton, pottery, rubber, radios and other electrical goods, wool, plywood, clothing, leather, handicrafts and miscellaneous goods,[11] and the list was later expanded. The composition of exports drastically changed from simple manufactured goods to heavy and electronic goods in the following 30 years. The export-promoting organization, the Korea Trade Promotion Corporation (KOTRA), was established, and general trading companies were encouraged. Exporters received direct tax incentives, indirect subsidies through policy loans (low interest loans), import duty exemptions for production inputs and some non-pecuniary awards.[12] It is estimated that these direct and indirect subsidies cancelled out the adverse effect of currency overvaluation in the late 1960s.[13] Export targets were set commodity by commodity, and export activities were closely discussed between government officials and business leaders. The highest achievers in exports were rewarded with more allocation of policy loans, less surveillance on tax assessment and non-pecuniary national awards.

Taiwan also successfully implemented an export-oriented policy after failure in the import-substitution programme in the 1950s. Export-promoting measures and targeting industries introduced from the 1960s included free trade zones, preferential loans, tax exemptions and tax holidays. Although some trade import protection was maintained until the mid-1980s, the list remained short. Banks are state-owned and provided capital to serve political purposes. Toward the end of the 1980s, the export share of GDP reached 60 per cent.

Singapore also tried import substitution in the 1960s, in vain. Toward the end of the 1960s, policy reform occurred. The Development Bank of Singapore expanded the amount of loans and shareholdings, with emphasis on the electrical machinery and petroleum products industries.[14] Singapore also encouraged inward FDI, in contrast to Korea which received foreign capital but not in the form of direct investment. Regulations on behaviour of foreign multinational firms, such as repatriation of profits and local content of products, were avoided. Tax incentives, such as tax holidays, were introduced in 1967. Foreign firms (with more than 50 per cent foreign equity) accounted for 82 per cent of manufacturing exports in 1984.

In sum, the East Asian countries succeeded in their rapid economic growth due to strong exports. The reasons seem obvious. It is necessary to expand externally for an industry with strong scale economies if domestic markets are small. For resource-poor countries, it is imperative to find exporting industries if the countries' growing needs for imports are to be financed without being heavily indebted. It is desirable to find-export items with high income elasticities so that exports will grow with the income of the importing countries. Upgrading of export industries is desirable.

The basic findings of the World Bank study and other background papers (including Ito, 1993) are twofold. First, a successful introduction of industrial policies is based on several prerequisites in the social and political environment as well as economic conditions. These prerequisites are derived from facts observed in Japan and the East Asian countries. It is most important to have the infrastructure (electricity, road and rail, literacy, safe and clean living conditions) in place. Second, there are four fundamental factors for the successful design of an economic system, whether a competitive, free market economy or a system with government intervention. (It should be noted that even among the industrialized countries today, there are many government programmes, and we do not observe a 'pure' competitive free market economy. In this sense, the comparison is not fair. The question may be better phrased if it asks what is the most effective, least costly way of government intervention.) Any successful economic system should have a reward system to motivate economic agents for efforts and hard work (*incentives*), a monitoring device so that the reward system is free from cheating (*monitor*), a politico–economic structure for correcting mistakes based on some balance of power (*check and balance*) and a mechanism for competition, although it is not necessarily in 'markets', (*competition*). A successful industrial policy is an alternative to the market mechanism to achieve these principles.

Export promotion is a subsidy (directly or indirectly) to a sector that the government identifies as having the possibility to export its products. There is a key reason why export promotion, as opposed to import substitution or some other type of industrial policy, works. In any government intervention, monitoring effort is a difficult task. Without competition and judgement in the market, producers tend to be lax in their efforts for innovation and quality control. In the case of exports, 'judges' of successful product development and quality control are in the world market. It is relatively easy for a government to determine whether the project was successful. In the case of a closed, planned economy, or import substitution, domestic consumers and users become captive customers and producers may not have incentive for effort. Since the firm is exposed to competition in the world market, and success is judged by customers in foreign countries, limiting entry to, or competition in the domestic market does not lessen market pressure. As long as the industry is exposed to competition from abroad or in foreign markets, an attempt to limit competition to nurture an industry with scale economies has a better chance of succeeding.

Of course, there are opposing views, both theoretical and empirical, to the export promotion strategy. It is hard to decide which industry to promote. However, for a developing country that follows the 'flying geese' pattern, it is easier to pick an industry that is losing competitiveness in countries similar in factor endowments and economic environment, just ahead of this country. In this sense the 'flying geese' pattern plays an important role. Peer pressure and competition from neighbouring countries work better than a model in a different part of the country. Regional development, either in Europe in the nineteenth century, or in Asia in the 1980s, benefits from market pressure from neighbouring countries.

4   INDUSTRIAL POLICY IN JAPAN: EMPIRICAL PERSPECTIVE[5]

Meiji Government in the Late Nineteenth century

The Meiji government, after more than two decades of isolation policy, opened Japan to the rest of the world. Having realized that Japan had been

left behind, due to the isolation policy, in terms of western power in technologies, the Meiji government embarked on an 'industrial policy', under
the national motto of 'wealthy nation, and strong army'. The Meiji government sent government missions to Europe and the United States to
study and import modern machines and technology for infrastructure, such
as railroad, electricity, water supply, mail and telegram services and port
facilities, as well as public institutions such as a central bank. In fact, these
infrastructure investments are credited by economic historians as a policy
that propelled Japan into a growth path, compared to Thailand (Siam) that
was in a similar initial condition in the 1870s but did not grow.[16]

In addition, the Meiji government encouraged the textile industries to
become competitive by building 'model' factories. Although raw silk was
the most important commodity to earn foreign exchange, the domestic
cotton industry was not competitive. The government aimed at developing
silk products, adding value to raw silk before exporting, and substituting
imports of cotton yarn. The government built 'model' factories for silk
reeling (the Tomioka mill in 1872, and two others in the decade), and
small-scale, water-powered cotton-spinning factories in the 1870s.

These model factories were later sold to private enterprise, mainly
because the government had a budget deficit problem (and resulting
inflation in 1878–80). Model factories were never profitable. For example,
the real success of the cotton-spinning industry came when the privately-
financed Osaka Spinning Mill (*Osaka Boseki*) introduced large-scale operation with steam power. This was the beginning of the long road for
'flying geese'. Although the model factories were not successful as business ventures they may have provided the training centre for managers
and workers who later went to the private sector. The government also
pointed the direction of industrial development – i.e. picking the winners –
although it failed to become a manager itself.[17] Policies by the Meiji government are usually credited as successful in laying the foundations for
sustained growth. The average annual rate of economic growth from the
Meiji Restoration to the 1930s exceeded 3 per cent per annum. However,
human capital, commercial capital, the national road network and agricultural technology accumulated during the Tokugawa period cannot be un-
derestimated.[18] The literacy rate at the end of Tokugawa period was
probably higher than some of the developing countries in the 1990s.
Commercial wealth was accumulated by merchants and money exchang-
ers, who were at the bottom of the Tokugawa social pecking order, especially in the Osaka area. The road system was established through the
local lords' periodic travels to the Tokugawa Shogun capital Edo (now
Tokyo). The technological level in the silk industry was competitive even

from the beginning of the Meiji era. The success of the Japanese economic development, from the 1870s to the 1930s is thus rooted in the foundation established in the early years of the Meiji government in addition to the legacy of the Tokugawa society.

Priority Production System (*Keisha seisan hoshiki*)[19]

The industrial policy after the Second World War, which destroyed a half to two-thirds of productive capacity, was the priority production system (*keisha seisan hoshiki*). Coal and steel were the two industries to be promoted. Production of coal, which was the major source of energy at the time, had to be increased for economic growth at large. Coal production in 1946 was down by 40 per cent from the peak during the war, partly due to the shortage of coal miners and bad maintenance. All imported oil, although a very small amount, was allocated to the steel industry. Produced steel was used in the coal industry to build coal mines and then coal was allocated back to the steel industry. Funds from the Reconstruction Bank were allocated to the coal industry. The growth cycle of coal and steel continued until 1948 with a goal of 30 million tons of coal, up by one-third in three years. This plan was much like socialistic quantitative planning, rather than any type of industrial policy. It served quickly to regain production levels of coal and steel necessary to provide for other industries. The policy is usually credited in the literature with establishing a good start for postwar industrialization.

Industrial Policy in the 1950s

After transitional instability, first high inflation and then the tough anti-inflation measures that caused recession in the late 1940s, more normal conditions had been restored by 1951. The Korean War that started in 1950 created an unexpected rise in demand for goods produced in Japan. Several measures were taken to promote steel, coal, electric and shipping industries. These industries were identified as growing and potentially leading industries to earn foreign exchange. Capital accumulation was encouraged in the key industries. Four types of policies were important: low interest rate loans, tax incentives, foreign exchange allocation and technology imports.[20] The policy was crafted by the Ministry of International Trade and Industry (MITI), but regulated by the Ministry of Finance (MoF), the budget agency.

First, for the targeted industry, low interest loans from the Japan Development Bank (*Nihon Kaihatsu Ginko*), established in April 1951 as a Government Agency, were allocated. Commercial banks (city banks) also lend to those industries, taking lending from the Japan Development Bank as a signal of a growth industry. As the banking industry is under the control and supervision of the Ministry of Finance, a major part of financing industrial policy had to be approved by the Ministry of Finance. The Export–Import Bank provided exporters with financing. The Enterprise Rationalization Promotion Law, enacted in 1952, gave an accelerated schedule for depreciation of plants and equipment.

The foreign exchange allocation system, which was put in place at the time the single exchange rate of 360 yen/dollar was introduced in April 1949, played an important role for industry to obtain imported raw materials. This system effectively acted as an import control, since the government had discretion to limit imported goods and parts of particular industries. The automobile industry was protected by this system throughout the 1950s.

Foreign technology imports were encouraged. Introduction and dissemination of foreign policy was coordinated by the MITI. The objective of the control was both to disseminate information of foreign technology for further growth and to keep competition among the oligopolies alive.[21]

Industrial Policy in the 1960s

The decade of the 1960s is known as a heyday of high-speed growth. The income-doubling plan set out by the Ikeda cabinet was not only achieved but carried out in seven rather than 10 years. The challenge was to promote a sequence of industries as prime exporters in order to expand continuously. Japan was required to abandon import restrictions and other types of quantitative measures as it became a member of multilateral institutions for industrial countries (such as the OECD) and an IMF Article VIII member. Infant industry protection, consciously or subconsciously employed to ensure domestic market protection, had to be modified, but just in time for many industries which had turned into exporting industries. It seems that only after domestic manufacturers became strong enough were import restrictions lifted: the restrictions on buses and trucks were lifted in 1961, those on colour TVs in 1964, on passenger automobiles in 1965, on colour film in 1971, on cash registers in 1973, on large-memory integrated circuits in 1974, and on computers in 1975. Could these Japanese industries have achieved the same dominance in world markets without import protection during their infancies?

The objective of industrial policy in the 1960s was to structurally strengthen several key industries, through mergers and the orchestration of 'orderly' capacity expansions. The specialization and coordination of small and medium-sized companies were encouraged. These measures were taken for fear that Japanese industries were too small in scale and were not competitive in the world market.

Industrial Policy in the 1970s and 1980s

Many researchers agree that industrial policies underwent great transformation in the 1970s. The floating exchange rate system made industrial policy through foreign exchange controls impossible. Many Japanese firms in manufacturing sectors became top-ranked in the world market, so that their needs for protection and promotion became less important. Then, MITI's policy objectives in the 1970s included environmental protection (or pollution control, as it was called then), and stricter application of anti-trust policies. The role of MITI gradually shifted toward using the market mechanism and deregulation. However, the process of dismantling some import protection and cartel protection was slow to proceed. For example, gasoline imports became possible only in the late 1980s (a legacy of a policy promoting petrochemical processing in Japan). Industries, such as coal mining and shipbuilding, were in the long process of restructuring. These industries, once 'sunrise', became 'sunset' industries, and MITI was involved in drafting their long-term readjustment.

MITI's aim in the 1970s and 1980s gradually shifted to promoting high-tech industries, for example, computers and semiconductors. However, tools to promote high-tech are quite different from the tools used to promote heavy industries. Cooperative research between government and industries plays an important role in high-tech industries rather than quantity planning and low interest loans. However, import restrictions – not by import permits or tariffs but by non-tariff barriers such as technological standards and government procurement procedures – seem to have helped domestic computer makers. This set the stage for trade conflict with the United States in the 1980s.[22]

Industrial policy has thus changed its objectives and tools over time, both in selection of industries and tools of the policy. Japan has constantly upgraded its main engine from textile to light manufacturing, to heavy manufacturing and to high-tech industries. The sequencing of industries is important.

The socialist quantitative controls disappeared in the 1960s and even the low interest policy and import restrictions had become obsolete by the end of the 1970s. In the 1990s, MITI's industrial policy is indirect (or market-friendly) and more 'catalytic' to private sectors. Which tools should be employed depends on a number of factors: how certain (or risky) the industry is to become a sunrise one; how the domestic and financial markets are willing to lend to the industry; and what the exchange rate regime is, to name a only few.

Motivations

Did the MITI in the 1950s and 1960s employ Japanese industrial policy after weighing the costs and benefits of industrial policy? Did the MITI pick winner after winner in finding targeted industries? It may not have done.

I will suggest a new interpretation – that industrial policy had the priority goal of earning foreign exchange. The utmost concern of the Japanese economy from the end of the Second World War to the mid-1960s was the constraint of foreign exchange. Since Japan is poor in natural resources, it is necessary to import raw materials and some foodstuffs. In order to pay for necessary imports, import controls were imposed for non-essential goods, such as 'luxury' consumption durables. Limiting imports of non-essentials is not enough, however, because as the economy grows, it needs ever-increasing raw materials, such as iron ore and oil for manufacturing production.

Four kinds of policy directions were sought. First, any exports were promoted, because the foreign exchange earned was used to purchase more raw materials. Second, in order to minimize spending of foreign exchange to pay for imports, it was better to import goods as raw as possible, and manufacture in Japan. This led to a policy of importing crude oil but banning petroproducts, such as gasoline. Importation of technology had also to be coordinated to save foreign currency expenditure. Third, a policy preference was given to manufacturing industries with higher value-added content. As Japan imported raw materials and exported finished goods, it was perceived desirable that industries contained a higher amount of the value-added, that is the difference in value between finished products and raw materials. Fourth, for the long-run growth of the economy, it was perceived necessary to develop products with a higher income elasticity. If Japan specialized in products for which world demand would not grow in the future, exports would not expand. If industries are nurtured for products for which world demand increases at a rate exceeding the income growth rate, then exports will automatically increase.

In sum, Japan's industrial policy was a result (or a by-product) of export-oriented and growth-oriented policies when the exchange rate was overvalued and no sovereign loans were available in the world financial market.

5 LESSONS

One of the interesting features of East Asian economic development is industrial sequencing, or the 'flying geese' pattern. Many countries have upgraded their industries in an orderly fashion. First, the textile industry flourishes. Light industry follows. Usually, heavy industries, such as steel, shipbuilding, transportation vehicle industries, and various chemical industries, have to wait for the appropriate time – the textile and light machinery industries' success in the world market. In fact, this pattern was initiated by England, the first nation to achieve industrial revolution, and was copied by Japan, Korea and Taiwan as discussed in the preceding section. Latecomers usually speed up the process, but the intermediate steps seem not to be missed.[23] This kind of industry sequencing still seems to be necessary, as argued above. Industrial policy is only a part of the overall strategy for development. The success of industrial policy depends on the political and economic infrastructure. If applied in the wrong context and environment, the policy is bound to fail.

Ito (1993) argued that the basic principles for success are the same for the 'free-market' approach. The market mechanism works because it encourages manufacturers on the supply side to generate innovation based on monetary incentives, because competition forces them to put in their best effort. Any successful economic system should have these elements: A reward system which works as *incentive*, *competition* and *monitoring* to encourage effort, and a *check and balance* of power to prevent any political corruption and distortion in resource allocation.

Industrial policy features in some East Asian countries are linked to these four principles. The basic mechanisms for success are common, and this aspect should be emphasized. Industrial policy is an alternative way to achieve the same outcome (efficient allocation of resources) as the market mechanism. 'The difference is whether decisions are left entirely to the market or whether government guidance should be provided at the key stage of economic development. The trade-off comes in specific circumstances.

The strongest argument for government intervention is that the market mechanism is known to be deficient in achieving efficient allocation in terms of long-term, risky projects. Risk should be hedged in the contingent contract markets in order to achieve dynamic, efficient allocation of resources. It may also be difficult for the market to achieve an optimal allocation of resources if technology has increasing returns to scale.

Other arguments for government intervention include the case of social infrastructure (known as public goods), and regulations when the quality of goods and services is uncertain. These cases are known as market failure.

Of course, markets can be created and expanded to correct for these market failures in specific environments (risks, public goods, uncertainty and scale economies). However, in the particular stage of economic development, government intervention seems to offer an alternative. In the following, the link between the four principles, market failures, and common features of industrial policy in Japan and East Asia will be discussed.

Although they may not be exhaustive or fail-safe, four principles summarize the common elements of success. Export promotion and sequencing seems to conflict with the principles least, while the government intervenes to accelerate economic development. The reasons behind these principles and the possibility of applying them to other countries were also discussed. Industrial policy is judged helpful in a certain development stage, when it is administered correctly. The key is *export promotion* (not protection from imports). Exports provide competition in the world market and quality monitoring, when domestic markets may be in less developed states to provide competition and monitoring. Managers and employees will be trained to become competitive and innovative in the world market, and initial incentives for exports are justified on these grounds.

Notes

*   This chapter is based largely on my previous work, referred to in the text. The views expressed in this chapter are the author's own, and do not necessarily reflect those of institutions which the author has been affiliated with in the past or present.

1. This chapter reiterates views given in my earlier work (Ito, 1992, 1993) without attribution in every instance.
2. See also an example presented in Ito (1992, pp. 24–6) without mentioning the name 'flying geese'.
3. See also Rostow (1960) for the idea of 'take-off'.
4. See Minami (1986, Chapter 5).
5. The list is from Westphal (1990, p. 47).
6. '[B]y the early 1980s, the real return on Singapore's massive capital stock was below 10 per cent [per] annum ... U.S. corporations in Singaporean manufacturing in the early 1980s enjoyed a return well over 30% per annum. This suggests that the return on the Singaporean-owned segment of the capital stock is well below the average return estimated further below' (Young, 1992, p. 24).
7. This section draws on Ito (1993).
8. See, for example, Romer (1986, 1990).
9. See, for example, Romer (1986, 1990), Murphy, Shleifer and Vishny (1989), and Shleifer and Vishny (1988) for early contribution to this literature, and see Ito and Krueger (1995) and Barro and Sala-i-Martin (1995) for recent surveys and contributions.

10. See Noland (1990), Young (1992) and Westphal (1990), to name only a few.
11. See Kim (1993) and Amsden (1989).
12. 'Exporters were provided exemptions from duties on imported inter-mediates, tax incentives, preferential access to capital, special depreciation allowances on imported capital equipment, and a variety of nonpecuniary awards' (Noland, 1990, p. 41).
13. As quoted in Westphal (1990, p. 45); Westphal and Kim (1982, pp. 217–45) estimated that benefits amounted to more than 8 per cent of total merchandise exports, while the degree of currency overvaluation was about 9 per cent. Thus, it is argued that exports were encouraged through 'neutral policies' (Westphal, 1990) with the exception of infant industries. Westphal uses the term 'neutral' to mean 'the absence of differential effects on the allocation of resources among activities relative to the putative circumstances of perfectly free trade'.
14. See Young (1992).
15. See a similar summary in Ito (1992, pp. 196–205).
16. The following excerpts from Yasuba and Dhiravegin (1985) summarize their findings:

> Siam [Thailand] and Japan shared striking similarities when they entered the modern period. In the preceding period, both had closed themselves to most western contact, and then were more or less forced open to trade, Siam in 1855 and Japan in 1859; yet both remained independent. Both started to modernize (westernize) in contemporary reigns. In Siam, this took place under Chulalongkorn (1868–1910), in Japan, during Meiji (1968–1912). For most of the period, both had to trade under procedures prescribed by the western powers. In the late 19th century, trade expanded rapidly and the terms of trade improved considerably. Initial trade patterns were similar; both exported mostly primary commodities in exchange for manufactured goods.
>
> Yet development was widely divergent. Siam gradually gave up most of its early industries and became more and more specialized in the production of a few primary commodities, particularly rice. Commercialization proceeded, but neither economic development nor industrialization occurred to any significant degree. In Japan, domestic producers soon offered substitutes for imports and eventually some of these industries became exporters. (p. 19)
>
> The Japanese government was very heavily involved in developmental policy, whereas relative inaction characterized the Siamese government. Both invested in infrastructure, but Japan went much further.
>
> The Meiji Restoration and related changes drastically redistributed income and opportunity, laying the foundation on which the private sector grew. Development was enhanced by such measures as model factories, subsidies of early private factories, and provision of extension and exposition services in an effort to close the gap in knowledge, as well as a strong emphasis on infrastructure and education. (p. 30)
>
> In contrast, a base for economic development appears to have been lacking in Siam … The government did not actively create a base for development. The infrastructure was far from adequate and serious efforts to learn from abroad or to propagate knowledge domestically

were lacking. Moreover, patrimonial institutions reduced initiative. (p. 31)

17. See Ito (1992, pp. 31–3) for the *Osaka Boseki* and the cotton-spinning industry and Minami (1986, p. 140) for the Tomioka silk-reeling factory. See also Minami (1986, pp. 131–40) and Francks (1992, pp. 40–6) for the textile industry development and the role of policy in general.
18. See Ito (1992, pp. 18–19) and references thereof.
19. This section summarizes Nakamura (1982, pp. 32–5).
20. See Nakamura (1981, p. 45) for these arguments.
21. Licences to import foreign technology were used to restrict entry into various industries and keep individual oligopolists from gaining excessive leads over their rivals.
22. See Prestowitz (1988) and Tyson (1992) for US–Japan competition in the semiconductor industry.
23. An analogy is the idea that 'ontogeny recapitulates phylogeny' (see Ito, 1992, p. 38, n. 18). Another analogy is that if a gradient of aircraft ascent is too steep, the aircraft loses the lift, and crashes. Although an analogy helps us to visualize the concept, it does not help too much in economic analysis.

References

Akamatsu, Kaname (1961) 'A Theory of Unbalanced Growth in the World Economy', *Weltwirtschaftliches Archiv*, Heft 2.
Amsden, Alice H. (1989) *Asia's Next Giant: South Korea and Late Industrialization* (Oxford: Oxford University Press).
Barro, Robert and Xavier Sala-i-Martin (1995). *Economic Growth* (New York: McGraw-Hill).
Francks, Penelope (1992) *Japanese Economic Development* (London: Routledge).
Ito, Takatoshi (1992) *The Japanese Economy* (Cambridge, Mass.: MIT Press).
———(1993) 'Industrial Policy for Development: 'Japanese Experience and Replicability', World Bank, part of Asia's Economic Miracle project, unpublished document.
——— (1994) 'Comments on John Page 'The East Asian Miracle: Four Lessons for Development Policy', *NBER Macroeconomic Annual*, pp. 274–80.
——— (1995) 'Comments on William Easterly, "Explaining Miracles: Growth Regressions Meet the Gang of Four"', in T. Ito and A. O. Krueger (1995).
Ito, Takatoshi and Anne O. Krueger (eds) (1995) *Growth Theories in Light of the East Asian Experience* (Chicago: NBER and University of Chicago Press).
Itoh, Motoshige, Kazuharu Kiyono, Masahiro Okuno-Fujiwara and Kotaro Suzumura (eds) (1991) *Economic Analysis of Industrial Policy* (New York: Academic Press).
Kim, K.S. (1993) 'President Park Chung Hee's Economic Development Policy', presented at the World Bank Colloquium on 'Lessons from East Asia' (25–26 March).
Komiya, Ryutaro, Masahiro Okuno and Kotaro Suzumura (eds) (1987) *Industrial Policy of Japan* (San Diego: Academic Press).
Kuznets, Simon (1959) *Six Lectures on Economic Growth* (New York: Free Press).
——— (1971) *The Economic Growth of Nations* (Cambridge, Mass.: Harvard University Press).

Minami, Ryoshin (1986) *The Economic Development of Japan: A Quantitative Study* (New York: St Martin's Press).

Morishima, Michio (1982) *Why Has Japan 'Succeeded'? Western Technology and the Japanese Ethos* (Cambridge: Cambridge University Press).

Murphy, Kevin M., Andrei Shleifer and Robert W. Vishny (1989) 'Industrialization and the Big Push', *Journal of Political Economy*, vol. 97, no. 5, pp. 1003–26.

Nakamura, Takafussa (1981) *The Postwar Japanese Economy* (Tokyo: University of Tokyo Press).

Noland, Marcus (1990) *Pacific Basin Developing Countries: Prospects for the Future* (Washington, DC: Institute for International Economics).

Prestowitz, Clyde V. Jr. (1988) *Trading Places* (New York: Basic Books).

Romer, Paul M. (1986) 'Increasing Returns and Long-Run Growth', *Journal of Political Economy*, vol. 94 (October), pp. 1002–37.

——— (1990) 'Endogenous Technological Change', *Journal of Political Economy*, vol. 98, no. 5, pt 2, pp. S71–S102.

Rostow, W. W. (1960) *The Stages of Economic Growth: A Non-Communist Manifesto* (Cambridge: Cambridge University Press).

Shleifer, Andrei and Robert W. Vishny (1988) 'The Efficiency of Investment in the Presence of Aggregate Demand Spillovers', *Journal of Political Economy*, vol. 96 (December), pp. 1221–31.

Tyson, Laura D'Andrea (1992) *Who's Bashing Whom? Trade Conflict in High-technology Industries* (Washington, DC: Institute for International Economics).

Vernon, Raymond (1966) 'International Investment and International Trade in the Product Cycle', *Quarterly Journal of Economics*, vol. 80.

Westphal, Larry E. (1990) 'Industrial Policy in an Export-Propelled Economy: Lessons from South Korea's Experience', *Journal of Economic Perspectives*, vol. 4, no. 3 (Summer), pp. 41–59.

Westphal, Larry and Kim, Kwang Suk (1982) 'Korea', in Bela Balassa *et al.* (eds), *Development Strategies in Semi-Industrial Countries* (Baltimore Md: Johns Hopkins University Press for The World Bank), pp. 212–79.

World Bank (1993) *The East Asian Miracle: Economic Growth and Public Policy* (New York: Oxford University Press).

Yasuba, Yasukichi and Likhit Dhiravegin (1985) 'Initial Conditions, Institutional Changes, Policy, and Their Consequences: Siam and Japan, 1850–1914', in Kazushi Ohkawa and Gustav Ranis (eds), *Japan and the Developing Countries* (Oxford: Blackwell).

Young, Alwyn (1992) 'A Tale of Two Cities: Factor Accumulation and Technical Change in Hong Kong and Singapore', *Macroeconomic Annual 1992* (Cambridge, Mass.: National Bureau of Economic Research and MIT Press).

3 Factor Endowments and Policies in South Asian Growth

Ashok Guha

SCHOOL OF INTERNATIONAL STUDIES, JAWAHARLAL
NEHRU UNIVERSITY, NEW DELHI, INDIA

1 INTRODUCTION

A notable common feature of the South Asian economies has been their uniformly rapid growth over the last decade or so. Through the 1980s and 1990s, South Asia's growth performance as a region ranks next only to the miracle economies of the Pacific rim (including, of course, China). Set against the canvas of protracted stagnation in the OECD countries, of the 'lost decade' in Latin America and of the perpetual crisis of most of Africa, South Asia's economic success is both spectacular and surprising.

Between 1980 and 1993, the GDP of South Asia grew at an average rate of 5.2 per cent, far above the world rate of 2.9 per cent. The rich countries meanwhile grew at 2.9 per cent, a rate buoyed up by the inclusion of the East Asian economies of Singapore, Hongkong and Japan. The less affluent countries of sub-Saharan Africa achieved only 1.6 per cent, Latin America and the Caribbean only 1.9 per cent and North Africa and the Middle East only 2.2 per cent. Only the astronomical 7.8 per cent of East Asia and the Pacific surpassed the South Asian record (World Bank, 1995).

The rapid growth of South Asia was not closely linked to any specific policy regime. India developed through the entire decade of the 1980s at 5.5 per cent under a policy regime which, if less regimented than in the 1970s, still included the highest rates of tariff and the most byzantine system of trade and industrial regulation outside the socialist world. After the crisis of 1991 and two years of stabilization, it resumed its former trajectory of growth at a very similar rate, though within a radically transformed policy framework. The Indian experience merely repeats the South Asian pattern. Bangladesh (1987) and Pakistan (1988) both passed through major policy turning points induced by conditionalities on IMF loans needed to tide over desperate foreign exchange crises. In both cases, the crisis and its management produced a temporary pause in growth. But after this two-year blip, economic growth returned to its former pace without notable acceleration or deceleration – Bangladesh to a 4.5 per cent rate, Pakistan to a much faster tempo of 6.5 per cent.

None of this indicates that economic policy is unimportant. Indeed the evidence may be interpreted to imply that the rates of the earlier period could not be sustained within the narrow confines of the earlier policy framework, that this was what produced the crisis and the policy transformation which made subsequent growth at the same rate possible. However, it does appear that the momentum behind South Asian growth is not policy-generated. Other factors have driven the growth process though the adaptability of the economy to the tempo of growth has been conditioned by policy.

2 THE ARGUMENT

It is our argument that factor endowments, particularly the abundance of labour, has been the basis of South Asian growth, as indeed of East Asian growth in an earlier period. The point may be illustrated very simply. In a two-good two-factor constant returns to scale closed economy, the profit rate is inversely related to the wage level; the wage profit rate ratio in turn is directly related to the price of labour-intensive goods relative to capital intensive goods. Further, by the modified Rybczynski theorem (Rybczynski, 1955, Guha, 1963), the relative composition of output at any commodity price ratio is a monotonic function of the factor endowment ratio; the more abundant is labour relative to capital, the larger at any given commodity price ratio will be the proportion of the labour-intensive output to the capital-intensive one.

This, of course, is only a supply effect. The impact on equilibrium commodity prices depends also on demand factors, specifically on the income elasticity of demand. If the income elasticity of demand for labour-intensive goods is equal to or greater than unity, a high labour: capital ratio will lead to a low equilibrium price of labour-intensive goods relative to capital-intensive ones. It is of course more likely that the demand for labour-intensive goods will be relatively income inelastic. In that event, a higher labour: capital ratio will lead through lower *per capita* income to a pattern of demand more biased towards labour-intensive goods: the demand effect will then work against the supply effect, and the impact on prices depends on the balance of the two.

The empirical generalization is that relatively labour-abundant economies would have relatively lower prices of labour-intensive goods under autarchy. They would in consequence have lower wages but higher rates of profit. A high rate of profit induces a high propensity to save and invest. Low wages encourage labour-intensive techniques in each industry while lower prices of labour-intensive goods induce consumer substitution in their favour (in addition to the income effect mentioned in the previous paragraph). Both factors reduce the capital: labour ratio. A higher propensity to save and invest and a lower capital: labour ratio both accelerate growth.

The argument is not in any way linked to a Kaldor–Pasinetti savings function with high rates of profit implying high profit shares and, therefore, an income distribution favourable to saving. The Cambridge logic in this context would require a less-than-unit aggregate elasticity of substitution; otherwise, lower wages may end up producing a higher share of labour and a lower aggregate saving ratio *à la* Pasinetti. Our argument runs not in terms of the supply effect of income distribution on capacity to save, but on its demand effects on incentives to save and invest. The rate of growth is thus an increasing function of the labour: capital endowment ratio.

However, if the economy is now opened up to free international trade and begins to export labour-intensive goods precisely because the relative world price of such goods exceeds their domestic price under autarchy the consequence predicted by the Stolper–Samuelson theorem (Stolper and Samuelson, 1941) is a fall in the rate of return to capital. Real income will certainly rise. But this will be a once-for-all effect. The abiding consequences will be rise in wage rates but a decline in the rates of profit and of growth.

This is, of course, an artefact. We have assumed that the autarchic economy was functioning on its production possibility frontier and that returns to scale are constant. We have also assumed that the growth rate is primarily a function of the rate of profit so that the increasing affluence of labour in an open economy does not accelerate growth. It is of course in the areas of scale economies and increase in X-efficiency that the principal gains of a liberalised economic regime may lie.

Further, a model with constant returns to scale offers no clue to the prolonged stagnation of British India, despite its abysmal wages. Increasing returns phenomena are essential to an understanding of our colonial backwardness. They also underlie the logic of the earlier regime of the typical South Asian process of import-substituting industrialization (ISI) which was most fully articulated in Indian planning strategy over nearly 40 years.

3 MARKET FAILURE AND THE ORIGIN OF ISI

The ISI regime developed primarily as a prescription for the forced development of a poor densely populated economy. Industrial markets in such an economy were small and inelastic: domestic manufacturers could not achieve economies of scale in such markets, and if they sought to export for this purpose, they encountered high distribution costs (on account of transport and information), exchange risks and the uncertainties of dependence on a foreign market in which they had no influence on policy formation. They tended therefore to be ousted by large-scale producers located in rich markets abroad. They did, of course, have the advantage of low costs of unskilled labour: but in modern manufacturing this was seldom decisive, and given the externalities involved in skill formation rarely translated into cheap skills. The few industries which were intensive in unskilled labour – garments and textiles for example – were also the strongholds of organized labour in the advanced countries and tended therefore to restrict exports from the poor to the rich countries. Poor countries, therefore, were believed to lack the potential for comparative advantage in manufacturing.

In primary production, on the other hand, population pressure on natural resources limited the range and variety of export possibilities. It was the emptier countries and continents, whether rich or poor, that dominated the world's primary markets.

Populous, backward regions were therefore seen to be ill equipped for large-scale production and export of either manufactures or primaries. Investment and profit opportunities appeared limited and the possibilities of growth through the market accordingly circumscribed.

But the pressures for development in independent India brooked no such constraints. They arose from two sets of imperatives: (1) the pressure of an exploding population on *per capita* income, living standards, nutrition and health, and (2) a revolution of rising expectations induced by the demonstration effect of advanced consumption patterns on the Indian psyche. Given these compulsions, in a milieu of market failure, forced development through state action became a political necessity.

Development policy involved infrastructural investment to widen supply bottlenecks in agriculture as well as the stimulation of demand in industry. Four main strategies of demand expansion were employed.

(1) the direct injection of government demand at key points of the economy
(2) support of the industrial profit rate through comprehensive protection of manufactures, subsidies, etc.

(3)   redistribution of income through the massive expansion of govern-
       ment and semi-government employment to create a homogeneous
       middle class market for manufactures
(4)   synchronisation through planning of investment over a wide spec-
       trum of industries (balanced growth), with each supporting the
       market for the others.

All this added up to the classic 1SI model with a nearly autarchic
economy pervaded by a nearly omnipresent state. In the Indian case, the
model if it functioned well was compatible with a fairly high rate of
growth because of two factors: (1) low wages which, for any given technology, implied high rates of profit, and therefore of savings, investment
and growth; (2) the possibility of achieving reasonably large scales of production in the domestic market, because of the relatively large size of the
Indian economy. However, the performance of a model of state-sponsored
industrialisation was necessarily a function of the efficiency of the state.

4   THE FAILURE OF GOVERNMENT IN A HETEROGENEOUS SOCIETY

Unfortunately, the efficiency of the Indian state was severely limited by
the extreme heterogeneity of Indian society. India is, and has always been,
a museum of the species, a storehouse of an infinite variety of races, castes,
languages and religions. Diversity on this scale fostered compromise and
concession and nurtured democracy. But it also generated a 'soft state' in
which central authority was hostage to a multitude of sectional interests.
    The power of such interest groups arose from the fact that, in a society
as far-flung and diversified as India, the centre had necessarily to depend
on a host of agents, linked to it through a network of patronage. The
agents could control the flow of information to the principal: they could
also demand and receive much discretionary power. The more complex
the society, the greater the bargaining power of the agents until the principal was virtually eclipsed and the political order became a bargaining
equilibrium between different organised interests. India was in fact an
Olsonian state (Olson, 1965).
    Pranab Bardhan (Bardhan, 1983), in an analysis which seeks to blend
Marx with Olson, suggests that Indian politics is essentially the interplay
of three proprietorial classes – big business, rich farmers and a white-
collar educated middle class, the owners of human, as distinct from physical, capital. Organisation potential, however, appears to be a more crucial

feature of successful groups than ownership of capital. A fourth class must therefore be added to Bardhan's trinity – organized labour. These four classes together dominated policy-making in India's strongly interventionist state. They enjoyed astronomical subsidies on exports, on food procurement, on fertilisers, irrigation and power, on transport rates, on education and on the public distribution of food to urban consumers. Capital and organized labour in industry were sheltered by an average protective tariff rate of 117 per cent (the highest in the world) and a formidable battery of quantitative import controls. Government jobs mushroomed, public enterprises sprouted endlessly and the explosive growth of the army, the bureaucracy and the university establishment created a high-wage low-productivity island within the economy for the urban middle class. In this lotusland of government employment, Parkinson's law ruled and the average wage was nine times that in the rest of the economy. Each of the organized groups resisted taxation with much success; farm income was totally tax-free and special interests could always carve out loopholes and exemptions for themselves. Finally, labour law guaranteed total job security in the organized sector; and productivity in consequence lagged behind wages, particularly in public employment.

Caste, ethnic, religious and linguistic interest groups added to the pressures of economic classes. The locations of industries, universities, government offices, etc. were determined by regional pulls and pressures rather than by functional efficiency. Politically influential groups secured preferential employment and promotion for their members, whether through formal quotas or through political and union pressure on the employers. The allocation of licences was likewise distorted.

The Olsonian state had all the standard Olsonian characteristics. There was the asymmetry in distribution of benefits between the organized and the unorganizable, between producers and consumers, between unionized labour and the landless rural work force. between concentrated large scale industry and small business. There was the consolidation of monopoly through entry barriers erected by established groups. There was the retardation of innovation as competitive pressures were diluted, as resources were diverted from research into rent-seeking and as vested interests succeeded in aborting change. There were the delays in decision-making that resulted from the cumbersome nature of group decision-making procedures, and the bureaucratic routine and political bargaining that preceded every decision. There was the byzantine character of regulation, reflecting the play of sectional pressures and counter-pressures and the need to draw a veil of unintelligibility over the sectional purposes that regulation serves. Even the administration and policing of regulation by government and compliance or evasion by firms became time-consuming and expensive.

All this led through many tangled paths to a common outcome – low and stagnant productivity. There were at least eight distinct factors that pointed in this direction: (1) the neglect of static comparative advantage in an ISI regime; (2) the exclusion of foreign and domestic competition; (3) the manipulation of industrial location; (4) appointments based on non-merit considerations; (5) the diversion of resources into rent-seeking; (6) the delays in decision-making; (7) the elimination on account of labour laws of the threat of dismissal as a worker-disciplining device; and (8) the belief that employment alone is socially valuable, not productivity, with its consequences for the morale of workers and supervisors.

Inefficiency was concentrated in, but not confined to, the public sector. The incompetence of the public sector had a twofold result. First, it hampered the supply of infrastructural inputs – coal, steel, electricity, railway transport, etc. – to the rest of the economy and retarded output growth everywhere. Second, it ensured large losses in most public enterprises which became in consequence a drain on the exchequer.

The operational inefficiency of public enterprise represented only a part of the problem of the public sector. The other part was its high capital cost. This reflected the capital-intensive character of many of the investments mandated by ISI. But it also reflected massive capital cost inflation due to corruption and cost escalation due to the dilatoriness of government decision-making.

The lavish scale of subsidies, the proliferation of government employment, the losses of public enterprise and the extravagant cost of public investment added up to an enormous strain on budgetary resources. Revenues, however, were limited both by resolute resistance to taxation and by the low level and slow growth of output. The initial impact of this was on public investment, which was severely compressed in the late 1960s and early 1970s. But the consequent running down of the infrastructure intensified its chronic inefficiency and precipitated a whole series of inter-related crises in steel, in cement, in energy, in transport. The consequence was a decade or more of industrial stagnation from the mid-1960s. This came at a time when the problems of the early years of development appeared to be abating: the Green Revolution had eased food shortages; the savings rate had shot up to respectability from its humble origins; even the scarcity of foreign exchange seemed near resolution, thanks to the inflow of remittances. The myth of 'the Hindu rate of growth', a maximum of 3.5 per cent to which the Indian economy was religiously devoted, gained currency. In the late 1970s, this compelled a revival of public investment, and in particular a restoration of the infrastructure. But revenues remained inelastic and government consumption rose inexorably. Thus budget deficits became endemic. This public impecuniousness contrasted strangely with the private frugality implied by a 22–24 per cent rate of private saving.

Deficit budgets implied a mounting public debt and rising interest rates as government competed with and crowded out private borrowers. Servicing costs thus rose more than proportionately to borrowing, further swelling the deficit in a vicious cycle.

The excess demand generated by government deficits was absorbed in part by the restraint on private spending due to higher interest rates. In part, however, it overflowed abroad in large trade deficits. Throughout the 1970s, the resulting pressure on foreign exchange reserves was eased by remittances from Indian emigrants, particularly from migrant workers in the Middle East in the wake of the oil boom. In the 1980s, however, things changed. The growth of the deficit necessitated artificial stimulation of the inflow of remittances. Large-scale borrowing abroad began, particularly from non-resident Indians attracted by exceptionally favourable terms on bank deposits in foreign currencies. The rate of growth accelerated quite sharply to 5.5 per cent, a level sustained throughout the decade by debt-financed investment in infrastructure on the one hand and the creeping liberalization of the 1980s on the other. The price of this was the accumulation of high interest debt. By the end of the 1980s, the mountain of indebtedness was large enough to make international confidence in India's ability to repay somewhat shaky. Political instability, the fiscal irresponsibility of the short-lived governments that accompanied it, and finally the Gulf War which imposed on India the cost of repatriating hundreds of thousands of Indian workers from the Gulf while depriving her of their foreign exchange earnings, precipitated the crisis of confidence which, in 1991, drove India into the arms of the IMF and down the road of reform.

The moral of this story is that the South Asian growth model, despite its many inefficiencies, was capable of generating a momentum that surpassed all other regions of the world except East Asia. This was largely due to its low wage levels. Low wages meant relatively high rates of profit, inducing high rates of private investment, and savings, given an essential minimum of infrastructure and some room for profit-oriented decision-making, at least in the domestic market. Both these conditions existed in the India of the 1980s so that rapid, if autarchic, growth could occur.

However, the system could not finance its infra-structural requirements internally. Massive government borrowing was needed, leading by 1991 to a terminal crisis of confidence for the ISI model.

5   THE ECONOMIC BASIS OF AN OPEN REGIME

Between the elaboration of the ISI model in the 1950s and 1991, the world had changed. Ocean transport costs had dropped dramatically (due to containerization, etc.); so had communication costs (the Information Revolution). The share of transport cost in delivery price fell as changes in tastes (in favour of light high-value products like diamonds and electronics) and technology (miniaturization and microelectronics) reduced the material intensity of output. Affluence spread from the Atlantic to the Pacific and the Middle East so that the geographic spread of the world market widened. As living standards rose, demand became more differentiated with quality, variety and exclusiveness counting relatively more than before, and mere cheapness (and therefore economies of scale) for less. The increased uncertainty and variability of the business environment (due to intensified global competition) discouraged large commitments in specific fixed assets (which are the basis of economies of long runs). 'Flexible specialisation' through microelectronically controlled general purpose machinery made it possible to produce small batches of differentiated products almost as cheaply as long production runs.

The upshot of this unification of the global market was that domestic market size began to count for less as a determinant of export advantage and relative factor costs far more. The East Asian economies were the first to exploit this opportunity. In the quarter century since 1965, their spectacular success at export-led growth had set up a novel development paradigm.

The opening up of India in 1991 to the world did not perhaps amount to a complete conversion of South Asia to the East Asian development paradigm. But it certainly represented a major policy switch. While the older growth strategy did generate respectable rates of saving, investment and growth, it used existing assets inefficiently. The new regime improves productivity through (1) intensified specialization according to comparative advantage, (2) economies of scale as export markets expand, and (3) heightened competition as participation in world trade grows. It also accelerates accumulation by attracting foreign capital.

Against these factors is counterpoised the Stolper–Samuelson effect. How strong is this effect likely to be? Stolper and Samuelson assumed that factor supplies are completely inelastic, rigidly defined by endowments. At the opposite pole from this is the Arthur Lewis postulate of an unlimited supply of labour at current wages (Lewis, 1955). In a Lewis economy, the Stolper–Samuelson effect vanishes and the impact of trade liberalization on the growth rate is entirely favourable. Later work avers that all real-life economies lie between the two poles. The increased demand for labour due to the freeing of trade raises wages and depresses the profit rate. However, in large labour-surplus economies, particularly China and the South Asian region, the effect may not be enormous.

A South Asia immersed in the mainstream of world trade is necessarily part of the new international division of labour. The main feature of this is the shift first of labour-intensive industries and then of standardized manufacturing to low-wage economies and the concentration of the West on services, research-intensive technologies and high-tech manufacturing. The prime movers of this process have of course been wage differentials. In an increasingly integrated world wage differentials have persisted because of migration restrictions which have made labour far more immobile internationally than goods or even capital, and they have become today a far more important source of export advantage than they ever were before. Thus, openness to world trade today accentuates the growth advantage of the low-wage economy: it adds to the growth potential implied by the South Asian wage level even under the older ISI regime.

However, the pattern of export advantage even in labour-intensive industry diverges somewhat from that of low labour cost because of the infrastructural requirements of modern export activity. A dense network of rapid transport and communication, a smooth and efficient legal and administrative framework, and an educated and disciplined work force are necessary, if not absolutely essential, ingredients of export success. Infrastructure is by and large non-tradeable; much of it consists of public goods which cannot, by definition, be marketed. Like labour, therefore, it constitutes a basis for export advantage in all industries which require it. The existence of such infrastructure in advanced countries and its absence in most low-wage economies retards the shift of export advantage towards the latter. Also, once a low-wage economy has built up its infrastructure, this advantage persists even when it ceases to be a low-wage economy and delays the growth of other economies where wages are still low. In modelling the development of international comparative advantage one must combine Francois Perroux's analysis of 'growth poles' with Heckscher–Ohlin endowments theory.

It is the infrastructural backwardness of South Asia relative to East Asia that holds its growth rates below East Asian levels, though its wage levels are substantially lower. Infrastructure also explains the success of East Asian economies where wages have of late risen to high levels (Singapore, Hong Kong, Korea) in continuing to grow at a relatively rapid pace.

Crucial factors in infrastructural development are the economies of scale associated with it. Efficient infrastructure generally requires huge investment. Such massive mobilization of capital in an imperfect capital market may well be beyond the domestic capacity of a poor country: neither its local producers nor its generally impecunious and inefficient public sector is likely to inspire the confidence of investors on this scale. International investment then may become indispensable and a welcoming attitude to foreign capital a necessary recipe for accelerated growth. An alternative of course is the Korean strategy of building up the financial capacity of domestic producers through elaborate government support of the *chaebol*, even at the expense of all equity considerations.

6   SOUTH ASIA IN THE INDIAN MIRROR

Up to this point we have referred primarily to India's development process. The Indian experience with economic development policy is not, of course, unique. Indeed, the broad contours as well as the twists and turns of economic policy-making in India, Pakistan and Bangladesh represent variations on a common South Asian theme, with many striking parallels in chronology despite the obvious differences. Nor is this surprising. Sharing as they did a composite culture, a colonial past, a legacy of intense poverty and population pressure and a common date of birth as independent states (though the separation of Bangladesh did take place much later) the large South Asian neighbours were very similar in aspirations, in inherited endowments and in the international milieux in which they developed. Their common early commitment to ISI was a consequence. So was the emphasis on extensive public ownership of basic industry and infrastructure, though in Pakistan this was delayed till the trauma of 1971 and the advent of popular democracy and Zulfikar Ali Bhutto. As state-sponsored autarchic industrialization in each country became enmeshed in its own contradictions, there was the slow contraction in the decade of the late 1970s and 1980s of the economic domain of the state. In each of the three countries, the retreat from regulation was slowed down by vested interests sufficiently to precipitate a growing budgetary and payments deficit in the late 1980s and a consequent crisis. In Bangladesh, this occurred in 1987, in Pakistan in 1988 and in India in 1991. In each case, the IMF was resorted to and stabilization and structural adjustment initiated under its vigilant gaze. An accelerated liberalization of trade and a programme of privatization have resulted, particularly in Pakistan.

While in broad outline, events in the three economies have been roughly parallel, differences of detail have been quite substantial. The differences may be traced, at least in part, to differences in the composition of the three populations. Pakistan is ethnically heterogeneous (but less so than India) with Punjabi, Sindhi, Baluch and Pathan sub-nationalisms as well as the Mohajir immigrants from India. However, unlike India, there is a preponderant Punjabi majority which dominates demographically, and controls the army and the bureaucracy as well. Unlike India, again, there are no religious divisions; even the sectarian divisions within Islam are subdued with the orthodox Sunnis overwhelming the Shias, Ahmediyas, Ismailis, Bohras and other heterodox groups both in number and influence.

Bangladesh is ethnically and linguistically more homogeneous than Pakistan, with Bengali being spoken by over 90 per cent of the population. In contrast to Pakistan, however (though not to India), it does have a strong religious minority (the Hindus) as well as a smaller minority of Buddhists.

The relatively more homogeneous character of Pakistan and Bangladesh is accentuated by the strong Islamic message of brotherhood within Islam. This discourages stratification by class despite strong feudal traditions. Hence central authority is much stronger in Pakistan and Bangladesh than in India. By the same token, democracy is far more fragile and precarious.

Apart from their Islamic heritage and relative homogeneity, Pakistan and Bangladesh are distinguished from India by their relatively smaller size. This disparity in size has major strategic implications on account of the economies of scale in defence. It has compelled both Pakistan and Bangladesh to build up a military apparatus which in relation to population and economy is comparatively larger than India's. This, in turn, has strengthened the voice of the military in the international politics of both countries. Both countries, in striking contrast to India, have been ruled by military dictatorships for most of their independent existence. Democratic interludes have been short-lived sequels either to the total discrediting of the military (as happened in Pakistan after the Bangladesh war of 1971) or to the decimation of its leadership (as in the plane crash that killed President Ziaul Haq and most of his army top brass). Bangladesh, of course, is at present enjoying a return to civilian democracy; but this was at least in part the product of a rift in the army which undermined the support base of the erstwhile military dictator General Ershad.

The greater influence of central authority and of the army in the two Muslim states makes for flexibility of policy. It smooths and speeds up policy reform since the painful, prolonged and often impossible process of consensus-building is not an essential preliminary. Sectional interests, though articulate, are not overwhelming. All this is reflected in the more radical character of some of the reforms that Pakistan in particular has experimented with recently, especially its large-scale privatization programme.

India, despite much rhetoric, has shied away from anything remotely resembling this. By the same token, there is an element of instability and reversibility about the Pakistani reforms. There is also the risk that, without effective outlets, the discontent generated by the reforms will erupt in forms even more violent and convulsive than those that India is experiencing.

Another major factor which has affected the development of the South Asian economies, though differentially, is population pressure. Population growth has been most explosive in Pakistan at the rate of 3.2 per cent, as compared with Bangladesh's 2.6 and India's 2.1. This reflects, among other things, the levels of female illiteracy (81 per cent in Pakistan, 78 per cent in Bangladesh and 71 per cent in India) Though the rate of growth for Bangladesh is substantially lower than that for Pakistan, it is by no means negligible, and in fact poses the most acute problems of all because of the almost suffocating density that already exists. With the exception of the city-states of Hong Kong and Singapore, Bangladesh with its 771 persons per km^2 is by far the most densely populated country on the face of the earth. The most populous advanced economy, the Netherlands, supports, by contrast only 400 persons per km.^{2} Fertile and well-watered though it is, a poor agrarian economy cannot possibly bear a burden so colossal. Labour-intensive industrialization, even on a massive scale, is unlikely in the immediate future to touch more than the fringes of this problem. Meanwhile the overflow of this still proliferating population in the form of large-scale migration into eastern India is inevitable.

Perhaps the most interesting of the factors differentiating the South Asian countries is the wide scatter of savings rates and even of investment rates and their highly imperfect correlation with rates of growth. Pakistan's savings ratio in 1993 was just half the Indian (12 per cent as against 24 per cent), Bangladesh's (8 per cent) just a third of India's. The discrepancies in investment rates, though substantially lower due to large-scale capital inflows into the two Muslim countries, were still significant. Nor was 1993 an atypical year in this regard. Yet India, despite continuously higher rates of saving and investment, has lagged continuously behind Pakistan in rates of growth (5.2 per cent for India as against 6 per cent for Pakistan in 1980–93). Bangladesh's growth rate has been lower than India's, of course, but certainly not to an extent commensurate with the gaps in investment rates (Table 3.1).

A look at the relative compositions of output in the South Asian economies dispels most of the mystery. The Pakistani and Bangladeshi economies have far more labour-intensive structures than the Indian. Services accounted in 1993 for over half the GDP of Pakistan and Bangladesh, as against only 40 per cent for India (Table 3.2). Even more

Table 3.1   South Asian economies: growth rates, 1970–93

Country	GDP growth rates		Investment/GDP		Saving/GDP	
	1970–80	1980–93	1970	1993	1970	1993
India	3.4	5.2	0.17	0.24	0.16	0.24
Pakistan	4.9	6.0	0.16	0.21	0.09	0.12
Bangladesh	2.3	4.2	0.11	0.14	0.07	0.08
Sri Lanka	4.1	4.0	0.19	0.25	0.16	0.16
Nepal	2.0	5.0	0.06	0.21	0.03	0.11

Note: GDP growth rates are given as percentages. Investment and Saving refer to gross domestic values.
Source: World Bank (1995).

Table 3.2   South Asian economies: percentage shares in GDP, 1970–93

Country	Agriculture		Manufacturing		Industry		Services	
	1970	1993	1970	1993	1970	1993	1970	1993
India	45	31	15	17	22	27	33	41
Pakistan	37	25	16	17	22	25	41	50
Bangladesh	55	30	06	10	09	18	37	52
Sri Lanka	28	25	17	15	24	26	48	50
Nepal	67	43	04	09	12	21	21	36

Source: *World Bank Report* (1995).

significant is the distribution of value-added by manufacturing. In 1988, the heavier industries (chemicals, petroleum, rubber and plastics, ferrous and non-ferrous metals and metal products, machinery and transport equipment) contributed 65.3 per cent of value-added by manufacturing in India. The same groups accounted for just 38.5 per cent in Pakistan and 32.6 per cent in Bangladesh (Table 3.3). Thus capital: output ratios were substantially higher in India.

The Indian emphasis on heavy industry is no doubt in part a function of her natural resource endowment, particularly her strong mineral base in fossil fuels and ferrous metals. But it is also largely a consequence of policy. India's much deeper commitment to import substitution dictated a heavier structure of production and an accordingly lower productivity of capital. There can be little doubt that this is a burden which India has inherited from her more autarchic past – a burden that is not shared to the same extent by her neighbours.

Table 3.3   South Asian economies: percentage shares of heavier industries
in value-added by manufactures, 1988

India	65.3
Pakistan	38.5
Bangladesh	32.6
Nepal	19.6

Source: World Bank Tables.

Additional explanatory factors include the possibly larger role of the public sector (with its less efficient use of capital) in India, the heavier infrastructural investment there (particularly in railways and water supply) and the larger share of human capital investment (particularly in education). Since the last two have long gestation lags, their immediate impact on the productivity of capital is limited though their eventual influence may turn out to be substantial. In any event, these differences are policy-induced and reflect the wide diversity of political economic compulsions in South Asia.

7   CONCLUSIONS

To sum up, in an autarchic or near-autarchic environment, labour abundance generally implies low relative prices of labour-intensive goods, low wages and high rates of profit, saving and growth (provided demand is sustained). Opening up such an economy while it promises many growth advantages also induces a Stolper–Samuelson effect, raising wages and eroding profits. However, if labour supply is highly elastic, what ensues is less a Stolper–Samuelson process than an Arthur Lewis process: wages hardly rise, rates of profit are sustained and the expansion of the labour-intensive export sector rapidly increases employment. For regions like South Asia and China, it is perhaps the latter model that is relevant, though wage pressures have already emerged in a number of specific areas even in these economies.

Apart from factor endowments, however, there are other influences on the rate of profit, the productivity of capital and therefore on the rate of growth. These include economies of scale, intensity of competition and X-efficiency. They also include the availability of infrastructure. While the abundance and elasticity of labour supply have ensured high growth rates throughout South Asia over the last 15 years it is policy differences (e.g. on openness or public investment) which account for significant disparities in these, and therefore for intra-regional differences in growth rates. Of course, factors like physical and human infrastructure are built up over time and tend to favour established growth processes rather than late-comers. They therefore add a third dimension to the explanation of growth differentials, particularly of those between the East and South Asian economies.

References

Bardhan, P. K. (1983) *The Political Economy of Development in India* (Oxford: Basil Blackwell).

Guha, A. (1963) 'Factor and Commodity Prices in an Expanding Economy', *Quarterly Journal of Economics*, vol. 177, no. 1, pp. 149–55.

Lewis, W. A. (1955) 'Economic Development with Unlimited Supplies of Labour', *Manchester School*, vol. 22, pp. 139–91.

Olson, M. (1965) *The Logic of Collective Action* (Cambridge, Mass.: Harvard University Press).

Rybczynski, T. M. (1955). 'Factor Endowment and Relative Commodity Prices'. *Economica*, N. S. vol. 22, no. 4, pp. 336–41.

Stolper, W. F. and P. A. Samuelson (1941) 'Protection and Real Wages', *Review of Economic Studies*, vol. 9, no. 4, pp. 58–73.

World Bank, (1995) *World Development Report* (New York: Oxford University Press).

4 Tunisia's Economy since Independence: The Lessons of Experience*

Christian Morrisson
UNIVERSITY OF PARIS–SORBONNE, FRANCE
and
Béchir Talbi
UNIVERSITY OF TUNIS, TUNISIA

1 INTRODUCTION

Tunisia offers an original example in the Arab world. Despite a number of handicaps such as a rather small territory, which is partly semi-desert and has few natural resources, in 30 years the country has managed to increase the population's standard of living by 160 per cent, greatly slowed population growth, eliminated extreme poverty and created a large middle class so that inequalities have clearly diminished by comparison with those observed under the former Protectorate.

It might be assumed that this success derives from a single policy steadfastly followed for 40 years, but an uninformed observer would be surprised to learn that this was not to be the case. The Tunisian authorities carried out very differing policies between 1956 and 1995, ranging from frankly liberal to collectivization with central planning. Thus after independence, the state maintained a relatively liberal framework although it took control of the economy's key sectors because they were controlled by foreign enterprises. During a second phase, from 1961 to 1969, there was a drive towards socialism which, during 1967–9, accelerated to the point where the situation in Tunisia in August 1969 could be likened to that of a communist country of eastern Europe. Tunisia returned to a capitalist market economy in 1970–1, but the state maintained a tight control over prices and private investment as well as a protectionist regime. This mixed economic system became less and less efficient in the 1980s, and the macroeconomic disequilibria led to the 1987–8 adjustment, with a stabilization programme and structural reforms at the same time. The latter set

54

Tunisia on the way toward a liberal system without restrictions either in its domestic market or its openness to imports.

This apparently paradoxical case can be better understood by recalling the country's past and two features – namely that whatever the economic strategy being followed, since 1960 the state has always given priority to education and public investment.

Tunisia's history since antiquity has been a factor in its development for several reasons. The past provided the country with an awareness of having had one of the world's richest civilizations and it bequeathed its monuments, which represent a precious capital for tourism. Then a succession of civilizations give rise to an open-mindedness to foreigners combined with a natural Muslim and Arab identity. The new government established at independence was marked by this open-mindedness. From the beginning, President Bourguiba embraced modernization in all domains: reorganization of government administration, accelerated development of education, a status for women modelled on European laws, establishment of a secular society and education, and the introduction of birth control.

Consequently, from 1960 Tunisia met the preconditions for growth described by Rostow:

- a relatively modern administration
- a strong sense of national unity among the population
- independence and a politically stable government
- a minimum of modern infrastructure
- a modern agricultural export sector
- a modern legal system adapted to individuals (on the status of women) and to enterprises.

The fulfilment of these conditions, like the desire for modernization, are indisputable factors for a success whose significance is now recognized, for the recent history of developing countries has shown that as an incentive to growth, institutional framework, in the broadest sense, counts as much as investment, if not more.

Nonetheless, investment has not been neglected as we will show. In fact, Tunisia's history since 1960 has been marked by a continuity of two elements in public finance, namely a high level of public investment and the priority given to education. This priority had a determining effect on growth because the quality of labour completely changed between 1960 and the present; the average schooling of the labour force increased from 1.5 to 6 years. Moreover, the accumulation of public capital in infrastructure increased the private sector's total factor productivity.

To explain these two policies, some basic characteristics of Tunisia's public finance should be noted:

- Public expenditure has always represented a higher proportion of GDP than the average of countries at the same level of development
- In the public sector, in the broadest sense (state + local authorities + social security), the state has always had a preponderant role, with its share of receipts being greater than 80 per cent
- The proportion of public expenditure for sovereignty (civilian and military) has always been low while the proportion for education, infrastructure and economic interventions has always been high.

In the context of a voluntarist policy giving the state a determining role in development, the Tunisian authorities rapidly increased public expenditure after independence. This expenditure rose from 14 per cent of GDP in 1957 to 22–24 per cent during the 1960s. After the first oil shock, the state's receipts were greater and public expenditure attained 29 per cent from 1977. The second oil shock and an expansionist policy, despite the fall in oil prices, propelled public expenditure to 38–39 per cent of GDP before the stabilization programme reduced it to 35 per cent in 1992–3. What is remarkable in this history is not the rapid rise of spending in the 1960s, a development that was entirely consistent with the socialist option, but the fact that the state continued to play a key role even after Tunisia changed policies and returned to a liberal option. Public expenditure as a proportion of GDP increased during the 1970s and declined only slightly after the 1987–8 adjustment. Consequently, its share remained much larger than in southern European countries with a greater GDP/*per capita*, and it is also larger than in a majority of countries with a comparable GDP/*per capita*.

Secondly, public expenditure for sovereignty has never been a priority. To be sure, military expenditure increased from 4–6 per cent of the budget initially to 9 per cent in 1980s, but these figures are low compared to many other countries. This is also the case for civilian sovereignty expenditure, which declined from 13–14 per cent of budget in 1960s to 8–10 per cent in the 1980s and 1990s. The sum of civilian and military spending on sovereignty has been becoming an increasingly smaller part of the budget, its share having declined from 23 per cent in 1961 to 17 per cent in 1990. This was an essential choice which made it possible to finance the accumulation of human and physical capital, while the share of these sovereignty expenditures in other countries at the same level development has been two or three times greater.

It has been shown (cf. W. Easterly and S. Rebelo, 1993) that investment in infrastructure has a positive effect on directly productive investment and growth of GDP. However, the state permanently financed this investment in Tunisia whatever the development strategy being followed. Investment by the government has regularly increased since 1960, so that its volume has multiplied by 2.5 in 30 years. To be sure, its share of total investment has tended to decrease, dropping from 20–30 per cent during 1963–9 to 18 per cent in 1991. This investment has been 4 per cent of GDP in the 1990s as compared with 6 per cent during the 1960s. This decrease is much less than might be expected, considering that in the interim there had been a transition from a socialist economy to an economy liberalized by a structural adjustment conforming to the 'Washington consensus'. Thus the state has always remained a major actor with respect to capital accumulation. This is all the more true as the state also controls other investment, since investment in the public enterprises has not been taken into account.

Two categories of this investment have had a crucial effect on private sector productivity. They are investment in agriculture, which was about half of the total during the whole period, and in transportation and telecommunication, whose share increased from 10 per cent to 33 per cent at the expense of construction of administrative buildings.

Education, the second budgetary priority, played an even larger role in stimulating growth. It was an absolute priority during the 1960s. In a few years, educational expenditure increased from 4 per cent to 8 per cent of GDP, so that in 1969 this percentage placed Tunisia ahead of most developing or developed countries. This emphasis has continued to the present. Of course, education has dropped from a maximum of 24 per cent to 16 per cent of the budget, and from 8 per cent to 7 per cent of GDP in 1990. This 7 per cent of GDP still leaves Tunisia among the front-runners of the developing countries. On the other hand, some needs have diminished. The total number of pupils in primary education has reached a ceiling as the percentage of children enrolled has attained 90 per cent and the birth rate is falling. A few figures will give an idea of the exceptional effort here. The percentage of children enrolled in primary education has increased from 33 per cent in 1957 to almost 90 per cent. The number of pupils in secondary education was 600 000 in 1992, in contrast with 43 000 in 1956. Finally, there are now 80 000 students in higher education as compared with 1500 in 1956. Furthermore, only 20 per cent of students in secondary or higher education were female in 1956, while today there is almost parity. In terms of enrolment in secondary and higher education, Tunisia is already ahead of the level of some European countries in the 1960s. This emphasis on education, as already noted, explains the very rapid increase in the average number of years of schooling from 1.5 in 1960 to 6 in 1990. This was a performance difficult to achieve for it refers to stocks (working-age population) and not to flows.

2   ESTIMATE OF THE GROWTH OF TOTAL FACTOR PRODUCTIVITY

As Tunisia permanently invested a large proportion of GDP, it was possible to attain some growth whatever the policy being followed. However, this growth was no guarantee of the policy's soundness, since even if inefficient, an exceptionally large investment will necessarily produce some effects. Thus it seemed that the best criterion for evaluating the efficiency of policies was not the growth rate of GDP but that of total factor productivity (TFP). If it is assumed that a Cobb–Douglas production function with constant returns is relevant for an economy, the growth rate of TFP equals the GDP *minus* the growth rates of L and K:

$$\overline{TFP} = \overline{Y} - 0.3\overline{K} - 0.7\overline{L}$$
(growth rates are indicated by a bar)

The growth rate of TFP can be either positive or negative. The first case produces a sort of bonus as GDP grows faster than the factors of production. The second case is a failure since TFP is less than should be obtained in relation to $\overline{K}$ and $\overline{L}$. These positive or negative differentials are sometimes due to exogenous shocks, such as an exceptional drought which sharply reduces agricultural output. It can be assumed, however, that they can often be explained by efficient policies or management errors.

A very simple example shows the superiority of this approach. Assume that both capital stock and labour both grow 2 per cent a year in an economy in which GDP grows by 4 per cent. In a neighbouring economy, assume that GDP as well as capital stock and labour all grow by 4 per cent. It is clear that the first economy is managed better, since it has the same growth rate with a much smaller increase in factors of production – 2 per cent instead of 4 per cent.

We recall first how we calculated the growth rate of TFP.[1] During the period studied, 1960–93, GDP increased by an average of 5.3 per cent, estimating the growth rate by a regression. Even though the population doubled during this period, GDP/*per capita* growth remained fairly high at 2.9 per cent, which was higher than that of Algeria and Morocco. However, this growth was relatively unstable, with a succession of phases of high and low growth. Consequently, the standard deviation of the GDP growth rate is clearly much greater than in other countries having high growth, like those in Southeast Asia.

A series of the Institut d'Economie Quantitative (IEQ), corrected to take into account the decrease in working hours, was used to estimate the variable L, which led to a growth rate of 1.74 per cent.

Three IEQ series on capital were used. The first includes only productive capital, K_1 (including transportation, telecommunications and energy), the second K_2, covers administrative buildings, and the third, K_3 family housing. These series have been estimated by the perpetual inventory method with:

$$K_t = (1 - \delta)K_{t-1} + I_t$$

where a depreciation rate (δ) of 4.6 per cent was used.

Having calculated the necessary data, some free estimates were made of the production function

$$Y_t = AK_t^\alpha L_t^\beta$$

which was tested in logarithmic form.

With K_1, the sum of coefficients α and β is not significantly different from 1, and the two coefficients were close to their usual order of magnitude. On the other hand, for $K_1 + K_2$ the sum is greater than 1, but if rents are subtracted from GDP (which is consistent since K_3 was excluded), the sum of the coefficients is very close to 1.

A second problem raised by the estimate of a production function concerns the 1965–9 period, when GDP growth was low although the capital stock increased 56 per cent in four years. After several attempts, it turned out to be impossible to obtain plausible and significant coefficients for L and K if the exceptional nature of the period were not taken into account with a dummy variable.

Satisfactory results were obtained with coefficients for α and β close to 0.3 and 0.7, while the dummy variable has a significant coefficient on the order of –0.08.

These results then made it possible to estimate production functions with constant returns of the form $Y/L = f(K/L)$. These estimates are given in Table 4.1. Equations (3) and (4) gave the most satisfactory results, with an elasticity of capital of 0.38. Inasmuch as an estimate of the same elasticity without constraint on the returns led to a lower figure, 0.32, on the same order (0.30) used by other studies, we used two values, 0.30 and 0.35.

Table 4.2 shows the growth rate of TFP[2] using these two values. Taking the sum of the growth rates of $K_1 + K_2$ and L, weighted by their elasticities (0.3 and 0.7, or 0.35 and 0.65), one can obtain the difference between the growth rate of the GDP and this sum, which corresponds to the growth rate of TFP. That enables the contributions to GDP growth to be calculated. The growth of capital stock played a determining role in long-term growth since its contribution always exceeded 50 per cent. The contribution of L was about one-quarter, the remainder (between one-quarter and

Regional Experience

Table 4.1 Estimate of the production function for (Y/L)

Equation	(1)	(2)(a)	(3)(a)	(4)(a)	(5)(a)	(6)(a)	(7)(a)	(8)
Dependent variable	Y/L^*	Y/L^*	Y/L^*	Y/L_c^*	Y/L_c^*	Y/L^*	Y/L^*	YM/LM
Constant	-01	0.004	0.004	0.004	0.009	0.003	0.01	0.01
	(1.6)	(0.4)	(0.4)	(.4)	(0.4)	(0.2)	(4)	(0.7)
K_1	0.32	0.36	–	–				
	(8.6)	(6.0)						
$K_1 + K_2$			0.38	0.39(5.7)	0.34			
			(6)		(3.3)			
$K_1 + K_2 + K_3$				–	–	0.52	0.40	
						(4.5)	(2.2)	
							(b)	
KM								0.28
								(2.8)
Dummy	-0.08	-0.06	-0.06	-0.07		-0.05	-0.03	-0.05
(1965–69)	(4)	(2.5)	(2.6)	(2.7)		(1.7)	(1.1)	(1.3)
R^2	0.73	0.79	0.79	0.78	0.75	0.77	0.76	0.65
DW	1.21	1.88	1.86	1.87	1.82	1.92	1.97	2.07
No. of observations	33.0	32.0	32.0	32.0	32.0	32.0	31.0	31.0

a   = Cochrane–Orcutt procedure.
b   = K_2 and K_3 (–2) means the stock of capital (K_2 and K_3) on 1 July two years ago instead of 1 July in year t.
c   = GDP, excluding rents.
*   Detrended variables.
KM = Capital stock in the manufacturing sector per employee.
YM/LM = Added-value in the manufacturing sector per employee.

Table 4.2 Contributions to growth (GDP), 1960–93

	Growth rate[a] 1960–93	Contributions	
		Elasticity of capital = 0.30	Elasticity of capital = 0.35
GDP	5.33%		
K_1 and K_2	8.93%	50.3%	58.5%
L	1.95%	25.5%	23.5%
TFP	1.29 (elast. = 0.30)	24.2%	18%
	0.94 (elast. = 0.35)		

Note: a = Rate calculated from regressions on 34 observations.

Table 4.3 TFP growth rate, 1962–92 (annual average)

Period	TFP	TFP corrected for quality effects
1962–9	–1.06	–2.8
1970–81	+2.6	+0.8
1982–8	–0.2	–1.2
1989–92	+3.0	+1.7

Note: Annual data from Appendix, p. 74.

one-fifth) being ascribable to TFP. The figures show that without any TFP growth (which corresponds to $\bar{Y} = 0.3\bar{K} + 0.7\bar{L}$), GDP growth would not have exceeded 4.3 per cent. Thus the improvement in the standard of living would have been much slower, and the growth rate of the GDP/*per capita* would have been reduced to 1.6–1.9 per cent instead of 2.9 per cent. The contribution of TFP is thus fairly satisfactory, even if it less than in Southeast Asian countries, for example, 38 per cent in Taiwan.

As was noted above, Tunisia's growth has been especially unstable. This is demonstrated by Table 4.3 which gives the GDP and TFP growth rates by period. The GDP growth rate ranges from 3 per cent to 7.1 per cent, while the variations are more striking for TFP, from –1.06 per cent to + 3 per cent. This breakdown into four periods brings out some striking contrasts, since the cumulative variations of TFP range from –8.6 points during 1962–9 to +31.5 points during 1970–81.

The abnormality of the 1962–9 period appears clearly: GDP growth during these seven years was much less (a loss of almost nine points) than it should have been for the growth of K and L (and with no TFP growth). That proves the inefficiency of the economic policy carried out during this period.

If the record figure attained in 1970–81 is explained by the radical policy changes, nonetheless it should be noted that the large investments in infrastructure undertaken during the 1960s also played a role, for there is some delay before these investments can have a favourable impact on production.

Next, the growth rate of TFP was almost zero from 1982 to 1988: the observed growth of GDP was slightly less than the theoretical growth in relation to K and L. This relative failure led to a policy change. A group of consistent reforms under a structural adjustment programme accelerated the GDP growth rate, thanks to a high growth rate of TFP (+ 3 per cent per year).

These striking contrasts in TFP from one period to another makes Tunisia very interesting for an economist to study. Indeed, this country appears to be a privileged field for testing economic policies since there was a succession of very different development strategies with contrasting results. Section 2 attempts to explain these different performances by the structural and short-term policies followed.

Until now we have assumed that labour is a homogeneous factor of production, but it is evident that this is not the case in a country where the average number of years of schooling increased from 1.5 to 6 in 30 years. This progress led to a rise in the quality of this factor which should be taken into account when TFP is estimated. Indeed, the growth of L is clearly more rapid than it appears, if this improvement labour quality is taken into account. If the growth of L is greater, TFP growth is automatically lower. Thus the impact of this quality effect was calculated by a regression of the logarithm of TFP on the logarithm of the average number of years of schooling. An elasticity on the order of 0.30–0.37 was obtained, which proves that the effect of labour quality made a significant contribution to TFP growth, justifying the policy of giving priority to education since independence. This choice, which had political, social and cultural justifications, also turned out to be a very pertinent economic decision. During the 1970–92 period the growth rate of TFP attained 1.9 per cent. Knowing that the average number of years of schooling increased 4.1 per cent per year and assuming that the elasticity of TFP with respect to this number is 0.3, it follows that:

$$\frac{0.3 \times 4.1}{1.9} = 0.66 \text{ or } 66 \text{ per cent}$$

Thus during this period the improvement of labour quality accounts for two-thirds of TFP growth, which shows the decisive role of the educational policy followed continuously since independence.

If a labour quality effect is taken into account, capital has to be treated similarly. Indeed, it well known that the quality of capital goods has constantly improved since the end of the Second World War. As Tunisia produces very few capital goods, this quality effect depends on imports of foreign goods. First the effect of technical progress on TFP growth in Tunisia was estimated (TFP net effect of education). Customarily, the United States is used as the country of reference, and by assuming that it is on the optimal production frontier, the only rise in productivity can come from technical progress. Thus the relationship between TFP in Tunisia and the United States was estimated. Then the evolution of imports of capital goods was taken into account. This was necessary because it is not possible to benefit from US technical progress if a country does not import capital goods, or imports very few. These imports are an indispensable vector of transmission.

Import statistics were used to construct a series on imported capital[3], then the difference ΔK_E between the growth rate of the imported capital stock and the productive capital stock (K_1) was calculated. A regression of the TFP in Tunisia on this difference confirmed that an acceleration of imports of capital goods indeed has a significant effect on TFP. From estimates of the elasticity of TFP in Tunisia in relation to TFP in the United States and in relation to ΔK_E, the contribution of the capital quality effect on TFP was calculated in the same way as for labour quality effect. A contribution of 19 per cent was found. Thus this quality effect accounts for about one-fifth of TFP growth in Tunisia.

Having estimated the effect on TFP of labour and capital quality, the growth rate of TFP net of quality effects was calculated. For example, if the average number of years of schooling increases 4 per cent per year and if the elasticity of the TFP with respect to this number is 0.3, the product of the elasticity $\times$ growth rate is $0.3 \times 0.04 = 0.012$, or 1.2 per cent, and 1.2 points are deducted from the growth rate of TFP to obtain a rate corrected for the effect of labour quality.

If the economy is on the production frontier and the best combination of K and L has been chosen on this frontier in terms of their relative prices, then TFP increases only according to the quality effects. This amounts to saying that in principle TFP corrected for the quality effects will be zero if the economic management is the most efficient possible.

Table 4.3 gives TPF corrected for the quality effects for each period. Thus during 1962–9 the growth rate of TPF was –2.8 per cent. That means that taking into account the growth of L and K, and the improvement in quality of L and K (it being understood the labour quality effect for L was due to the government), GDP growth should been 2.8 points greater each year. As the observed rate was 4.9 per cent, it should have been 7.7 per cent per year with an efficient economic policy. GDP should have been about 20 per cent higher in 1969. Thus it can be concluded that the cost of economic policy errors during this period represented 20 per cent of GDP at the end of the period. The fact that TPF corrected for the quality effects was clearly positive during the 1970–81 period is linked to these errors in the 1960s. Indeed, from the moment that an economy is not on the production frontier, a policy change as at the end of 1969 and in 1970 makes it possible to come closer to this frontier, which translates into a corrected TFP greater than 0.

The four corrected growth rates for TFP (Table 4.3) reflect large differences in efficiency from one period to another and the aim of the next section is to explain these differences by the successive, more or less contradictory economic policies.

ECONOMIC POLICIES AND PERFORMANCES

The 1962–9 Period

Economic growth of 4.9 per cent per year appeared to be satisfactory during this period which, however, was marked by the worst performance of TFP corrected for quality effects. The explanation of this failure thus merits special attention.

The two decisions that were most costly for efficiency were collectivization of land and the development of a capital-intensive industrial sector. These errors were compounded by a highly protectionist trade policy and a policy which discouraged private saving, both being a logical consequence of the socialist option. The state had a complete hold on all sectors. From 1956, all modern activities – mining; electricity, water and gas; railroads; trucking; maritime and air transport; and the banks were progressively put under state control. Next in the 1960s, the state nationalized wholesale trade and it rapidly developed a parastatal industrial sector, which represented half of production by 1964. From 1964 to 1968 most shopkeepers and some craftsmen were compelled to enter cooperatives. Thus between 1956 and 1969 the state took control of 80 per cent of the non-agricultural sector, without causing major disadvantages. The nationalization of enterprises belonging to foreigners was popular and managing the enterprises did not create serious problems. Collectivization of retail trade was disliked by most shopkeepers, but they were unable to oppose the cooperatives.

On the other hand, collectivization of land had a major economic cost for several reasons:

- Management of farms by an agency in the capital instead of decentralized management by the directors of cooperatives.
- Collectivization was unpopular in regions of market gardening and fruit growing where the peasants were very attached to their own individual farms. In regions of large-scale farming, the peasants were opposed to cooperatives because they led to a fall in the standard of living.
- Finally, it was unrealistic to try to adopt modern farming methods on several million hectares with a lack of financing and skilled personnel.

Management difficulties which followed the nationalisation of the *colons'* lands in 1964 (450 000 hectares), then the threat of collectivization which discouraged private investment, and finally the collectivization measures themselves (gradual in 1967–8, accelerated in 1969) all largely explain the stagnation of agricultural production: +2.7 per cent in eight years from 1961 to 1969. As other sectors were then still fairly dependant on the situation in agriculture, this stagnation slowed growth in the whole economy.

The second cause of inefficiency was the creation and development of a state industrial sector with low productivity. This failure is not explained by the public status of the enterprises. As mentioned, the management of foreign firms nationalized after 1956 did not present any special difficulty and some public enterprises like the STEG were well managed. However, the state made errors in its industrial investments. A comparison by Stolper (1980) of public and private enterprises proves this. On average, public enterprises had a capital: output ratio (K/Q) four times higher than private enterprises. To meet the argument that the same types of production had not been compared, Stolper also compared four sub-sectors of engineering and electrical industries producing identical goods and found that the productivity of public capital (Q/K) was one-eighth–one-sixteenth that of private capital. Most of the industrial investments by the state during the 1960s wasted capital, since considerable investment had resulted in a small rise in production and employment. Waste was favoured by interest rates that were too low, leading to use of capital-intensive techniques; by an overvalued exchange rate which reduced prices of capital goods; and by effective rates of protection of from 100 per cent to 470 per cent, which permitted inefficient enterprises to survive. However, according to Stolper, the primary reason for this failure was due to the centralized management of the economy. Directors of public enterprises were not free to manage their enterprises, but had to obey their supervisory ministry. As a result, what mattered most to the directors was not market conditions but their relationship with the administration, for obtaining import licences, operating subsidies and investment funds. It should be added that even if they had been unconstrained, their task would sometimes have been difficult, because investment decisions were not subject to a cost-benefit analysis, but were based on technical coefficients under planning based on physical quantities. In these conditions, negative growth of the industrial sector's TFP was inevitable since there was only a small increase in production while capital stock grew very fast.

As just shown, this industrial failure was linked to the trade policy. The self-centred development strategy followed in the 1960s was especially unsuited to the Tunisian economy, which was handicapped by its small size. The domestic market was too small for many industrial sectors. Instead of aiming at self-sufficiency, it would have been preferable to conquer foreign markets in some sectors in order to benefit from increasing returns to scale, even if that meant renouncing all domestic production of other manufactured goods. The policy carried out during the 1960s did just the opposite, by establishing and protecting domestic enterprises in all sectors with the aid of quotas and very high customs duties, without taking into account the problem of returns to scale and the many instances of underutilization of capital goods. Moreover, there was an inefficient system of supplying enterprises with intermediate goods and imported capital goods as the government administration authoritatively made the decisions on the allocation of foreign exchange.

There was also a problem of financing investments, because the state raised the rate of investment to a high level of about 25 per cent, while the saving rate remained low (14.4 per cent on average), which was less than before independence. In fact, growth was financed by borrowing: the foreign debt as a percentage of GDP doubled from 1961 to 1967, and at the end of the period Tunisia experienced difficulties in long-term borrowing and had to use suppliers' credits at very high interest rates. Despite this need for financing, financial savings remained very low during this period, actually less than 4 per cent of total savings in 1969.

Nothing was done to stimulate these savings: deposit rates were less than the inflation rate one year out of two, the number of banking offices hardly increased, and collectivisation did not encourage investments. To be sure, the socialist development strategy was not based on a rapid growth of financial savings, but on massive use of foreign financing which left the risk that the lenders, especially international organizations, would ponder the cost-effectiveness of investments and draw the consequences.

The combination of these errors with high rates of investment and rapid capital accumulation explains the twofold nature of this period: a fairly rapid GDP growth and a negative growth rate of TFP of −2.8 per cent per year.

The 1970–81 Period

On taking office, H. Nouira, the new prime minister, clearly stated the government's development policy in his programme speech of 17 November 1970:

● Except for the basic sectors, the economy should be entrusted to private enterprises
● Market mechanisms should be restored

- Agriculture whose development is a precondition for all growth should be a priority
- In industry, large projects and heavy industry should be abandoned and investment based on returns on capital and number of jobs created
- Industry should be oriented towards foreign markets.

By March 1971, the economy was completely decollectivized, the state conserving only the management of public land. Authoritarian planning was abandoned and a 1972 law provided major incentives for exports.

However, this picture has to be qualified. On the one hand, the state retained control of the large parastatal sector which existed in 1960; moreover, the two oil shocks provided the state with ample resources, enabling it to invest massively in the productive sector. Thus in 1978 public and parastatal investment was 62.2 per cent of total investment, which was greater than the corresponding share of 61.8 per cent in 1968. Moreover, prices remained largely controlled, with only a third of consumption goods in category outside price controls, and a much smaller proportion of intermediate and capital goods. In industry most manufacturing products were subject to a price authorization regime, or to self-authorization (the price was fixed at the production cost *plus* a margin by the Direction des Prix, or in agreement with it). The prices of public services (water, electricity and transportation) were fixed by the administration at levels which did not even cover operating costs, as was the case with the railroads.

Of course, the state henceforth encouraged exports: exporting enterprises were granted facilities for importing intermediate goods and the customs duties on these goods were reduced. Exports were also given tax benefits. However, a highly protectionist system with quotas and high customs tariffs was preserved, in place until the structural adjustment programme of the late 1980s. In 1986, for example, 93 per cent of imports were subject to licensing and the effective rate of protection was 124 per cent for manufactured goods.

The state retained an equally ambiguous policy with respect to saving. On the one hand, the state encouraged saving by creating new financial products like a housing–savings programme in 1973, and foreign capital was encouraged to participate in joint ventures by tax exemption. The process of increasing banking operations was successful, since the number of banking offices nearly tripled in 12 years. From 1971, banks were requested not to engage direct transactions among themselves, but to use the money market, which functioned normally from 1975. The authorities encouraged the banks to use a maximum of liquid resources for medium-/long-term financing. These measures led to a rapid rise in financial savings (whose proportion of total savings more than doubled) and of loans.

On the other hand, this policy was ambiguous because the authorities rejected financial liberalization. A repressive policy was maintained by fixing interest rates at a low level. From 1970 to 1981 interest rates on 12–18-month deposits were less than the inflation rate, except in two years. In particular, from 1975 inflation accelerated while interest rates were not raised, or only slightly.

This picture shows the *mixed* character of this development strategy: despite decollectivization, public investment was greater than private investment; some prices were liberalized, but the major part remained controlled; exports were encouraged, but a highly protectionist system was maintained; financial savings, the banking sector and the money market were developed, but negative real interest rates were imposed and the allocation of bank credits was controlled.

Initially, a combination of favourable factors brought about rapid GDP growth, and the abandonment of the socialist policy of the 1960s led to major efficiency gains, as proven by the growth of TFP corrected for the quality effect of +0.8 per cent per year. Among the favourable factors were greater than average rainfall, the two oil shocks, the benefits from investments in infrastructure, and the first fruits of the expenditure on education during the 1960s. It is clear that the 1969–70 policy change brought the economy close to the production frontier, and then favourable factors stimulated the economy for the whole decade. However, the development strategy reached its limits in the 1980s, after the 1969–70 gains no longer counted and the favourable factors had disappeared.

The 1982–8 Period

This period was marked by unfortunate conditions, unfavourable exogenous shocks and a lax macroeconomic policy. Among the shocks were the fall in the price of oil, years of drought and a fall in foreign remittances due to the dismissal of expatriate workers in Libya. Instead of taking into account the new conditions, the state wanted to continue making large public investments, which increased 22 per cent (in volume) from 1982 to 1985, causing a budget deficit and growing indebtedness. The foreign debt reached 46.5 per cent of GDP in 1985 and debt service was 32 per cent of exports in 1986.

The counter-performances in this period are not surprising, with GDP growth rate barely greater than population growth and a clearly negative growth of corrected TFP. The experience of other countries has shown clearly that there can be satisfactory growth rates when the environment is favourable despite the existence of many distortions in the allocation of resources and other inefficiency factors. On the other hand, when faced with a series of exogenous shocks like the rise in interest rates in 1982, only economies managed as efficiently as possible can maintain growth.

In this respect, a comparison of the Southeast Asian and Latin American economies during the 1980s is enlightening. The former rapidly adapted to an unfavourable environment and resumed growth while the latter suffered much more from the exogenous shocks at the beginning of the 1980s because they had conserved many inefficient factors. Tunisia experienced the same situation for several reasons. Decollectivization and the partial liberalization of 1970–1 had a very stimulating impact. Then the two oil shocks provided fairly large benefits to Tunisia. Consequently, the 1970s were happy years marked by very rapid growth under easy conditions, even though structural inefficiencies remained. These weaknesses were revealed at the beginning of the 1980s during the exogenous shocks just mentioned. Thus Tunisia's experience conformed completely to that of many other developing countries during this critical period, which harshly selected countries according the efficiency of their policies.

It is evident that Tunisia's economy at the beginning of the 1980s was not marked by efficient policies. The system of largely controlled prices did not allow a rational allocation of resources; it encouraged enterprises to maintain inefficient practices, it encouraged collusion between producers and it discouraged innovation and improvement of quality. This pricing policy was combined with strong protectionism and strict control of private investment (which was subject to administrative authorization), preventing the functioning of a competitive economy. The system favoured the existence of 'private hunting grounds', benefiting certain interest groups. Manufacturers were satisfied with having guaranteed profits and the administration, which totally controlled the economy in August 1969, still conserved a significant part of its old powers.

Similarly, negative real interest rates satisfied large farmers who borrowed (even if they had funds available), exporters and especially the authorities, because the state could borrow at low rates to finance its deficit. This explains several characteristics of the financial sector: the state controlled four of the five main deposit banks, there was no competition between banks since the state fixed the rates and the allocation of credit, and the sector was segmented, different bodies each had a monopoly of a financial product. As can be seen, many interest groups were satisfied by this situation, which had a high cost in efficiency at the national level.

As the government and administration were among the beneficiaries of this situation, it was difficult to make structural reforms and liberalize the Tunisian economy. However, the government committed an error which

made the status quo untenable. It continued to make large public investments despite the conditions requiring borrowing; moreover, some of the
projects were too capital-intensive and had low returns. Furthermore, all
the gains brought about by the 1969–70 policy change had long been ex-
hausted. Thus the Tunisian economy experienced slow growth during this
period, despite a high rate of investment and rapid accumulation of human
capital. It can be understood that in these conditions the growth of TFP
corrected for quality effects was clearly negative. Indeed, production increased slowly despite a rapid growth rate of capital stock and skilled
labour, because of the unfavourable environment combined with an
economy with little competition and a macroeconomic policy unsuited to
new realities.

The 1989–92 Period

Because of the financial crisis some drastic stabilization measures were
adopted from 1985–6, but it was necessary to go much further by an in-
depth reform of economic structures, which was undertaken in the structural adjustment programme of 1987–8. During four–five years a set of
consistent measures was implemented:

● Liberalization of most prices and adoption of legislation in respect of
  competition
● Liberalization of imports
● Liberalization of the financial sector
● Reform of parastatal enterprises.

The state of course continued to play a very large role because of the
weight of the public sector in infrastructure, energy, mining, industry and
banking, but for the first time since independence competition regulated
the functioning of the economy.

From 1987, growth resumed with the abolition of the authorization required for all industrial investment, permitting the entry of new producers.
Then prices were decontrolled: from 1986 to 1990, the percentage of controlled prices in agriculture and industry was reduced from 95 to 40 per
cent. Finally the management of parastatal enterprises was reformed so
they functioned competitively: some enterprises were privatized (in hotels
and textiles), others were given greater autonomy while abolishing their
operating subsidies, which had undermined competition and was costly to
the state (these subsidies and the financing of the investment concerned
reached 12 per cent of the GDP in 1984).

The liberalization of the financial sector was the second element of the adjustment programme. Henceforth interest rates were uncontrolled, except for medium-/short-term credit for priority sectors. The banks could now make loans up to 10 million dinars without prior approval. Moreover, a large range of new financial instruments was introduced to stimulate savings. In 1988 they included certificates of deposit (issued by banks to obtain liquidity on the money market) and commercial paper of enterprises. In 1989 Treasury bonds were introduced as a substitute for *bons d'équipement*, but requiring that the state pay much more to borrow. The reform of 18 January 1988 reorganized the money market so that all agents (banks, large enterprises and insurance companies) could use it and freely fix the interest rate, with banks henceforth obliged to refinance on this market. New instruments continued to be offered in the 1990s: stocks without voting rights, convertible stocks and investment funds.

The decontrolling of rates resulted in a large rise, and real rates became clearly positive. This policy stimulated financial savings, which doubled from 1989 to 1993. In 1993 these savings (including Treasury bonds) reached 15 per cent of the total savings flows. These reforms also stimulated stock exchange transactions: the volume of transactions was multiplied almost by eight from 1990 to 1994. All these figures prove that the liberalization of the financial sector mobilized savings which potentially existed, but had been discouraged by certain forms of financial repression.

Liberalization of foreign trade, the third element, was probably the most important for its effects on TFP growth. The effective rate of protection was reduced from 70 per cent to 44 per cent between 1986 and 1990, the proportion of imports subject to licensing fell from 93 per cent to 35 per cent. From 1985, several measures encouraged exports: the abolition of export licenses and export taxes, and facilities for temporary admission and for customs formalities. However, the depreciation of the dinar was the greatest incentive (see Lahouel, 1996). A 10 per cent devaluation in 1986 had been followed by a depreciation of 30 per cent between 1987 and 1991. While exports formerly increased at the rate of domestic demand, they rose twice as fast between 1986 and 1991 (7.6 per cent instead of 3.5 per cent), so that one could speak of export-led growth.

This policy of openness (the export: GDP ratio rose from 30.7 per cent in 1986 to 39.8 per cent in 1993) changed the functioning of the Tunisian economy because, for first time since 1956, foreign competition prevented certain errors of management or misallocation of factors between sectors. This is proven by the allocation of capital. From 1960 to 1986, the share of the sectors having the highest capital productivity (agriculture, agricultural and food industries and tertiary industries) continually decreased in favour of sectors whose capital productivity was lower. However, this reversed from 1987, with capital going first and foremost towards the activities where it was most profitable.

The efficiency gains explain TFP growth (+1.7 per cent per year from 1989 to 1992), after the below-average performance of 1982–8. It is significant that this success coincided with a sharp slowing down of the accumulation of physical and human capital. The rate of investment, which had exceeded 30 per cent, returned to 22 per cent for 1987–93. Education's share of budgetary expenditure decreased as the fall in the birth rate clearly slowed the growth of primary school enrollment.

There was a sort of transition from an extensive-growth model, based on rapid increases in capital stock and labour (after correction for the quality effect), with a high GDP growth rate and a low, even negative, TFP growth rate, to an intensive-growth model, based on better management and allocation of resources, while K and L increased less quickly. That led to a much higher TFP growth rate.

PRELIMINARY CONCLUSIONS: MUCH OR TOO MUCH
STATE INTERVENTION?

To the question of whether there was too much state intervention, we can answer that there was 'fortunately much state intervention and unfortunately too much state intervention'. Indeed, we saw how the state weighed on the Tunisian economy since independence. This intervention had many beneficial effects for growth: the large investment in infrastructure increased TFP in the private sector, the first public investment in industry contributed to the training of a skilled labour force and managerial personnel in a sector which had been managed mainly by foreigners, and the aid to the tourism industry and public facilities stimulated the growth of tourism while respecting the environment more than in other Mediterranean countries. Above all the rapid improvement in the quality of labour (the average number of years of schooling was multiplied by four in 30 years) would not have been possible without exceptional state expenditure for education. Some other decisions had an equally important impact on the country's balanced development such as the extensive system of student grants and the advancement of women by a modern legal system and female equality in the rate of schooling enrollment.

All these examples show that after the Protectorate and a weak regime under a Bey, Tunisia needed a strong state to modernize the society and economy, and in this sense 'much state intervention' has been beneficial.

On the other hand, it significant that the two periods when the TFP growth was negative there was 'too much state intervention'. The first failure will not surprise all those who have studied socialist economies. By collectivizing up to 80 per cent of the economy and imposing the supervisory ministries' direct management on agricultural cooperatives and industrial enterprises, Ben Salah's policy was destined to fail. The second failure also involved 'too much state intervention', even though the error is less obvious. By accumulating large budget deficits, in part financed by foreign loans, for public investment in productive sectors and infrastructure, and by maintaining strict control of all levels of the economy (controlling prices, investment, credit, foreign exchange, foreign trade), macroeconomic disequilibria were combined with structural inefficiency. A stabilization and structural adjustment programme became the only way to restore sustainable growth.

For a better understanding of the reasons for the two failures a political analysis of the economy is very useful. We showed how the status quo was defended by a coalition of interests groups in the 1982–8 period. The errors of the 1960s had also political causes. At independence, a large proportion of the modern sector's capital was held by foreigners. By nationalizing many companies from 1956 to 1960, establishing exchange control in January 1959, by influencing farmers and heads of enterprises of foreign origin to withdraw, 'Tunisification' provoked capital flight. In order for development to continue in a liberal framework with public enterprises in key sectors, it would have been necessary to have a Tunisian entrepreneurial class capable of taking over from foreign capitalists. However, there was none so that there was a great temptation to go to the limits of state control. That strategy had been advocated since independence by the Union Générale Tunisienne du Travail (UGTT), and its leader Ben Salah. This economic choice had an obvious political dimension, for the socialist strategy more or less provided benefits in form of power, income and job creation to the employees of the public and parastatal sectors, who were Ben Salah's political base.

In this sense, Tunisia's honourable performance for 35 years, while less impressive than that of some Southeast Asian countries, is explained more by the excessive weight of interest groups during certain periods (in contrast with Southeast Asian countries) than by economic handicaps. From the end of the Second World War to the 1987 adjustment, Tunisia's economic policies were always subject to interest group pressures. That is obvious for the colonial period when there were two key groups, the *colons* in agriculture and the large foreign companies which controlled the railroads, electricity, mining and banking. During the 1960s there was a gradual conquest of economic power by employees of the public and parastatal sectors, especially by the senior civil servants and directors of nationalized companies who controlled the major part of the Tunisian economy in 1969. Finally, the mixed economy of the 1970s and 1980s served the interests of a composite group: manufacturers under protectionism, large farmers, senior civil servants who retained part of their powers, and directors of parastatal enterprises and, to some extent, their personnel who benefited from 'private hunting grounds'. It is probable that until 1987 the political weight of these interest groups slowed the reforms which have increased the economy's efficiency and thus stimulated growth in the interest of the whole population. Concern for this interest had counted for more in Southeast Asian countries than in Tunisia, where these successive groups vigorously defended the rents they benefited from.

Appendix: TFP, Annual Data

1962	–10	1978	+1.8
1963	+7.4	1979	+1.9
1964	–3.2	1980	+3.2
1965	–0.6	1981	+0.9
1966	–3.5	1982	–4.8
1967	–5.3	1983	+0.6
1968	+6.6	1984	+2
1969	+0.1	1985	+2.2
1970	+2.5	1986	-3.7
1971	+7.2	1987	+4.6
1972	+13.5	1988	–2.1
1973	–5.1	1989	–0.5
1974	+3.4	1990	+5.4
1975	+1.8	1991	+1.7
1976	+2.3	1992	+5.5
1977	–1.7	1993	–0.2

Notes

*   This analysis is largely based on the authors' study, *The Tunisian Economy's Long-Term Growth* (OECD Development Centre, 1996). That study was carried out under a Development Centre research programme on long-term growth, directed by J.-C. Berthélemy.

1.   Our figure for the growth of TFP (1.3 per cent) is lower than the estimate of J. Page and J. Underwood (1995) (2.1 per cent if quality effect for labour is included). The main factor explaining this discrepancy is the rate of growth

of *L*. From Page and Underwood's data – and assuming an elasticity of *L* of 0.7 – this growth rate is 1.3 per cent instead of our estimated 1.95 per cent (Table 4.2). We must recall that this figure (1.95 per cent) comes from IEQ data base, and is in better agreement with the population growth.

2.   As note 1 above.
3.   By using the perpetual inventory method and assuming that imported capital goods have a 15-year lifetime.

References

Easterly, W. and Rebelo, S. (1993) 'Fiscal Policy and Economic Growth: An Empirical Investigation', paper presented at a conference on 'How do National Policies Affect Long-Run Growth?', World Bank, Washington, DC.

Lahouel, M. (1996) 'Trade and Exchange Rate Policies and the Performance of the Tunisian Economy in the Eighties', ADB Development Seminar, Abidjan, mimeo.

Page, J. and Underwood, J. (1995) 'Growth, the Maghreb and the European Union', IEA Congress, Tunis, mimeo.

Stolper, W. (1980) 'Le Développement en Général et en Particulier: Le Cas de la Tunisie 1961–71', *Annales économiques*, Université de Clermont, Clermont-Ferrand.

5 Economic Policy and Economic Development in Tunisia

Hassouna Moussa

HOSEI UNIVERSITY, JAPAN, AND
ACADIA UNIVERSITY, CANADA

1 INTRODUCTION

Since the end of the Second World War, we have witnessed a continuous expansion of the club of developed countries. The process accelerated during the 1970s and 1980s. Some countries, the newly industrialized countries (NICs), like Japan, South Korea, Taiwan and Singapore, achieved phenomenal growth rates. Others, like Tunisia, despite remarkable efforts achieved only moderate but fluctuating growth rates. The mean growth rate was 5.1 per cent and the standard deviation 3.6 per cent (see also chapter 4 in this volume).

Tunisia began its development effort at the end of the 1950s with low wages and a development strategy based on industrialization through learning from imported technology. A cursory look at Tunisia's economic policy during the period 1960–91 shows that it bears a great resemblance to those pursued by the NICs during the same period. In the beginning, Tunisia pursued an import-substitution (IS) policy. The government created and protected infant industries with high tariffs and trade barriers. It embarked on an ambitious investment policy in the industrial and tourism sectors and in education. The investment policy was buttressed by a financial policy of credit selection, nominal interest rate controls and an industrial policy based on a careful choice of priority sectors. Later government attention was extended to exports. The government granted various incentives to exporters including low interest rates, elimination of tariffs on imported inputs and raw materials, tax exemptions and holidays and reduction of corporate profit taxes, free trading zones and various incentives to domestic and foreign investors. The government controlled prices, exchange rates and financial capital movements. The government was omnipresent – created, destroyed, distorted relative prices, implored, offered carrots and wielded sticks just like the governments of other NICs.

In his comparison of the performances of the NICs of Asia to those of Latin America, Balassa (1991) noted that the two groups of countries had similar investment GDP ratios. Thus he attributed the mediocre and some-times poor performance of the latter to wastage of capital. The NICs of Latin America had decidedly higher incremental capital output ratios. The NICs of Asia had a robust and aggressive export sector which contributed to a more efficient use of capital. With the exception of Hong Kong, the NICs of Asia went through the same stages of development as all other NICs including Tunisia. They followed an IS policy during the first stage of their development. In the beginning, consumption goods produced locally using imported simple technologies with limited economies of scale and unskilled labour replaced imports in the domestic market. Such was the case for textiles, leather and shoes. Once the domestic market was saturated, Balassa observed that the NICs had two choices – extend IS further up to include sectors of durable goods and capital equipment, or conquer new foreign markets of consumer products. The NICs of Latin America chose the first alternative. The NICs of Asia chose the second; they decided to compete on international markets.

To succeed, the NICs of Asia had to become more competitive, both on international and domestic markets. The symbol of their development policy became competitiveness instead of self-sufficiency on all fronts. They devalued their respective currencies many times despite the advice of many pundits to be prudent, especially in view of the J-curve phenomenon and adverse elasticities. Early in this second stage they granted fiscal incentives to exporters based on their performance in export markets. At the same time, they reduced substantially tariffs and quantitative trade barriers on imports of inputs and raw materials used in export industries. They reduced tariffs and quantitative trade barriers to low levels on imports of all products. Later the wages the NICs of Asia increased substantially, and other competing countries with low wages appeared in international markets, following the example of the NICs. Following the same policy of search for improved competitiveness, the NICs of Asia gradually abandoned the markets of consumer goods with low capital: labour ratios. Aware of the importance of high-technology products, they changed their niches, gradually targeting new products, technologically more advanced, for production and export.

During many long periods, just like Tunisia, the NICs of Asia (with the exception of Hong Kong) practised an inflationary monetary policy with cheap credit and nominal interest rates controls, often with negative real

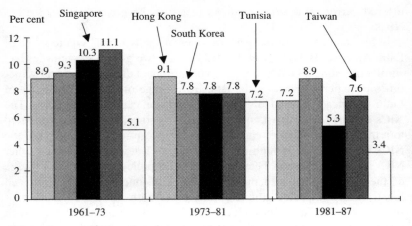

Source: Balassa (1991); IMF, *International Financial Statistics*.

Figure 5.1   Real GDP growth rates: Tunisia and the NICs of Asia, 1961–87

interest rates. To re-establish positive real interest rates, just like Tunisia, the majority of them embarked in the 1980s on financial reforms: liberalizing credit and nominal interest rates and reducing inflation through monetary and fiscal austerity programmes.

Despite the striking resemblance in many areas, there are a few fundamental differences in the conduct of economic policy between Tunisia and the NICs of Asia. As Figure 5.1 shows, the NICs achieved growth rates often double those achieved by Tunisia with the exception of the 1970s. The oil shocks of the 1970s benefited the Tunisian economy, but had negative effects on the economies of the NICs. Tunisia's oil production reached its peak during the 1970s and the NICs of Asia are not oil producers. Thus it is interesting to examine the economic development policy of Tunisia in detail in order to isolate those factors responsible for the difference in growth performance.

2   MONETARY POLICY AND INFLATION

During the period 1961–91, the government assigned to the central bank of Tunisia (BCT) the mission to support the development effort by supplying the Tunisian economy with the credit and investment funds it needed. BCT had the power to fix a plethora of interest rates and to control credit, the exchange rate and foreign exchange. To help it with this task, and for other social reasons, the government imposed extensive price controls. In its effort to discharge its mission and provide investment funds to priority sectors, BCT maintained negative real interest rates for many short periods of time. Despite this exorbitant power, BCT behaved reasonably well. Throughout the period and with a few exceptions, it maintained inflation within tolerable limits. Price controls probably helped BCT to control inflation, but due to their mechanics, they cannot by themselves explain satisfactorily BCT's success. Rather, as illustrated by (1) and (2), its relative success in controlling inflation can be credited to the efforts of BCT to follow a responsible monetary policy:

$$GrM = 0.45GrM_{-1} - 1.18GrGDP_{-1} - 1.02Inf_{-1} - 0.6ResM_{-1} \qquad (1)$$
$$(2.62) \qquad (-3.93) \qquad\quad (-1.55) \qquad (-4.02)$$

$$ResM = LM - (-6.27 + 0.9LRGDP + 0.67\,LP - 0.07\,R) \qquad (2)$$
$$(-3.93)\ (4.36) \qquad\quad (2.95) \qquad (-2.39)$$

$$\overline{R}^2 = 0.44 \qquad SER = 0.05 \qquad F = 4.26 \qquad DW = 2.2$$

Cointegration test: Logarithm of maximum likelihood = 58.25
                     Critical value at 1 per cent   = 54.46

where GrM = growth rate of the stock of currency in the hands of the public
$GrGDP$ = growth rate of real GDP
Inf = inflation rate of the consumer price index
LM = Logarithm of the stock of currency in the hands of the public including banks
$LRGDP$ = Logarithm of real GDP
LP = logarithm of the consumer price index
R = Discount rate of BCT
Numbers in parenthesis are t-statistics; estimation period: 1961–1991

(1) and (2) were estimated in a single stage in the form of an error correction model. (2) is the long-run demand for money. The cointegration test of Johansen shows that we can reject the null hypothesis that there is no cointegrating relation at the 1 per cent confidence level. Thus we accepted the hypothesis that its residual *ResM* is stationary. We can use (1) to derive a few characteristics of the behaviour of BCT during the 1961–91 period.

First, (1) shows that BCT assigned a heavy weight to inflation control in its utility function. When the inflation rate increased by 1 percentage point, BCT reduced the money supply growth rate in the following year by an amount slightly greater than 1 per cent. Second, (2) and (1) show that BCT acted to maintain equilibrium between the long-run demand for money and its supply. When an excess money supply appeared, BCT reduced the growth rate of money supply in the following year by 60 per cent of the excess. Third, (1) shows that BCT tried to lean against the wind

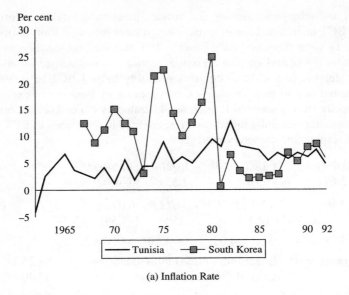

(a) Inflation Rate

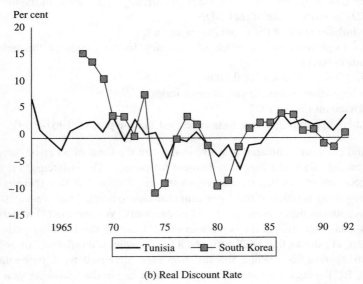

(b) Real Discount Rate

Source: IMF, *International Financial Statistics*.
(a) Inflation rate   (b) Real discount rate

Figure 5.2   Tunisia and South Korea: inflation and real discount rates, 1965–92

in an effort to reduce the fluctuations in economic activity. Figure 5.2 describes the behaviour of the inflation rate and the discount rate in Tunisia and South Korea. The figure shows that in the long run both countries have similar propensities to tolerate inflation. It shows also that both central banks tolerated negative real interest rates for similarly short periods of time. In fact, the central bank of South Korea had tolerated inflation rates much greater than those tolerated by BCT. We conclude that the monetary policy of Tunisia by itself was no worse, if not better, than that practised by many NICs of Asia. Thus we must look elsewhere for differences in economic policy responsible for the differences in growth performance.

3 INTERNATIONAL TRADE AND COMPETITION IN DOMESTIC MARKETS

Taiwan began its development effort in the early 1950s. It started with an import-substitution (IS) programme protected by high tariffs and trade barriers. Soon it realised that despite a 10 per cent growth rate of the manufacturing sector output, there were enormous excess capacities. In 1959, many industries operated at less than 50 per cent capacity. Balassa (1991) attributed the excess capacity to exchange controls, protection of local markets and a system of import licences. To solve the problem, the government introduced incentives to exporters designed to reduce overcapacity. It devalued domestic currency several times. Henceforth, exporters were reimbursed customs duties on imports of intermediate products and were allowed to deduct 2 per cent of the value of their exports from their taxable income. They could deduct 10 per cent if they exported more than 50 per cent of their production. They benefited also from substantial reductions in interest rates, 6 per cent as compared to 22 per cent on ordinary loans. The association of manufacturers was allowed to collect a certain tax on sales in the domestic market in order to subsidize exports. Starting in 1959, the government reduced tariffs on many occasions. Balassa's calculations show that the ratio of income from customs duties to the total value of imports decreased from 30 per cent in 1958 to 17 per cent at the end of the 1960s to 10 per cent in 1975. By the end of 1972, there was no more prohibition on imported products. The new regulations introduced in 1960 allowed domestic producers to demand the imposition of restrictions on similar imported products if their prices did not exceed the prices of the imported products by more than 25 per cent and their imported intermediate products did not represent more than 70 per cent of their price.

The important lesson we learn from this brief review of Taiwan's international trade policy is that Taiwan not only encouraged exports but it opened up the country to international competition. Starting in 1972, Tunisia has encouraged exports and investment in the exporting sector but did not encourage Tunisian firms to compete in international markets. It discouraged competition in domestic markets.

Realizing the failure of the IS policy, the government of Tunisia enacted the 1972 Law in an effort to encourage exports. The law allowed exporters to dispose of their foreign exchange cash flow after repatriation of the cost of inputs bought in Tunisia. Companies, less than one-third of whose capital was controlled by Tunisian nationals, could not borrow in Tunisian dinar, the Tunisian currency. Since 1981, exporters have benefited from a 50 per cent reduction of the corporate profit tax. Since 1982, exporters have enjoyed a reduction of interest rates on long and medium-term credits proportional to the share of their exports in their total sales. In addition, the government reimburses the totality of the indirect taxes paid on intermediate products and they can obtain credit to finance their exports.

Incentives were thus slow to come to exporters. Despite the failure of the IS policy, the Tunisian dinar preserved its value in terms of the French franc from 1964 to 1985. Between 1970 and 1980, the dinar appreciated by 70 per cent with respect to the Italian lira, slightly less than the differential inflation rate between the two countries. During the same period, the Tunisian dinar depreciated by about 40 per cent with respect to the German mark, slightly more than the differential inflation rate between the two countries. Indeed, an exchange rate equation estimated for Tunisia shows that apart from the devaluation of 1985–6, BCT essentially adjusted the exchange rate of the dinar from 1970 to 1991 according to the relative version of the purchasing power parity (Moussa, 1994). It is to the credit of BCT that it did not cause the real exchange rate of the dinar to appreciate. However, the Tunisian economy had to wait until 1985 to have a true devaluation that would test the true equilibrium exchange rate of the dinar.

Before 1986, only 10 per cent of imports were exempted from tariffs and non-tariff barriers covered 97 per cent of GDP. Only a few industrialists could import raw materials, a few merchants could import finished products and some state monopolies imported certain necessity products. Tariffs on most manufactured products exceeded 100 per cent and were over 200 per cent on some products.[1] In 1982, the spectrum of tariffs extended from 5 per cent to 236 per cent. The government tightened price controls in 1972, thus stifling competition. The majority of industrial products were subjected to a price control regime called 'régime d'auto-homologation'.[2] Under this regime, the government fixed the profit margin as a proportion of total cost. The producer fixed his price as equal to the sum of the profit margin and the average total cost. Since every industry is protected against foreign competition, one sure way to increase profits is to behave like a monopoly. It is profitable to inflate costs so as to increase profits, until marginal revenue is equal to marginal cost. With a negative or very small real interest rate, a policy of cheap money and credit control, an overvalued dinar and BCT guarantees which prevent commercial banks from going bankrupt, to inflate costs it suffices to borrow and import redundant equipment. Thus the creation of excess capacity, the excessive indebtedness of public and private enterprises and the government.

According to a 1989 survey of industrial firms, the majority of them did not operate at full capacity. Only 42 per cent of firms in the textile and leather sector operated at full capacity, and the percentage of firms in other sectors that operated at full capacity was even lower. On average, only 32 per cent of all enterprises in the manufacturing industries operated at full capacity in 1989, a relatively good year. The authors of the Seventh Plan (1987–91) were conscious of this shortcoming. However, instead of recommending measures to help reduce excess capacity by encouraging exports, liberalizing the domestic market and integrating the export sector into the rest of the economy, they recommended more of the same thing – measures to reduce inflation and reinforce price controls.

After the 1985 crisis, the government embarked on a profound reform programme. The dinar was devalued in 1985 and 1986 by approximately 40 per cent. A gradual liberalization programme was initiated in 1986. In the first stage, the programme called for a reduction of tariffs on imports of capital equipment, raw materials and semi-finished products. Yet in 1990, the imported products which benefited from tariff reduction represented only 28 per cent of GDP. The elimination of tariffs on raw materials and semi-finished products alone does not reduce monopoly power. The reduction does contribute to a reduction of marginal costs and prices of finished products, but this would happen both in competitive and monopoly dominated markets. Competition in the markets of intermediate and finished products remained relatively restrained and the quality of products continued to suffer. The substandard quality of certain Tunisian made intermediate products explains why the exporting sector buys only 10 per cent of its inputs domestically. In 1995, more than 75 per cent of wholly-exporting firms uses intermediate products supplied by their foreign parents because of inadequate quality of products available locally or local unavailability of needed intermediate products. This fact shows the lack of integration of the export sector in the rest of the economy and the lack of competition in the domestic market.

Before 1986, high tariffs and negative real interest rates encouraged investment in marginal projects.[3] To remedy the situation, the 1987 *Loi de Finance* introduced several measures:

- institution of a minimum tariff of 15 per cent on all imports
- immediate reduction of tariffs between 26 per cent and 35 per cent to 25 per cent and reduction of tariffs between 31 per cent and 55 per cent by six percentage points.

In addition, the law provided for a further reduction of those tariffs between 26 per cent and 34 per cent to 25 per cent and the reduction of those exceeding 34 per cent by 9 percentage points. The objective was to reduce the effective rate of protection on all products to 25 per cent by 1991. However, even in 1995, the average tariff rate was still 43 per cent.

Many other measures were undertaken to improve access to credit for exporters and quality improvement. In 1987, quantitative restrictions were removed on 30 per cent of imports. Quantitative restrictions were lifted on imports of raw materials, unfinished products and parts for firms exporting more than 15 per cent of their production. Before the 1986 reform, the effective protection rate varied from 5 per cent to 234 per cent. Consumer products received the highest level of protection. One of the objectives of the reforms was to unify all tariffs. In 1990, the average tariff on consumer products was 35 per cent, 19 per cent on capital equipment and agricultural products. Despite this reduction in tariffs, protection continued in the form of quantitative restrictions which produced rents. Imports in direct competition with domestically produced products as well as other products such as cars were practically excluded from the liberalization programme. In 1990, restrictions were eliminated completely on only 30 per cent of all imports compared with an objective of 48.5 per cent.

Even in June 1992, only non-residents could keep foreign exchange during trips outside of the country. Residents, with the exception of a certain margin, must surrender to BCT all or part of foreign exchange earned from exports. Foreign exchange receipts must be repatriated within 10 days from the previously agreed date of payment. Only enterprises exporting more than 15 per cent of their output and operating in sectors covered by laws encouraging investment are exempt, and even these privileged firms can keep only a maximum of 20 per cent of their foreign exchange receipts. As an incentive, exporters and importers can purchase foreign exchange risk cover from BCT. Non-residents can open so-called 'capital accounts', where they may deposit revenues of sales of securities or real estate without prior authorization of BCT but under certain conditions. These accounts can be debited freely only in favour of other capital accounts or to pay for management fees of business with a domicile located in Tunisia. Until the end of 1992, regulations were thus still overwhelming. They were reduced somewhat after the government introduced current account convertibility of the dinar in 1994.[4]

We set this brief review of Tunisian regulations of trade and reform measures against the background of the reforms undertaken much earlier by Taiwan. We discover a difference in philosophy. Taiwan has chosen to use competition as an engine of development. Tunisia has chosen to rein in competition for the longest time possible by creating as many regulations as possible and sometimes taking contradictory measures such as the 1972 Law and the simultaneous tightening of price controls. Despite the benefits reaped from the 1972 Law, 10 years elapsed before fiscal incentives were granted to exporters based on performance in international markets, 13 years before reducing seriously the bias against domestic exporters by a devaluation and 20 years before seriously reducing tariffs and quantitative restrictions and dismantling price controls to allow for more competition in domestic markets. In fact, the newly established industries (NIEs) under the 1972 Law were not integrated in the rest of the Tunisian economy. It appears that the Law was conceived mainly to reduce the unemployment of unskilled workers and reduce emigration to Europe. It was not part of a general development strategy based on conquering new markets.

There is plenty of evidence of what benefits the Law brought about. The manufacturing sector output *per capita* increased from US$ 90 in 1970 to US$ 157 in 1976 in constant 1970 prices. In the same period, the value-added of the manufacturing sector rose from US$ 115 million in 1970 to US$ 212 million in 1976 in 1970 constant prices. More specifically, we recognize the positive effects of the law in the following equations. (3) shows the positive effect of the 1972 Law on the exports of textiles, leather and shoes, *XTEX*, represented by a dummy variable *Dum*72.[5] (4) shows the positive effect of the 1972 Law on the exports of phosphates and chemicals, *XFOC*, represented by a dummy variable *Dum*72. In both equations, all variables are in logarithms except for *Dum*72. Numbers in parenthesis are *t*-statistics.

$$XTEX = -25.49 + 1.71\,Dum72 + 4.6\,PGDP - -1.76\,RPTexF \qquad (3)$$
$$\quad\ (-5.18)\ \ (6.38) \qquad\quad (5.15) \qquad\qquad (-3.20)$$

$$\bar{R}^2 = 0.97 \qquad SER = 0.22 \qquad DW = 2.32$$
$$SGE = -7.78 \quad \text{MacKinnon critical value at 5 per cent} = -5.50$$

where $PGDP$ = a weighted index of the GDP of the three main partners of Tunisia – France, Germany and Italy
$RPTexF$ = relative price of textiles in France
SGE = Granger–Engle cointegration statistics

DW = Durbin–Watson statistics

$$XFOC = -9.43 + 0.86\,Dum72 + 0.69\,PGDP - 1.12\,RPFOC \qquad (4)$$
$$\quad\;\; (-2.99)\;\; (3.98) \qquad\quad (1.09) \qquad\quad (-6.94)$$

$$\bar{R}^2 = 0.94 \qquad SER = 0.18 \qquad DW = 1.49$$
$$SGE = -4.15 \quad \text{MacKinnon critical value at 5 per cent} = -4.69$$

where $RPFOC$ = relative price of Tunisian phosphate and chemical products with respect to the corresponding French products.

After 1972, there was a profound and sustainable change in the structure of Tunisian exports. Textile, leather and shoes, the principal beneficiaries from the Law, grew in importance from close to nothing in 1970 to 28 per cent of total exports in 1991. Agriculture and foodstuffs decreased in importance from 40 per cent of total exports in 1961 to about 10 per cent in 1991. Energy products, after reaching a peak of 38 per cent of total exports in 1980, declined to only 10 per cent of total exports in 1991. However, this remarkable performance was not exploited to build a broader basis for increased competitiveness in international markets, as evidenced by the evolution of the geographic composition of Tunisian exports and imports. In 1991, Tunisia sold 21 per cent of its exports to France, 20 per cent to Italy, 16.5 per cent to Germany and 6 per cent to the Benelux countries. In total, the countries of the European Economic Community absorbed 68 per cent of Tunisian exports. The geographic distribution of imports was similar. This composition has changed very little over the last three decades. In contrast, South Korea sold 35 per cent of its exports to the United States, 15.5 per cent to Europe and 20 per cent to Japan. It has purchased 25 per cent of its imports from the United States, 13.5 per cent from Europe, 30 per cent from Japan and 6 per cent from Canada and Australia. Population-wise, the markets of the United States, Japan and Canada combined are three times the size of the combined markets of Tunisia's three main partners. Competition in these markets is more fierce. The economies of South Korea and Taiwan, more open than Tunisia's to international competition in domestic and foreign markets, benefited more from international trade. Competition and conquest of international markets constituted the engine of their development since the early stages of their development. Already in 1972, only 12 years after abandoning the IS strategy, Taiwan did away with all the tariffs and quantitative trade barriers and set out to compete all over the world. In 1981, South Korea's Fifth Plan declared that South Korea's development strategy would henceforth be based on competition inside the country and the liberalization of international trade policies (Balassa, 1991). The continued geographic concentration of Tunisia's international trade and the fact that Tunisia's exports to the EEC were protected by quotas suggested that international trade was little more than a safety valve against unemployment. It was also an indication of the lack of competition and innovative efforts. The policy of encouraging exports is not enough, it is necessary to integrate it in a competitive framework that encourages innovation in changing products and markets mixes.

4   INDUSTRIAL AND INVESTMENT POLICY

According to Balassa (1991), misallocation of resources caused in part by negative real interest rates was partly responsible for the lower growth rates achieved by the NICs of Latin America. Negative real interest rates discouraged savings and encouraged the accumulation of inventories. The saving rates of Brazil and Argentina dropped respectively from 26 per cent and 20 per cent during the periods 1961–73 to 20 per cent and 16 per cent during the period 1981–7. The analysis of Tunisia's monetary policy has shown that the records of Tunisia's inflation and real interest rates are similar, sometimes even better, than those of South Korea. As Figures 5.3(a) and 5.3(b) show, South Korea maintained a higher savings ratio than Tunisia after 1975, despite the fact that it tolerated higher inflation rates and lower real interest rates. Thus its higher savings ratio after 1975 was not due to higher rates of returns. Moussa (1994) estimated a savings function for Tunisia over the period 1961–90. The results show that the real interest rate coefficient is positive but not significantly different from zero.

It is probably true that negative real interest rates discourage financial savings. However, given the low level of the housing stock in Tunisia, there are ample opportunities of investment in this sector offering positive rates of returns. As Figure 5.3(b) shows, Tunisia maintained until 1985 an investment GDP ratio similar to that of South Korea. Thus the question is not that negative real interest rates discouraged savings, which in turn discouraged investment. The question is whether the observed level of investment in this sector is consistent with an optimal allocation of resources in the long run. Financial savings are that much more flexible. They can be easily collected to reach a critical mass necessary to undertake large industrial investment projects with higher rates of returns, allowing the country

Per cent

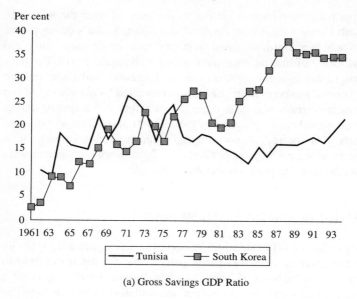

(a) Gross Savings GDP Ratio

Per cent

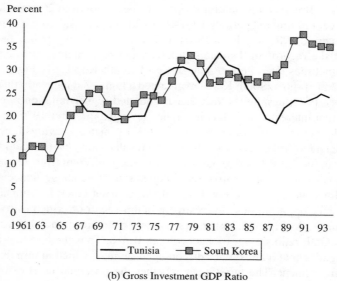

(b) Gross Investment GDP Ratio

Source: IMF, *International Financial Statistics*.
(a) Gross savings: GDP ratio   (b) Gross investment: GDP ratio

Figure 5.3   Tunisia and South Korea: savings and investment, 1961–93

to realize in the long run both its industrial and residential investment programmes. A nation's higher savings ratio may play the same role as a firm's higher retained earnings ratio. It allows a nation to manage its investment programme better by taking advantage of external circumstances which would not be possible if the country relied heavily on foreign investment. However, during the whole period Tunisia did not seem to have suffered from a lack of investment funds. As Figure 5.3(b) shows, the investment GDP ratios in Tunisia and South Korea are similar at least until 1985. Thus the poorer growth performance of Tunisia must be due to a misallocation of relatively similar amounts of capital resources, rather than to a dearth of savings. More direct foreign investment would have helped, but it is as important to make sure that the country is allocating its existing resources efficiently.

Tunisia invested heavily in tourism. From the private and social point of views, these investments are probably profitable. From the point of view of optimal development policy, they do not seem to constitute an efficient allocation of resources. As in other countries across the world, the tourism sector suffers from chronic underutilisation of capacity of the order of 50 per cent. Despite similar investment GDP ratios we observe different patterns of evolution of exports and GDP compositions in Tunisia and South Korea. Figures 5.4 and 5.5 describe the differences in evolution of the structure of exports.

Until 1970, the structure of Tunisian exports changed little. Even four years after the enactment of the 1972 Law, the manufactured products did not represent more than 26 per cent of Tunisia's exports in 1976, while they represented 88 per cent of South Korea's exports in the same year. As Figures 5.4 and 5.5 show, Tunisia's export structure in 1993 resembled that of South Korea in 1970.

In 1960, the manufacturing sector represented 8 per cent of Tunisia's GDP and 12 per cent of South Korea's. In 1977, the manufacturing sector represented 11 per cent of Tunisia's GDP and 25 per cent of South Korea's. In 1993, the manufacturing sector represented 19 per cent of Tunisia's GDP and 29 per cent of South Korea's GDP. Even in 1993, and despite approximately the same investment effort, Tunisia's manufacturing sector, while it has gained respectable ground, did not reach in terms of importance the same level as South Korea's had in 1977. In 1970, the output of the manufacturing sector *per capita* of Tunisia was equal to 81 per cent of that of Korea. In 1977, it was 56 per cent.

From this analysis, it appears that the rate of return on investment, as judged in terms of GDP growth, has been inferior to that in South Korea because of different allocation of resources or less successful management.

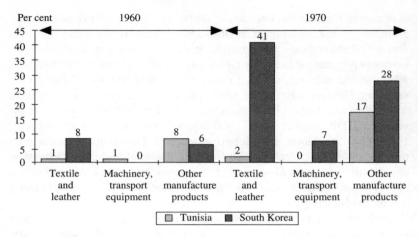

Source: World Bank, *World Development Reports*.

Figure 5.4   Tunisia and South Korea: structure of exports, 1960–70

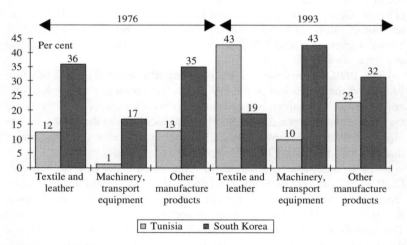

Source: World Bank, *World Development Reports*.

Figure 5.5   Tunisia and South Korea: structure of exports, 1976–93

The advantage of investment in the manufacturing sector is that it allows an improved utilization of human capital, learning-by-doing, better flexibility and wider access to international markets. Such an efficient deployment of resources requires a greater effort of geographic diversification of export markets, a sustainable increase in productivity and better product quality. However, Tunisia was interested only in the markets of the three large economies of the EEC. It reacted with long delays to changes in its environment rather than anticipating and/or inducing them. It granted investment incentives without *quid pro quo* conditions rather than rewards for innovation, thus reinforcing the status quo.

In Tunisia, government subsidies as a proportion of GDP have never stopped increasing. In 1961 they represented 3 per cent of GDP; in 1991, they represented 9.5 per cent. Had the government reduced them by a half, it would have wiped out its budget deficit. In 1972, government revenues from customs duties represented 14 per cent of the value of imports. In 1980, they represented 16 per cent, in 1985 26 per cent and in 1992 18.8 per cent. By way of comparison, after successive reductions of tariffs, government revenues from custom duties in Taiwan represented 30 per cent of the value of imports in 1957, 16 per cent in 1970, 10 per cent in 1975 and 8 per cent in 1986. Subsidies without *quid pro quo* conditions supported by an effective protection of the domestic market and price controls according to the markup plus formula have probably contributed to a less efficient allocation of resources. This inefficient allocation of resources, resulted in chronic excess capacity. The incremental capital output ratio exhibited large variations, from 135 to −135. Sometimes it was negative and sometimes it was more than double that of South Korea. However, on average it was about the same as those of South Korea and Taiwan.

Hikino and Amsden (1994) noted that many NICs in Asia distorted relative prices and subsidized industries, but they had *quid pro quo* conditions attached. Often those conditions are related to export performance of those benefiting from the subsidies. The government of Japan subsidized manufacturing firms indirectly in the form of allowing them control of domestic final goods markets at the wholesale distribution level with a *quid pro quo* condition related to their export performance. In Japan, the prices of many consumer goods are implicitly regulated by the association of wholesale and retail merchants (Lazarus, 1995). Consumer goods prices in Japan are almost double the OECD average (OECD, 1994). However, it is almost impossible for foreign competitors to penetrate Japanese markets despite the fact that Japan has the lowest tariffs in the world and has no quantitative restrictions. Cultural factors aside, we can explain this puzzle in terms of economic factors related to competition and industrial policy in Japan. These factors are urban planning laws, powerful retail trade associations, a law regulating the maximum number of large scale retail stores (*Dai ten Ho*), large trading companies, quality control and price maintenance agreements.

In Japan, the wholesale and retail trade distribution systems are dominated by large trading companies, conglomerates called *Keiretsu* and small shopkeepers' trade associations. Large trading companies have a monopoly on the imports of many products especially basic materials and are partly owned by a *Keiretsu* (Lawrence, 1991). Each *Keiretsu* is dominated by a group of large manufacturers and owns a certain proportion of the stocks of other *Keiretsu* (Ito and Maruyama, 1991). Manufacturers loan some of their employees to large department stores to help with sales of their products. Many manufacturers, including car makers, have their own retail stores system which sells their products exclusively (Ito and Maruyama, 1991). In a country where space is at a premium, location is important and can be used to collect monopoly rent. Similarly, thanks to price maintenance agreements and small shopkeepers' associations which are not illegal in Japan, monopoly rents can be easily collected and shared. The *Dai Ten Ho* reduces competition, favours insiders including *Keiretsu*, small store-owners and large stores which challenge the status quo. It allows each one of them to collect a certain share of the rents. Because large manufacturers own *Keiretsu* and large trading companies, they share in monopoly rents. Thus consumers subsidize large manufacturers (Okuno-Fujiwara, 1991, p. 294).

In contrast to the monopoly arrangements in the distribution sector, there is fierce competition in the manufacturing sector (OECD, 1994). In fact, *Keiretsu* purchase only 12 per cent of their supplies from their own manufacturer members,[6] they buy the rest from competitors. During the 1950s when the Japanese ministry of international trade (MITI) tried to consolidate the car manufacturing industry into a single firm in order to strengthen it against foreign competition, the car makers refused. MITI fixes implicit export targets for large Japanese manufacturers and exercises control on quality. To realize those targets and achieve the desired quality standards, Japanese manufacturers must allocate resources efficiently because they must compete in the domestic market with other Japanese manufacturers and on international markets with other international competitors. In exchange, the government allows access to low-cost financing and such monopolistic practices as price maintenance agreements, the use of the large-scale stores and urban planning laws to control domestic competition in the distribution sector and block access to foreign competition (OECD, 1994; Lazarus, 1995; Meerschwan, 1991). In the 1960s the government assisted those practices by high tariffs which it agreed to lower in 1970 to the same levels as those of other OECD countries. Later it lowered them even more so that Japan has now the lowest tariffs of any country in the world. To help Japanese firms small and large to compete in international markets, the Japanese government agreed early in the 1950s to help increase productivity and improve quality by creating and financing a Productivity Institute whose main objective was to adapt and diffuse imported technology and organize research and development of new production methods and new products. Many of the new research results were denied to foreign competitors (Okuno-Fujiwara, 1991).

In other words, the government of Japan encouraged competition among Japanese firms in the manufacturing sector and allowed the large firms who export to collect monopoly rents from Japanese consumers. These rents may be construed as indirect subsidies by the taxpayer to the producers. The government of Japan controlled the quality, but not the price. It used monopoly rents at the distribution level as an incentive to improve quality and reduce costs, thus allowing prices to perform their useful and natural functions of disseminating information about incentives. In contrast, the government of Tunisia controlled prices using a markup plus system, but did not control quality. Under such circumstances, producers have no incentives to improve quality or reduce costs. Those of them who exported operated under protection of a quota system granted by the EEC and under the watchful eyes of the European demanders who controlled quality and took advantage of low wages of unskilled workers and made little of their workers' skills. Now, faced with a reduction of tariffs and new international trade agreements to eliminate quotas, Tunisian producers are asking for new subsidies which they call 'compensation' within a restructuring programme called 'Programme de Mise à Niveau'. Such compensation might never have been needed if subsidies had been replaced by rewards and government had controlled quality with *quid pro quo* conditions related to an easily observable and verifiable performance such as exports.

5   INFRASTRUCTURE INVESTMENT POLICY

There is another important comparison to be made relating to investment in human capital and infrastructure. Table 5.1 shows that by 1970 Tunisia has caught up with South Korea in the field of primary education. However, while South Korea had virtually eradicated illiteracy in 1991, Tunisia's illiteracy rate was 35 per cent in that year. Tunisia's illiteracy rate in 1991 was higher than that of South Korea in 1960 despite a serious

Table 5.1   Education achievement levels in Tunisia and South Korea, 1960–91, percentage of the corresponding age groups

Year	Primary		Secondary		University		Illiteracy rate	
	Tunisia	S Korea	Tunisia	S Korea	Tunisia	S Korea	Tunisia	S Korea
1960	66	94	12	27	1	5	84	29
1965	91	101	16	35	2	6		
1970	100	103	23	42	5	16		
1975	118	109	20	59	6	10	45	9
1980	103	116	27	85	5	14		
1985	118	96	39	94	6	32		
1991	117	107	46	88	9	40	35	4

Source: World Bank World Development Reports.

effort by the Tunisian government. Table 5.1 shows also that the level of human capital formation in Tunisia at the secondary and university levels was 25 years behind that of South Korea. Secondary education is the cornerstone of the development strategy of the manufacturing sector in the NICs of Asia. In Japan, high school graduates are called 'Golden Eggs' in reference to their capacity to absorb the further recurrent training that makes them easily adaptable to changing conditions in the market place.

Road infrastructure relative to GDP in Tunisia is as good as in Korea in terms of quantity. In 1990, Tunisia had 17 500 km of paved road, 55 per cent of which is in good condition. South Korea had 34 250 km of paved road, 75 per cent of which is in good condition. In contrast, Tunisia lags in terms of electric generating capacity. In 1990, the electric generating capacity of Tunisia was 0.18 kW per person; South Korea's generating capacity was 0.55 kW per person. With respect to access to drinkable water, 49 per cent of the Tunisian population had access in 1970, 60 per cent in 1980 and 70 per cent in 1990. For South Korea these proportions were 58 per cent, 75 per cent and 93 per cent. With respect to access to sanitation, 63 per cent of the Tunisian population had access in 1970, 55 per cent in 1980 and 47 per cent in 1990. In contrast, 90 per cent of South Korea's population had access to sanitation in 1990.

Having access to essentially the same resources in terms of an invest-ment: GDP ratio, Tunisia improved its infrastructure but not to the same extent as South Korea. This suggests that South Korea achieved a more efficient allocation of resources long before Tunisia did. Thus it was able to achieve a significantly higher growth rate.

6 CONCLUSIONS

The Tunisian economy achieved respectable average growth rate during the last three decades. It has been able to increase its *per capita* income substantially. Now it ranks among the middle-income countries. This performance was associated with an investment: GDP ratio similar to that observed in the NICs of Asia who achieved a significantly higher growth rate during the same period. In this chapter, I investigated some of the factors that might be responsible for this difference. The difference cannot be attributed to a difference in the availability of resources, nor to a difference in monetary policy, nor to a failure to encourage exports or private initiative. Rather, I find that the difference is due to a lack of coordination of international trade, domestic trade and industrial policies. Tunisia did not recognize the role of competition and quality control nor the appropriate role of subsidies in development policy.

The Tunisian market is small. Yet, regulations from price control to tariffs and quotas were pervasive. These regulations can only stifle competition and promote monopoly. Their effects cannot be completely undone by privatization, elimination of price controls, devaluation and reduction of tariffs alone. In Tunisia, subsidies are used as compensation rather than rewards, reinforcing monopoly rather than competition. To resolve trade deficits, Tunisia used and still uses traditional Keynesian demand control policies, which require a host of unnecessary regulations. Early in their development, the NICs recognized that trade deficits could be resolved if exchange rates were set correctly and if the economy transformed increased imports into more rapidly increasing exports. They achieved this transformation by adopting a competition policy that emphasized quality control, productivity improvement through diffusion of newer technology and provision of adequate infrastructure and by using subsidies as rewards to workers and employers with *quid pro quo* conditions related to export performance. In this way, they harnessed the power of competition to promote development. Such a policy is not beyond the reach of Tunisia, and such a policy is now more necessary than ever, especially since Tunisia has now committed itself to entering into a free trade agreement with the European Union.

Notes

1.   Seventh Plan, p. 119.
2.   Seventh Plan, p. 125.
3.   Seventh Plan, p. 126.

4.   In January 1994, Tunisia introduced current account convertibility of the dinar. Among other things it increased the foreign exchange allowance of residents to an amount equivalent approximately to US$ 500.

5.   *Dum*72 is a dummy variable reflecting the effects of the 1972 Law of trade liberalization – *Dum*72 is equal to 0 from 1970 to 1972 and equal to one from 1971 to 1991.

6.   This is simple average of two figures reported by Saxonhouse, (Saxonhouse, 1991, p. 40). The first figure, 14.8 per cent, relates to *Keiretsu* with strong pre-Second World War roots. The second figure, 8.9 per cent, relates to *Keirestsu* created after the war.

References

Balassa, B. (1991) *Economic Policies in the Pacific Area Developing Countries* (London: Macmillan).

Enquête des entreprises (1989) Institut National de Statistiques, Tunis.

Hikino, T. and A. H. Amsden (1994) 'Staying Behind, Sneaking up, Soaring Ahead: Late Industrialization in Historical Perspective' in W. L. Baumol, R. R. Nelson, and E. N, Wolf (eds), *Convergence and Productivity* (Oxford and New York: Oxford University Press).

Ito, T. and Maruyama, M. (1991) 'Is the Japanese Distribution System Really Inefficient', in P. Krugman (ed.), *Trade with Japan*, National Bureau of Economic Research Report (Chicago: University of Chicago Press).

Lawrence, R. Z. (1991) 'How Open is Japan', in P. Krugman (ed.), *Trade with Japan*, National Bureau of Economic Research Report (Chicago: University of Chicago Press).

Lazarus, D. (1995) 'A Record Retailer's Lessons in Selling to Japan', *International Herald Tribune* (October 17).

Meerschwan, D. M. (1991) 'The Japanese Financial System and the Cost of Capital' in P. Krugman (ed.), *Trade with Japan*, National Bureau of Economic Research Report (Chicago: University of Chicago Press).

Moussa, H. (1994) *Politique Monétaire en Tunisie* (Tunis: Institut d'économie Quantitative).

OECD (1994) *Country Studies, Japan, 1991–1994* (Paris: OECD).

Okuno-Fujiwara, M. (1991) 'Industrial Policy in Japan: A Political Economic View', in P. Krugman (ed.), *Trade with Japan*: National Bureau of Economic Research Report (Chicago: University of Chicago Press).

Seventh Plan (1987–1991) Ministère du Plan et de Développement Régional (Tunis).

Saxonhouse, G. (1991) 'Comment on "How Open is Japan"', in P. Krugman (ed.), *Trade with Japan*, National Bureau of Economic Reseach Report (University of Chicago Press).

Data Sources

Base de Données Modèle Monat, Institut d'Economie Quantitative (Tunis)

International Financial Statistics (Washington, DC: IMF).

World Bank Development Reports (Washington, DC: World Bank).

Part II
System Reform

6 Strategies of Transition: A Political Economy Approach

Marek Dąbrowski
CASE – CENTER FOR SOCIAL AND ECONOMIC RESEARCH,
WARSAW, POLAND

1 INTRODUCTION

The transition to democracy and the market economy in Central and Eastern Europe (CEE) and in the former Soviet Union (FSU) may be the most important political and economic event in the world history of the last decade of the twentieth century. This chapter deals mainly with the problem of the optimal transition strategy and its political economy determinants.[1] The intention is to revisit the controversy of how quickly and radically the new market rules (and their individual components) should be adopted in the formerly communist countries (FCC). Particularly, the chapter deals mainly with two basic questions:

- Why a fast transition is better than a slow one
- What factors determine the speed, and therefore the effectiveness, of the transition process?

Arguments in favour of fast transition can be found in three areas: (1) technical requirements of some important components of transition process (e.g. macroeconomic stabilization cannot be done gradually); (2) the danger of a systemic vacuum (there are no effective coordination mechanisms half way between plan and market); (3) the political economy of the process (the so-called period of 'extra-ordinary politics' after the collapse of communism (Balcerowicz, 1994), the limited patience of society, the danger of rebuilding pressure groups and the credibility issue).

Answering the second question, we must look mainly at political factors. Those countries which managed to make progress in political reforms could bring about an environment conducive to successful economic transition. The quality of political elites and the consolidation of society around some basic goals and values (such as achieving and maintaining national independence or geopolitical reorientation) have also played a very important role in this respect.

The paper is organized in the following way. Section 2 classifies the transition strategies adopted in different countries in the period 1989–95. I also try to evaluate different strategies from the economic and political points of view. In section 3, I will return to the transition strategy debate, elaborating the technical, systemic and political arguments in favour of fast transition. Section 4 analyzes political and other factors determining the speed and therefore the effectiveness of transition process. Section 5 contains general conclusions.

2   TRANSITION STRATEGIES AND THEIR RESULTS

The last six years have given us a lot of very interesting evidence on how to manage the transition from central planning to market economics. There are three basic parameters for classifying the transition strategies:

(1)   The speed of actions in the main fields of transition: macroeconomic stabilization, liberalization and institutional changes, privatization and restructuring
(2)   The comprehensiveness and internal consistency of implemented policies, which create the so-called 'critical mass' of reform and avoid both macroeconomic mismanagement and a more serious systemic vacuum on the microlevel.
(3)   The cumulative progress in transition achieved so far.

With respect to all three factors, the countries of CEE and the FSU[2] may be classified into six broad categories. They are defined mainly along the third criterion – i.e. the cumulative progress in the transition process – although the two other criteria also play an important role. The proposed categories are.[3]

(1)   Overnight transition (East Germany), made possible through the rapid 'importation' of a stable currency and of most economic institutions from West Germany
(2)   First generation of fast and comprehensive reformers (Poland, Czech Republic, Slovakia, Hungary, Slovenia, Albania)
(3)   Second generation of fast reformers (Estonia, Latvia, Lithuania, Kyrgyzstan, Moldova, Croatia, Macedonia)

(4) Third generation of fast reformers (Armenia, Georgia, Kazakhstan)
(5) Gradual reformers (Bulgaria, Mongolia, Romania, Russia, Ukraine).
(6) Other countries – which suffer from armed conflicts (New Yugoslavia – Serbia and Montenegro, Bosnia and Herzegovina – Azerbaijan, Tajikistan) or have halted the reform process due to political reasons (Belarus, Uzbekistan, Turkmenistan).

The categorization proposed here gives, of course, a very general picture only. The real picture is much more complicated than this. Some cases escape neat classification. For example, Slovakia, after the dissolution of the Czecho–Slovak federation, slowed down the transition process in comparison with the Czech Republic, especially where privatization is concerned. This is also true of Lithuania, which in 1992 lagged behind Estonia and Latvia, especially with respect to macroeconomic stabilization and liberalization. Later, in 1993–4, Lithuania caught up with its Baltic neighbours. Moldova and Kyrgyzstan also joined the third group in 1994, after initial failures in the macroeconomic policy sphere.

By the end of 1994, Hungary and Slovenia had achieved a level of progress in the transition process similar to Poland and the former Czecho–Slovakia. They moved, however, much slower but in a rather well coordinated way. They had a better starting point, especially in terms of the earlier liberalization of the economy, institutional reforms (creating market institutions), in having smaller structural distortion, and in possessing more business experience in state-owned enterprises (SOEs) competing on the international market. This explains why the gradualist policy could give any positive results at all[4] – in contrast to other Eastern European countries (Romania or Bulgaria) and the FSU.

The two last categories contain, by definition, very different cases. Romania and Russia, for example, engaged in some important reforms (an example is the Russian voucher privatization) but have not had well coordinated transition policies (especially in the macroeconomic sphere) and have suffered macroeconomic mismanagement at least until the end of 1994.

In 1991, Bulgaria started a very radical liberalization and stabilization programme similar to the Polish and Czecho–Slovak ones. But later, it slowed down the transition process and did not achieve the critical mass of changes. Moreover, the inability to start large-scale privatization early enough has led to the return of a policy of 'soft budget constraints' for SOEs and to the significant erosion of macroeconomic policy in 1993–4.

At the beginning of 1994 New Yugoslavia started a very ambitious anti-inflationary programme (after one of the biggest hyperinflations in world history – see Rostowski, 1995) but its effect was limited due to the continuing Bosnian war and all its consequences in the economic sphere (such as UN economic sanctions against Yugoslavia).

Abstracting for now from all the above nuances one can say that fast and comprehensive reforms give better economic, social[5] and political results than a more gradual compromise scenario (not to mention cases where the real start of transition process has not even begun yet). This assessment is supported by the statistical data presented in Tables 6.1–6.3

The political advantages of fast transition are usually less obvious than the economic ones. The election defeat of democratic, pro-reform forces and success of populist anti-reformers in the second round of elections in many FCC serve very often as an argument against radical economic

Table 6.1   Increase (+) or decrease (–) in GDP, 1989–95 (in per cent in relation to the proceeding year and cumulatively for the whole period)

Group	Country	1989	1990	1991	1992	1993	1994	1995[a]	1989–95
2	Poland	+0.2	–11.5	–7.6	+2.6	+3.8	+6.0	+5.5	–2.4
	Czech Rep.	+0.4	–3.0	–10.0	–5.0	–0.9	+2.6	+4.0	–12.0
	Slovakia	–1.0	–2.5	–11.2	–7.0	–4.1	+4.8	+5.0	–15.9
	Albania	+9.8	–10.0	–27.7	–9.7	+9.6	+9.4	+7.8	–16.6
	Hungary	+0.7	–3.5	–11.9	–4.5	–0.8	+2.0	+1.2	–16.3
	Slovenia	–3.6	–2.6	–9.3	–6.5	+1.3	+5.0	+4.5	–11.5
3	Estonia	+3.3	–8.1	–11.3	–19.3	–6.6	+6.0	+6.0	–28.7
	Latvia	+5.7	–3.4	–8.3	–33.8	–14.8	+1.9	+0.4	–46.0
	Lithuania	+1.1	–6.9	–13.1	–37.7	–24.2	+1.7	+5.3	–58.1
	Kyrgyzstan	+3.8	+3.2	–5.0	–19.1	–16.0	–26.5	+2.0	–48.2
	Moldova	+8.8	–1.5	–18.0	–21.3	–8.7	–22.1	+1.5	–50.1
	Croatia	–1.5	–8.5	–28.7	–24.8	–3.7	+0.8	+5.0	–50.7
4	Kazakstan	–0.3	–0.8	–13.0	–14.0	–12.0	–25.0	–11.0	–56.5
	Armenia	+8.0	–7.2	–11.8	–52.0	–14.1	+5.3	+5.1	–59.7
	Georgia	+2.6	–11.1	–20.6	–42.7	–39.2	–35.0	–5.0	–83.4
5	Romania	–5.8	–5.6	–15.1	–13.5	+1.3	+3.5	+4.5	–28.4
	Russia	+1.5	–3.6	–12.9	–18.5	–15.0	–12.0	–4.3	–50.3
	Bulgaria	–1.9	–9.1	–11.7	–5.6	–2.4	+1.4	+2.3	–24.7
	Ukraine	+4.1	–3.6	–11.9	–17.0	–16.8	–23.7	–10.3	–58.2
6	Belarus	+7.9	–3.2	–1.9	–9.6	–10.6	–20.2	–13.8	–43.0
	Turkmenistan	–7.0	+1.8	–4.7	–5.3	–10.0	–20.0	–1.0	–39.1
	Uzbekistan	+3.7	+1.6	–0.9	–9.5	–2.4	–3.4	–4.0	–14.5
	Azerbaijan	–6.3	–11.7	–0.7	–26.8	–23.1	–22.0	–8.7	–67.1
	Tajikistan	–2.9	–1.6	–8.7	–30.0	–11.1	–21.4	–19.5	–65.7

Note: a = Forecast.
Source: IMF, World Bank and PlanEcon data bases.

transition. However, there is a danger of misinterpretation of these election results. Of countries where parties proposing anti-market programmes won elections, only Poland presents a case of the radical strategy. However, many non-economic factors, such as the so-called 'war at the top' in the Solidarity camp or a conflict about the place of the Catholic Church in political life, played important roles here. Other political stories in Eastern Europe are different. For example, the Lithuanian pro-democratic movement Sajudis which failed in the 1992 parliamentary election did not implement a radical economic transition (in contrast to Estonia and Latvia) and conducted a rather weak, pro-inflationary macroeconomic policy. The

Table 6.2 Inflation in selected post-communist economies, 1989–95
(CPI = increase in the average yearly indicator in per cent)

Group	Country	1989	1990	1991	1992	1993	1994	1995[a]
2	Poland	251.0	586.0	70.3	43.0	35.3	32.2	29.0
	Czech Rep.	2.3	10.8	56.7	11.1	20.8	10.2	9.0
	Slovakia	0.0	10.8	61.2	10.1	23.0	14.0	10.0
	Albania	0.0	0.0	35.5	225.9	85.0	28.0	9.0
	Hungary	17.0	29.0	34.2	22.9	22.5	19.0	29.0
	Slovenia	1306.0	549.7	117.7	201.2	32.0	19.8	13.0
3	Estonia	6.1	23.1	210.6	1069.0	89.0	48.0	26.0
	Latvia	4.7	10.5	124.4	951.2	109.0	36.0	25.0
	Lithuania	2.1	8.4	224.7	1020.3	390.2	72.0	36.0
	Kyrgyzstan	0.0	3.0	85.0	854.6	1208.7	280.0	44.0
	Moldova	0.0	4.2	98.0	1276.0	789.0	327.0	20.0
	Croatia	2520.5	135.6	249.5	938.2	1516.0	98.0	2.0
	Macedonia	1246.0	120.5	229.7	1925.2	248.0	65.0	18.0
4	Kazakhstan	0.0	4.2	91.0	1610.0	1760.0	1980.0	165.0
	Armenia	0.0	10.3	100.0	825.0	3732.0	5458.0	185.0
	Georgia	0.0	3.3	78.5	913.0	3126.0	18000.	163.0
5	Mongolia	0.0	0.0	208.6	321.0	183.0	145.0	25.0
	Romania	1.1	5.1	174.5	210.9	256.0	131.0	34.0
	Russia	2.2	5.6	92.7	1353.0	896.0	220.0	181.0
	Bulgaria	6.0	22.0	333.5	82.0	72.8	89.0	62.0
	Ukraine	2.0	4.0	91.2	1210.0	4735.0	842.0	321.0
6	Belarus	1.7	4.5	83.5	969.0	1188.0	2200.0	737.0
	Turkmenistan	2.1	4.6	102.5	492.9	3102.0	2400.0	226.0
	Uzbekistan	0.7	3.1	82.2	645.0	534.0	746.0	273.0
	Azerbaijan	0.0	7.8	105.6	616.0	833.0	1500.0	464.0
	Tajikistan	0.0	4.0	111.6	1157.0	2195.0	452.0	389.0

Note: a = IMF Forecast.
Source: De Melo, Denizer and Gelb (1995, Table 3); IMF data.

Table 6.3 Revenues, expenditures and budget balance of the general governmental in transformation countries, 1989–94 (in per cent of GDP)

Country/group	Indicator	1989	1990	1991	1992	1993	1994[b]
Albania (2)	Revenues	48.0[c]	47.0[c]	31.0[c]	25.5[c]	28.0[c]	27.7[b]
	Expenditures	57.0[c]	62.0[c]	62.0[c]	48.0[c]	44.0[c]	41.0[b]
	Balance	−9.0[c]	−15.0[c]	−31.0[c]	−22.5[c]	−16.0[c]	−13.3[b]
Czecho–Slovakia (2)	Revenues	69.5[a]	61.1[a]	55.0[a]	56.4[a]		
	Expenditures	72.3[a]	61.5[a]	57.1[a]	60.1[a]		
	Balance	−2.8[a]	−0.4[a]	−2.1[a]	−3.7[a]		
Czech Rep. (2)	Revenues	42.8[c]	42.4[c]	35.3[c]	49.5[a]	48.5[a]	51.2[b]
	Expenditures	42.4[c]	41.2[c]	37.0[c]	47.5[a]	47.5[a]	50.7[b]
	Balance	+0.4[c]	+1.2[c]	−1.7[c]	+2.0[a]	+1.0[a]	+0.5[b]
Slovakia (2)	Revenues				50.9[a]	48.1[a]	50.5[b]
	Expenditures				64.0[a]	55.1[a]	53.0[b]
	Balance				−13.1[a]	−7.0[a]	−2.5[b]
Hungary (2)	Revenues	59.6[a]	58.0[a]	56.1[a]	57.8[a]	54.1[a]	52.3[b]
	Expenditures	61.0[a]	57.5[a]	58.3[a]	63.4[a]	60.5[a]	58.8[b]
	Balance	−1.4[a]	+0.5[a]	−2.2[a]	−5.6[a]	−6.4[a]	−6.5[b]
Poland (2)	Revenues	41.4[a]	42.8[a]	41.5[a]	43.9[a]	45.5[a]	47.9[b]
	Expenditures	48.9[a]	39.8[a]	40.8[a]	50.7[a]	48.4[a]	50.4[b]
	Balance	−7.5[a]	+3.0[a]	−6.5[a]	−6.8[a]	−2.9[a]	−2.5[b]
Slovenia (2)	Revenues		48.9[c]	43.7[d]	46.6[d]	49.8[d]	43.1[d]
	Expenditures		49.3[c]	41.0[d]	46.4[d]	49.4[d]	44.1[d]
	Balance		−0.4[c]	+2.7[d]	+0.2[d]	+0.4[d]	−1.0[d]
Croatia (3)	Revenues			14.9[d]	20.4[d]	20.1[d]	27.2[d]
	Expenditures			19.5[d]	20.6[d]	20.7[d]	27.6[d]
	Balance			−4.5[d]	−0.2[d]	−0.6[d]	−0.4[d]
Estonia (3)	Revenues	43.0[c]	35.7[c]	38.5[c]	31.4[a]	32.5[a]	35.0[b]
	Expenditures	42.5[c]	33.3[c]	32.5[c]	31.0[a]	33.9[a]	35.0[b]
	Balance	+0.5[c]	+2.4[c]	+6.0[c]	+0.4[a]	−1.4[a]	0.0[b]
Kyrgyzstan (3)	Revenues	38.5[c]	39.5[c]	35.2[c]	15.8[c]	14.2[c]	24.3[b]
	Expenditures	36.4[c]	37.9[c]	27.3[c]	33.9[c1!]	23.0[c]	32.7[b]
	Balance	+2.1[c]	+1.6[c]	+7.9[c]	−18.1[c]	−8.9[c]	−8.4[b]
Lithuania (3)	Revenues	49.8[c]	45.0[c]	44.0[c]	33.3[a]	25.1[a]	25.1[b]
	Expenditures	53.8[c]	48.8[c]	36.7[c]	32.9[a]	30.4[a]	30.4[b]
	Balance	−4.0[c]	−3.9[c]	+7.3[c]	−0.4[a]	−5.3[a]	−5.3[b]
Latvia (3)	Revenues	31.0[c]	36.6[c]	26.5[c]			36.7[b]
	Expenditures	29.8[c]	35.8[c]	21.8[c]			38.7[b]
	Balance	+1.2[c]	+0.8[c]	+4.7[c]			−2.0[b]
Macedonia (3)	Revenues						42.8[b]
	Expenditures						45.4[b]
	Balance						−2.6[b]
Moldova (3)	Revenues	35.3[c]	35.2[c]	26.2[c]	20.3[c]	12.4[c]	17.1[b]
	Expenditures	33.7[c]	32.4[c]	26.3[c]	42.4[c]	18.1[c]	25.9[b]
	Balance	+1.6[c]	+2.8[c]	−0.1[c]	−22.1[c]	−5.7[c]	−8.8[b]

Sources: See p. 105.

Table 6.3   Continued

Country/group	Indicator	1989	1990	1991	1992	1993	1994[b]
Armenia (4)	Revenues	52.2[c]	42.7[c]	29.1[c]	21.5[c]	17.6[c]	37.0[b]
	Expenditures	49.8[c]	36.9[c]	36.4[c]	61.5[c]	66.4[c]	61.0[b]
	Balance	+2.4[c]	+5.8[c]	−7.3[c]	−40.0[c]	−48.8[c]	−24.0[b]
Georgia (4)	Revenues	31.5[c]	33.2[c]	30.0[c]	10.2[c]	2.7[c]	15.0[b]
	Expenditures	30.6[c]	32.0[c]	35.9[c]			24.0[b]
	Balance	+0.9[c]	1.2[c]	−5.9[c]			−9.0[b]
Kazakhstan (4)	Revenues	40.7[c]	41.4[c]	35.1[c]	24.6[c]	22.3[c]	19.0[b]
	Expenditures	39.2[c]	38.4[c]	44.1[c]	31.9[c]	23.5[c]	23.5[b]
	Balance	+1.5[c]	+3.0[c]	−9.0[c]	−7.3[c]	−1.2[c]	−4.5[b]
Bulgaria (5)	Revenues	59.6[a]	51.6[a]	42.3[a]	38.3[a]	37.4[a]	38.0[b]
	Expenditures	61.0[a]	60.4[a]	50.9[a]	45.3[a]	51.2[a]	44.1[b]
	Balance	−1.4[a]	−8.8[a]	−8.6[a]	−5.0[a]	−10.9[a]	−6.1[b]
Mongolia (5)	Revenues	48.6[c]	50.6[c]	47.4[c]	29.9[c]	36.2[c]	36.2[b]
	Expenditures	65.3[c]	64.1[c]	55.1[c]	42.7[c]	53.2[c]	48.0[b]
	Balance	−16.7[c]	−13.5[c]	−9.7[c]	−12.8[c]	−16.9[c]	−11.8[b]
Romania (5)	Revenues	51.0[a]	39.8[a]	39.4[a]	37.6[a]	30.8[a]	32.6[b]
	Expenditures	42.8[a]	38.7[a]	38.8[a]	42.2[a]	31.0[a]	35.6[b]
	Balance	+8.2[a]	+1.1[a]	+0.6[a]	−4.6[a]	−0.2[a]	−3.0[b]
Russia (5)	Revenues				37.6[a]	35.9[a]	36.3[b]
	Expenditures				44.4[a1]	41.9[a1]	45.1[b]
	Balance				6.6[a]	−6.0[a]	−8.8[b]
Ukraine (5)	Revenues	26.4[c]	27.4[c]	38.3[e]	44.0[e]	42.4[e]	42.3[b]
	Expenditures	25.7[c]	26.6[c]	51.9[e]	73.3[e]	52.1[e]	51.4[b]
	Balance	+0.7[c]	+0.8[c]	−13.8[e]	−29.3[e]	−9.7[e]	−9.1[b]
Azerbaijan (6)	Revenues	22.3[c]	26.4[c]	25.5[c]	23.4[c]		36.0[b]
	Expenditures	24.3[c]	31.9[c]	30.5[c]	27.5[c]		49.0[b]
	Balance	−2.0[c]	−5.5[c]	−5.0[c]	−4.1[c]		−13.0[b]
Belarus (6)	Revenues			47.5[e]	43.3[e]	43.6[e]	36.6[b]
	Expenditures			43.9[e]	46.8[e]	51.9[e]	38.1[b]
	Balance			3.6[e]	−3.5[e]	−8.3[e]	−1.5[b]
Tajikistan (6)	Revenues	40.3[c]	46.8[c]	40.7[c]	32.8[c]	27.2[c]	35.4[b]
	Expenditures	38.6[c]	43.4[c]	31.9[c]	69.8[c]	52.2[c]	38.1[b]
	Balance	+1.7[c]	+3.4[c]	+8.8[c]	−37.0[c]	−25.0[c]	−2.7[b]
Turkmenistan (6)	Revenues	32.4[c]	42.7[c]	44.7[c]	22.5[c]	13.4[c]	6.2[b]
	Expenditures	31.2[c]	41.1[c]	41.2[c]	32.6[c]	17.0[c]	7.3[b]
	Balance	+1.2[c]	+1.6[c]	+3.5[c]	−10.1[c]	−3.6[c]	−1.1[b]
Uzbekistan (6)	Revenues	35.2[c]	45.0[c]	45.5[c]	31.9[c]	41.0[c]	43.0[b]
	Expenditures	35.8[c]	45.9[c]	50.0[c]	42.1[c]	43.4[c]	45.0[b]
	Balance	−0.6[c]	−0.9[c]	−4.5[c]	−10.2[c]	−2.4[c]	−2.0[b]

Note: 1. Without hidden import subsidies.
Sources: (a) WEO (1994), table 14, and 15, (a); (b) de Melo, Denizer and Gelb (1995, table 8 (b); (c) PRD WB data base, (c); (d) MultiQuery Database (1995); (e) D'browski, and Antczak (1995).

Hungarian right-wing government ruling from 1990 to 1994 was very reluctant to implement a radical transition scenario. Successive Bulgarian and Russian governments between 1992 and 1994 failed to establish a transition agenda and avoid high or very high inflation. The election defeats of the Ukrainian President Leonid Kravchuk and Belarusian Prime Minister Vyacheslav Kebich in 1994 show that very slow transition and populist macroeconomic policies were not good political assets.

A rapid rotation of political elites is likely in a situation of deep economic crisis and a young, unstable democratic regime. But cyclical changes of political sympathies occur in every democratic society. In a young democratic environment with very weak political parties and very unstable public opinion, such a cycle may be much shorter.

3   WHY DOES A FAST TRANSITION GIVE BETTER RESULTS THAN A SLOW ONE?

The controversy about the most relevant strategy of economic transition dominated the political and intellectual debates in the first half of 1990s. It was formulated as the choice between the *radical* strategy of fast and comprehensive changes (very often called 'shock therapy') on the one hand and the evolutionary ('gradual') way on the other[6]. Now, the experience of more than six years of transition helps to solve this controversy on empirical grounds. In its best variant (such as Hungary), the gradual strategy only extends the duration of economic contraction and produces positive results later than the radical ones would have done. In its worse variant (such as Romania, Russia, Ukraine or Belarus), it fosters macroeconomic mismanagement and, often, a deep political crisis.[7]

As we mentioned earlier, arguments in favour of fast transition can be found in three areas: (1) the technical requirements of individual components of transition process (2) the danger of a systemic vacuum, (3) the political economy of the process. Below we will try to discuss all three aspects of transition process.

Recommended Speed of the Individual Components

Table 6.4 presents a general picture of the possible and recommended speed of the individual components of the transition process.

Macroeconomic stabilization, especially in the case of very high inflation or hyperinflation, must be a one-shot, comprehensive, and radical operation. Transition economies need a tough stabilization policy at the

Table 6.4   What can be done gradually?

Area	Can it be done gradually?	If YES, what are the main dangers or negative implications?
Macroeconomic stabilization	NO	
Domestic liberalization	NO; YES – in exceptional situations	Price distortions, inflationary expectations, fiscal problems, delayed demonopolization and privatization
External liberalization	YES	Price distortions, weaker competition, less pressure for restructuring
Privatization	YES	Delayed restructuring, pressure on macropolicy, intensive rent-seeking, informal privatization
Restructuring of the state sector (subsidization)	YES	Delayed restructuring, fiscal crisis, other pressures on macropolicy, intensive rent-seeking, informational and political barriers in monitoring, credibility problem

very beginning of the transition process to impede the conversion of one-time corrective inflation into permanent high inflation or even hyperinflation. Most of the countries must also solve the problem of current flow imbalances in fiscal and monetary policies.

Theoretically, *domestic and external liberalization* can be implemented either in one radical package or gradually, step by step. However, the specific features of post-communist transformation present arguments in favour of a more radical liberalization scenario. This is due, among other things, to the negative fiscal implications of price control, difficulty in privatizing an overregulated economy, and the necessity of building a competitive environment for state-owned enterprises. Price liberalization is absolutely necessary at the very beginning of the transition process. A postponed price liberalization will seriously hurt the budget and create inflationary expectations (as was the case in Ukraine in 1992–4). The development of the private sector is also unlikely in an economy in which practically all prices are controlled.

The liberalization of foreign trade and the introduction of a convertible currency become inseparable elements accompanying the liberalization of the domestic market and deregulation of domestic prices (because of the necessity of strengthening domestic competition and adjusting the structure of domestic prices to the structure of prices in the international market). However, the speed of external liberalization is controversial not only in post-communist countries (see Bruno, 1988, pp. 223–47). Many economists and politicians propose that external opening should be carefully 'dosed'. They argue that a radical opening of the economy (such as during the reunification of Germany) risks the sudden bankruptcy of a large number of enterprises, with all the unpleasant associated political and social consequences.

There are many arguments also against gradual external liberalization. First, the possibility of demonopolization of the domestic market (the only fast means in case of small and medium-sizes countries) would be lost. Second, putting off the opening only delays the moment of truth for ineffective factories and businesses. The general technological backwardness of post-communist economies does not provide, in principle, chances for significant reconstruction during the transition period. Third, in the meantime (before liberalization is completed), further investment decisions based on a distorted price system can be taken. Fourth, lobbies interested in the protection of specific industries are usually seriously weakened in the beginning of transition but after some time start to rebuild their political influence (see Gacs, 1994). Thus the idea of 'fine tuning' policy in respect to external liberalization is hardly feasible from the political point of view. The rationality of slow price and trade liberalization applies only in countries which had more open and deregulated economies before the post-communist transition started and inherited fewer price and structural distortions (Hungary and the former Yugoslavia).

More comprehensive *institutional changes* cannot usually be introduced overnight, especially in new democratic regimes where the legislative process needs some time. The former German Democratic Republic is the only exception, because it imported all market institutions from West Germany. The speed of institutional change is of great importance. The sooner institutional progress can be achieved, the better the results that can be expected in both macroeconomic and microeconomic policy spheres. Some examples of urgently needed institutional reform are the new tax system and tax administration, banking and insurance law, civil and commercial law, bankruptcy law, justice administration and budgetary law.

Privatization by its nature, is a gradual process. However, it can be implemented quickly or slowly. Arguments in favour of rapid privatization have a fundamental character. Quick market reform demands quick ownership changes. Progress in other aspects of the transformation process depends on the speed of privatization.

Bulgaria is an example of the negative consequences of delayed privatization which should be treated as a real warning to other countries in transition. Early in 1991, Bulgaria began with radical and quite successful liberalization and stabilization programmes. However, the privatization process was seriously delayed. Only small-scale privatization, based mainly on physical restitution, was carried out. The non-reformed sector of large, state-owned enterprises quickly increased pressure on the state budget and monetary policy, leading to significant erosion of the macro-economic situation at the end of 1993–4. Politically powerful groups involved in profit-shifting and asset-stripping from non-reformed SOEs to the private sector emerged. These groups were not interested in supporting progress in real privatization and liberalization, exploiting the unclear status quo and political uncertainty (see Bogetic and Hillman, 1995). A similar phenomenon can be observed in some FSU countries where privatization has been delayed.

The purpose of *restructuring* is to change both the sectoral and branch structure of the national economy and the internal structure and behaviour of individual firms. The restructuring of state-owned enterprises is not a one-step process (as price liberalization can be). However, as in the case of privatization, it can be done with varying speed. Faster restructuring (as in East Germany) can give a positive output response sooner than a slower one. Initially, however, it threatens a larger output decline, a larger number of bankruptcies, and higher unemployment that may have unpleasant political and fiscal implications. On the other hand, if governments want to slow down this process, open or hidden subsidization often becomes unavoidable. This involves the risk of fiscal crisis and negative pressure on monetary policy, intensive rent-seeking, and slower economic growth in the future. Governments in the FCC may also have information problems (who really needs support, and for how long?) with monitoring such a fine-tuning policy. It is very easy to lose political credibility and at the same time generate strong political pressure from different groups.

Summing up this part of discussion, there are only two advantages for slower transition in the microsphere and in the institutional sphere. First, more gradual changes makes accommodation to the new rules of game and institutions easier. This applies to producers, consumers and the public administration, which must also go through the complicated period of transition and have time to learn the new system. Second, slower restructuring of SOEs can, to some extent, dilute political resistance against change. Too large a number of bankruptcies in a relatively short period of time and too high a level of open unemployment is probably not acceptable politically, even for the most popular government. Generally, however, even in the microeconomic sphere, the advantages of fast transition approach seem to be bigger than those of slow transition.

The Danger of a Systemic Vacuum and Government Limited Regulating Capacity

The main microeconomic danger is associated with a systemic vacuum where the old rigours of the command economy no longer apply and the influence of the market mechanism is still too weak to change the economic behaviour of enterprises. This non-plan and non-market economy is practically unmanageable. Soft budget constraints allow SOEs to continue their excessive demand for various inputs and make them unresponsive to market signals. Additionally, an ownership vacuum is created when the state owner, for political and administrative reasons, has lost the capacity to enforce its property rights and too much state property has been left unprivatized. This usually results in the illegal transfer of profits and assets to private firms personally connected with SOE managers and (sometimes) with trade union activists.

The negative macroeconomic consequences of this vacuum manifest themselves mainly through a big budget deficit (resulting from continued open and hidden subsidization giving firms 'soft budget' constraints), various kinds of interventionism and excessive social obligations of the state. The budget deficit together with a soft credit policy in relation to the SOE sector results in a big monetary expansion. Excessive demand must lead to serious balance of payments difficulties. Although some elements of a systemic vacuum during the transition period cannot be completely avoided, the government should try to shorten this period as much as possible to avoid both macroeconomic and microeconomic mismanagement.

Unfortunately, the experiences of almost all delayed (group 4), slow (group 5) and very slow (most of group 6) reformers is very discouraging. Continuing market shortages (due to incomplete price liberalization), inflation or hyperinflation, decreasing output, and balance of payments crises have been the standard economic problems in countries such as the Ukraine, Belarus, Turkmenistan, Azerbaijan, Georgia, Armenia and Russia. Only a few gradual (but eventually quite fast and radical) reformers such as Hungary avoided these negative consequences because they started the transition with more advanced market regulation and with a better macroeconomic equilibrium (see section 2).

The necessity of constructing various substitute solutions for the transition period is another weakness of the gradual (slow) strategy. Palliative solutions, in general, do not bring the economy closer to final market solutions. These solutions start living their own lives and create an independent logic of behaviour of economic agents. Their unexpected side effects make additional intervention and regulation necessary. The energy of government is used not for the quick completion of reforms but for improving temporary instruments. The transformation period becomes extended, and economic policy gets into a vicious cycle of overregulation.

Moreover, if economic transition is slow and inconsistent it can create special arbitrage opportunities for intensive rent-seeking. Interest groups built around temporary regulation (e.g. government bureaucracy distributing export quotas and licences, management of *kolkhozes* and *sovkhozes* receiving heavily subsidized credits) will struggle strongly against real liberalization and macroeconomic stabilization (see Krueger, 1990; Havrylyshyn, Miller and Perraudin, 1994).

Post-communist governments that engage in excessive intervention have immediately encountered informational and administrative barriers. Informational barriers are well known from the centrally-planned economy. Central authorities have to rely on information received from the bottom level – from enterprises, their associations, etc. This information is, of course, heavily influenced by the micro interests of the economic agents trying to obtain as much as possible from the government. Strong political bargaining and intensive rent-seeking are unavoidable consequences of excessive government intervention (Dąbrowski, 1994).

FCC government administration connected with political and institutional transformation is extremely weak (Åslund, 1994; Dąbrowski, 1994). It has tremendous problems in providing basic public goods such as public security, justice administration, enforcement of contracts, protection of private property rights, etc. Overloading the government with additional tasks worsens its performance.

Political Economy Arguments

Analyzing the political economy aspects of transition, it is worth emphasizing two problems: the political window of opportunity for reforms and credibility issues.

The importance of the first problem is connected with the nature of any fundamental economic reform (not only in the post-communist countries) which must hurt many existing interests. The enormous agenda of post-communist economic transition makes this operation specially difficult. To be politically feasible economic transition from a centrally planned to a market economy needs a special window of opportunity which Balcerowicz (1994) call the 'period of extraordinary politics'. What factors create this window of opportunity will be considered in section 4. Here, I want to concentrate on the effective use of the window of opportunity already existing.

The main argument in favour of fast transition process is the fact that the period of 'extraordinary politics' is limited in time. Usually it lasts no longer than one, or a maximum of two years, sometimes even less. It is followed by a period of 'normal' politics where some old groups of special interests are rebuilt and many new ones are created. Social patience and support for reforms is usually reduced in comparison with the period just after the political breakthrough. Radical economic changes, though theoretically still possible, are far more difficult to implement.

This means that policy-makers in transition economies should be aware of the limited historical chance given them to change from the ineffective post-communist system to the stable free market economy. Once this chance is lost, it may not return quickly. This is true not only in relation to macroeconomic stabilization and liberalization but also to privatization and microeconomic restructuring. Like stabilization and liberalization measures, privatization requires political momentum. If the best political time is lost, privatizers will have to work in far less comfortable conditions. The history of Polish privatization is a good example here.

Every government, but especially a post-communist one, faces the problem of credibility. Faster, more dynamic, and consistent change increases this credibility in relation to macroeconomic and microeconomic policies. They create positive expectations, bring inflation down earlier, and push SOEs toward quicker restructuring. On the other hand, a slow pace of change, policy compromises, continued subsidization (even if it is claimed to be temporary), or attempts to bail out enterprises and banks (even if they are declared to be one-shot deals) increase illusions that the reforms are not definitive and can be reversed under political pressure.

Thus, a fast pace and good coordination of economic reforms may enlarge a political window of opportunity and extend it in time (creating a credible image of government and its actions). In contrast, slow and inconsequental changes undermine the credibility of government and make the period of 'extraordinary politics' shorter.

It is worth mentioning here the historical experience of the 'socialist market reforms' (mostly unsuccessful). It showed that partial and gradual changes did not have any perceptible effect. The old system quickly swallowed and adapted new instruments and institutions. The changes seemed to be temporary. This experience also created negative expectations of economic agents (particularly managers of SOEs) *vis-à-vis* any new economic reforms and made the task of post-communist governments more complicated.

4 REASONS FOR SUCCESS OR FAILURE

In this section I want to investigate the question why some countries managed to choose a fast transition track quite early (Poland, Czecho–Slovakia, Estonia, Latvia), some only after initial failures connected with slow and inconsistent reforms (Lithuania, Moldova, Kazakhstan), and others have still not done so. Among many possible factors I concentrate on two: initial and implementation conditions and political reforms.

4.1 The Role of Initial and Implementation Conditions

Some countries started and implemented their transition policy in relatively better circumstances: they inherited fewer macroeconomic imbalances from the communist system (Czecho–Slovakia, the former GDR and Hungary to some extent), fewer structural distortions (Hungary, Slovenia, Poland), a partially liberalized economy and some market institutions (Hungary, the former Yugoslavia, Poland), some enclaves of private economy (Poland, Hungary), some democratic traditions (CEE and the Baltics in comparison with the rest of the FSU and Albania), better quality of state administration and the legal system (Central Europe in comparison with the FSU). Some purely political and ethnic factors such as the strength of anti-communist and pro-independence movements, ethnic homogeneity and the absence of militant trade unions should also have helped in the transition process.

This cross-country differentiation also existed in the case of implementation conditions. The size of adverse shocks differed significantly across the region, with Bulgaria, Mongolia, and most of the European FSU countries except Russia bearing the biggest burden. Some countries suffered war destruction that stopped any reforms at all (Bosnia, Tajikistan) or delayed them significantly (Moldova, Croatia, the Caucasian countries). On the other hand, Russia, Turkmenistan, Uzbekistan and Kazakhstan, due to the presence of rich and easy tradeable natural resources, theoretically have an easier task of structural adjustment. The size of Western assistance has differed significantly, with Poland, Albania and the Baltic states as the relative leaders (see Kaminski and Wang, 1995; Dąbrowski, 1995).

All these factors have created different conditions of economic and political transformation across the region. Do better starting and implementation conditions help make the transition process more smooth and successful? There is no simple answer to this question. On the one hand, a comparison of Central European countries with Romania, Bulgaria,

Ukraine or Belarus suggests a positive answer. On the other hand we can find successful fast reformers among countries suffering extremely difficult starting and implementation condition (the Baltic states, Kyrgyzstan, Moldova) and very slow, rather badly performing countries with rich natural resources (Russia, Uzbekistan, Turkmenistan). This last factor (i.e. rich natural resources) very often has a demobilizing influence on the political elite. In contrast, more dramatic initial conditions (heavy external shock or war damage) may stimulate ruling politicians to decide in favour of radical and unpopular changes (because they understand that there is no other way out). This happened in the case of Albania, the Baltic states, Kyrgyzstan, Moldova, and more recently Georgia and Armenia.

However, sometimes worse starting and implementation conditions serve as a justification for a slower and less extensive economic transition. In countries such as Ukraine or Belarus one often hears the argument that 'we are a unique case and we must look for our own variant of transition'. In practice, this means rejection of a radical and consistent variant of transformation in favour of some version of gradualism with less macroeconomic discipline, gradual liberalization, greater government intervention, and slow privatization.

4.2 The Role of Political Reforms

I have already discussed the importance of the political window of opportunity for the successful economic transition. The question is: what factors may help to create this window of opportunity or, using Balcerowicz's terminology, the period of 'extraordinary politics'?

A broader comparative analysis of the transition countries in CEE and the FSU shows a strong correlation between the size of political change and achieved progress in economic transition (see Åslund, 1994; de Melo, Denizer and Gelb, 1995; Karatnycky, 1995). Countries which have achieved the biggest progress in the economic transition are usually the same ones that have been leaders in the democratization process. This is because sound democratization makes it possible to break up the political and economic domination of the former communist oligarchy (*nomenklatura*) and eliminate economic structures inherited from the communist systems, such as various types of branch organizations. Countries that have made only partial progress in democratization and political liberalization (most CIS countries and Romania) have serious problems with real demonopolization and deconcentration of domestic market structures, external liberalization, removing subsidies and implementing 'hard budget' constraints, avoiding organized clearing of inter-enterprise arrears, implementing a real positive interest rate policy, starting mass-scale transparent privatization, replacing SOE managers, etc. The economic policy of these countries is dominated by strong rent-seeking special interest groups, originating mainly from the former structure of the economy.

The above correlation is not surprising. The economic transition in FCC could not have started without political liberalization and democratization. All the experience of pre-transition reforms shows that they could never reach some critical point (like abandoning the monopoly of state ownership) because the communist political regime did not allow it (even in its most liberal version, such as in Hungary or Poland). When the communist system finally collapsed at the end of the 1980s two factors determined the speed and consistency of economic transition to capitalism: radicalism of political changes and the personal quality of the leadership of economic reform.

The importance of the first factor is connected with both the nature of any fundamental economic reform (not only in post-communist countries) and with the unclear economic preferences of the post-communist societies. Serious economic policy reforms must hurt many existing interests. The enormous agenda of post-communist economic transition makes this operation especially difficult. The success of economic transition depends both on a strong political stimulation and on the weakening of the expected political resistance of the lobbies which could lose as a result of the changes. Both are possible only if the political transformation is deep enough. This was the case in Poland, Czecho–Slovakia (especially the Czech Republic), Hungary and the Baltic states, where radical political change created a window of opportunity for radical economic transformation.

Radical political change can also assist economic transition in another way. Because of the long break with capitalism (see section I), a significant part of post-communist societies approved *de facto* many aspects of the communist economic system such as fixed low prices, guaranteed employment, quite substantial social welfare programmes, etc. even while being strongly politically opposed to the communist regime or not enjoying some other aspects of economic life in this system (e.g. market shortage, low quality of consumer goods). Thus most or even all the transition societies were not prepared to choose *expressis verbis* the tough pro-market and anti-inflationary transition strategy, even if they generally accepted capitalism and a Western style of living. The only possible way to gain temporary democratic support for carrying out difficult economic reforms was to utilize the general political credit vested in the new political elites who were breaking with communism and (in many cases) maintaining newly achieved national independence.

The quality of the new elites is the second important factor. The political opportunity to initiate radical reform is a necessary condition, but not a sufficient one. Political elites and technocrats must be able to use the existing window of opportunity, which is not automatically the case. The short history of transition gives us examples of lost chances – Lithuania under the Sajudis government (1991–2), Ukraine (1991–3), and to some extent Russia (1992–4). When lost, a political window of opportunity for substantial economic reform can come again only after some period of time. The negative social and political effects of economic mismanagement usually educate both society and political elites, changing their attitude to the economic policy priorities. However, such an education is very painful, and may last many years.

The optimal situation occurs when political reforms and economic reforms are actively promoted at the same time. The very impressive results of the Czech transition were possible due to the very close coordination of economic and political reforms.

5   SOME FINAL REMARKS

Generally, faster and more comprehensive economic reforms allow rulers to minimize the economic, social and political costs of the transition process and avoid chronic macroeconomic mismanagement. Only countries such as Hungary that had achieved some progress in market-oriented reform earlier (before the communist regime collapsed) and had less macroeconomic disequilibrium could go a little bit more slowly. Political liberalization and democratization helps the successful economic transition mainly because it contributes to the weakening of political positions of the traditional communist oligarchy (*nomenklatura*), interested mainly in parasitic rent-seeking.

The empirical experience of the period 1989–94 provides many valuable observations which can contribute to the initial discussion on the speed and sequencing of the transition process. Macroeconomic stabilization and liberalization play a crucial role and must be achieved quickly, otherwise we can hardly expect quick progress in microeconomic restructuring even if the privatization process is going very fast (as in Russia). The latter needs more time to take off, because a legal base and organizational infrastructure must be created. However, even in this case, a fast transition seems less risky than a slow one.

Practically, there is no way of avoiding a relatively large decline in output, especially of industrial production in the state sector. Its scale largely depends on the inherited structural distortions and adopted transition strategy. Those countries that were not afraid to undertake a radical transition programme were the first to arrest the output decline and restore economic growth. On the other hand, those countries that attempted to maintain previous production levels through subsidies, credit expansion, and protectionism have already recorded more dramatic GDP decreases than those that chose the radical scenario, and moreover they have few prospects for a return to economic growth. The decline has been accompanied by high inflation or hyperinflation, with all the attendant social costs, such as more unequal distribution of income and wealth or the deep criminalization of economic activity.

The policy of granting concessions to various pressure groups does not produce the expected political results and does not increase social acceptance of the changes under way. Here the experience of Russia, Romania, the Ukraine and Belarus is the best proof. On the other hand, where a strong institutional foundation of a market economy has been established, even when the political forces of the *ancien régime* return to power in elections, they have to continue the policy of reform. There are also lessons for political leaders in transition countries. They should focus more on exploiting the political window of opportunity (which usually opened at the very beginning of the transition process) for making as many reforms as possible for the benefit of the country rather than focusing on short-term personal political survival. A sound and responsible transition policy involves a risk of political failure in the short run, but may result in long-term credibility and popularity.

Notes

1. The topic and issues presented in this chapter are a continuation of my research and resulting papers since 1990 (see, for example, Dąbrowski, 1992). Particularly, this chapter is a shortened, updated and revised version of my working paper 'Different Strategies of Transition to a Market Economy: How Do They Work in Practice?', prepared at the beginning of 1995 under the World Bank Visiting Research Fellow Programme (Dąbrowski, 1996). I am very grateful to Alan Gelb, Martha de Melo and other colleagues from the Transition Economies Division, Policy Research Department of the World Bank for the stimulating suggestions, helpful comments and technical assistance which allowed me to work on this topic. Of course, I am solely responsible for the content and quality of this paper and presented conclusion. They reflect my personal views and not necessarily the World Bank official positions.
2. China and Vietnam are excluded from this classification for many reasons: continuation of communist dictatorship, less structural distortions and less

social obligations of the government inherited from the pre-reform period, etc. (see Sachs and Woo, 1994; Sachs, 1995).

3　This classification is similar to the one proposed by de Melo, Denizer, and Gelb (1995).

4.　However, whether Hungarian gradualism can be seen as a real success story remains an open question. The macroeconomic situation of this country at the end of 1994 seems to be worse than that of other Central European countries.

5　Macroeconomic instability and the lack of sufficient competition create greater income and wealth differentiation and often encourage criminal practices.

6.　The review of this discussion can be found, for example, in Åslund (1994) and Dąbrowski (1996).

7.　Other available comparative studies demonstrate the superiority of a radical, fast and comprehensive variant of transition strategy over other approaches (Åslund, 1994; Balcerowicz and Gelb, 1995; EBRD, 1994; de Melo, Gelb and Denizer, 1995).

References

Åslund, Anders (1994) 'Lessons of the First Four Years of Systemic Change in Eastern Europe', *Journal of Comparative Economics*, vol. 19, no. 1.

Balcerowicz, Leszek (1994) 'Understanding Postcommunist Transitions', *Journal of Democracy*, vol. 5, no. 4 (October).

Balcerowicz, Leszek and Alan Gerb (1995) 'Macropolicies in Transition to a Market Economy. A Three-Year Perspective', CASE–Center for Social and Economic Research, Warsaw, *Studies and Analysis*, no. 33.

Bogetic, Zeljko and Arye L. Hillman (1995) 'Privatizing Profits of Bulgaria's State Enterprises', *Transition*, vol. 6, no. 3 March.

Bruno, Michael (1988) 'Opening up: Liberalization with Stabilization', in R. Dornbusch, F. Leslie and C. H. Helmers (eds), *The Open Economy*, EDI Series in Economic Development New York, The World Bank and Oxford University Press.

Dąbrowski, Marek (1992) 'From Planned Economy to Market Economy: Rate and Stages of Transformation Process', paper for the 2nd EACES Conference on Problems of Transforming Economies, Gröningen, The Netherlands (24–26 September).

——— (1994) 'The Role of the Government in Postcommunist Economies', in Laszlo Csaba (ed.), *Privatization, Liberalization and Destruction: Recreating the Market in Central and Eastern Europe* (Brookfield, VT; Dartmouth Press).

——— (1995) 'Western Aid Conditionality and the Post-Communist Transition', Center for Social and Economic Research, Warsaw, *Studies and Analyses*, no. 37.

——— (1996) 'Different Strategies of Transition to a Market Economy: How Do They Work in Practice?', The World Bank, *Policy Research Department Working Papers*.

Dąbrowski, Marek and Rafal Antczak (1995) 'Róta procesów inflacyjnych w Rosji, Ukrainie i Bilorusi' (Sources of Inflation in Russia, Ukraine and Belarus), Polish Academy of Sciences, Institute of Economics, Warsaw (October), mimeo.

de Melo, Martha, Cevdet Denizer and Alan Gelb (1995) 'From Plan to Market: The Patterns of Transition', The World Bank, Policy Research Department (September), mimeo.

EBRD (1994) *Transition Report: Economic Transition in Eastern Europe and the Former Soviet Union*, European Bank for Reconstruction and Development (October).

Gacs, Janos (1994) 'Trade Policy in the Czech and Slovak Republics, Hungary and Poland in 1989–93: A Comparison', Center for Social and Economic Research, Warsaw, *Studies and Analyses*, no. 11 (February).

Havrylyshyn, Oleh, Marcus Miller and William Perraudin (1994) 'Deficits, Inflation and the Political Economy of Ukraine', *Economic Policy*, vol. 19 (October).

Kaminski, Barlomiej and Zhen-Kun Wang (1995) 'External Assistance and Finance for the Transition Economies', The World Bank, Washington, DC (January 11), mimeo.

Karatnycky, Adrian (1995) 'Democracies on the Rise. Democracies at Risk', *Freedom Review*, Freedom House (January–February).

Krueger, Anne (1990) 'Government Failures in Development', *Journal of Economic Perspectives*.

MultiQuery Data base (1995), prepared by Nancy Vandycke, under the Supervision of Luca Barbone, the World Bank, EC2 (March 15).

Rostowski, Jacek (1995) 'Giperinfljacia i stabilizacia v Yugoslavii v 1992–1994gg.', CASE–Center for Social and Economic Research, Warsaw, *Studies and Analyses*, no. 32 (February).

Sachs, Jeffrey D. (1995) 'Reforms in Eastern Europe and the Former Soviet Union in Light of the East Asian Experiences', CASE–Center for Social and Economic Research, Warsaw, *Studies and Analyses*, no. 39.

Sachs, Jeffrey D. and Wing Thye Woo (1994) 'Structural Factors in the Economic Reforms in China, Eastern Europe, and the Former Soviet Union', *Economic Policy*. vol. 18 (April).

WEO (1994) *World Economic Outlook*, International Monetary Fund (October).

7 Welfare in Economic Transition*

John S. Flemming
WADHAM COLLEGE, OXFORD, UK

1 INTRODUCTION

This chapter concentrates more directly on welfare than the transition. Only if the transformations fulfil certain conditions of political accept-ability will the momentum of the reform process be sustained and with it the growth it should eventually foster. A particularly simple model (Balcerowicz, 1995) suggests that the electorate's critical faculties are sus-pended for a predetermined period after the fall of communism and that anything could be done during the opening of this 'window of opportu-nity' (see also Chapter 6 in this volume).

While it is certainly true that oppositionist forces take time to regroup, the extent, and particularly the duration, of this opening must respond in part on the public's reaction to the measures being implemented and its as-sessment of their consequences. I shall focus on this as a potential problem rather than as an actual one whose operation has been observed and moni-tored. The potential problem can be summarized briefly.

Under Communism the transition economies were recorded (e.g. in World Bank tables) as delivering greater equality, better education, liter-acy and health than other economies with comparable levels of *per capita* income. Moreover while much of the old regime and its ideology were discredited and rejected, some validity was attributed to a greater concern with these matters than was believed to characterize market economies.

These (re)distributionist values confronted a post-communist situation in which performance on many of the relevant indicators was almost bound to decline. The liberalization of trade and prices created perfect op-portunities for well placed entrepreneurs while threatening the continued employment of some categories of workers in particular sectors over-expanded under the previous regime.

In the Former Soviet Union (FSU), where reform was typically rela-tively slow and partial, there were not only uneven responses to the oppor-tunities of market disequilibrium but also extensive opportunities for arbitrage between free and regulated markets for those with access to the necessary permits and licences, whether acquired legally or not.

Unemployment typically rose from negligible levels to the mid-teens in Central and Eastern Europe (CEE) while it was kept low in the FSU partly by retaining some people in nominal employment at a much lower wage (often the statutory minimum) than was being paid to non-redundant workers. Whether open or hidden in this way *de facto* unemployment contributed to a deterioration in income distribution as well as reflecting a fall in output and, generally, of average incomes. Layard and Richter (1995) attribute lower recorded unemployment in the FSU to greater downward flexibility of real wages there. One reason for the prevalence of the less open form of unemployment in the FSU was that only in this way could redundant workers and their families retain access to a wide range of social and other services and benefits supplied through enterprises. The equitable transfer of such services from the enterprise to some agency of government is a major challenge in itself.[1] In the meantime the quality of services offered initially varied to some extent with the diverse financial positions of enterprises.

Where the supply of social services has been shifted on to the government, they have been subject to acute budgetary pressures arising from several sources – from the need to rectify inherited fiscal deficits and to stabilize inflationary situations. The process of legitimizing private economic activity while the opportunities for monitoring and taxing it was embryonic created widespread and large 'shadow economies' which did not contribute to the budget. In several cases a key determinant of whether to stay (or come into the light, or to fade into the shadows) depended on whether, in the former case, the activity would be a net contributor to or a net recipient of tax money.

There are conflicting accounts as to the effect of these pressures on the quality, quantity and distribution of health care, education and similar services. Certainly academic staff whether teaching or researching in public institutions, have typically felt hard done by. It is more difficult to identify the discontent of their 'customers'. Equally the strongly negative UNICEF reports on health in transition economies may be influenced by discontented suppliers – nevertheless the circumstantial and other evidence reviewed below of a decline in both average quality and especially distribution of services, with consequences for aggregate morbidity and mortality statistics, is strong, especially in the FSU.

The rest of this chapter is organized as follows. There is a discussion in Section 2 of data on the indicators under the previous regime – *per capita* output, income and consumption since 1990; the distribution of these variables; unemployment; pensions; health; and budgetary problems. This is followed by a reconsideration in section 3 of policy issues under four headings – output and employment; liberalization, quasi-rents and rent-seeking; the (re)integration of the shadow economy; and the social safety net and the delivery of social services. The recommendations and reconsiderations may be more relevant, in several respects, to the countries of the CIS than to those of Eastern Europe, where the problems have already proved not to be insuperable.

2 DATA

Social Indicators under the Previous Regime

Table 7.1 draws on World Bank and UN sources, but is taken from the EBRD's 1995 *Transition Reports*. For reference, aggregate data is also supplied on low-, middle- and high-income countries, as classified by the World Bank. Subsequent development of some of these indications is shown in Figure 7.1.

Table 7.2 (from the EBRD's 1994 *Transition Report*) presents a very small sample of late-communist income distributions with the same comparators. Among the comparators equality is greatest in G-7 countries followed by the high-income group with South America next and both middle and low-income groups last with much lower shares in the bottom quintile particularly.

Against this background of middle-income countries' lowest quintile share being less than half that in the G-7 the few late-communist countries listed had lowest quintile shares on average three times those of middle-income countries (four times if Yugoslavia is excluded), twice those of our South American sample and 50 per cent higher than the G-7 countries that were three times richer. Almost as striking a story relates to the top end of the distribution, with the highest decile share, excluding Yugoslavia, half that in South America, at the bottom of the high-income range and significantly lower than that of the G-7 countries.

The claim about the persistence of egalitarian values derives partly from anecdote, partly from surveys (such as that by Richard Rose), partly from political developments. These take the form of parliamentary resistance to Acts on pensions (e.g. in Poland) or other benefits (e.g. in Hungary) even where on paper these benefits represent exceptionally high replacement rates. In practice, some such ratios are eroded by payment by inflation. There is also the electoral success of reform communists in the elections in Lithuania, Hungary and Estonia, for example.

Table 7.1 Social indicators for countries of the region

	Education indicators			Health indicators					Demographic indicators		
	PPP-GNP per capita in 1993[1]	Primary enrolment rate[4]	Secondary enrolment rate[4]	Immunisation rate[2]	Low birth weight[3]	Crude birth rate[5]	Male life expectancy at birth[6]	Female life expectancy at birth[6]	Infant mortality rate	Under-5 mortality rate	Aged 20–59 mortality rate[7]
Czech Republic	7,550	99.7	88.5	98.6	5.9[c]	10.4	68.9[a]	76.6[a]	7.9	11.6[b]	3.7[b]
Hungary	6,050	99.1[a]	81.4	99.8[a]	8.7	11.3	64.5[a]	73.8[a]	11.5	13.5	6.7
Poland	5,000	97.1	82.0	97.8[a]	7.2	12.5	67.4[a]	76.0[a]	15.1	17.3	4.3
Slovak Republic	6,290	99.5	90.2	na	6.7	12.4	68.3	76.5	11.2	13.2	3.9
Slovenia	10,585	95.5	84.7	93.9[a]	5.2[a]	9.8	69.4[a]	77.3[a]	6.5	8.2	3.6
Estonia	6,320[a]	94.2	84.6	78.2	5.0	9.5	61.0	74.0	14.5	17.4	8.0
Latvia	5,010	84.9	81.2	84.8	5.0	9.5	61.6[a]	73.8[a]	15.5	20.1	9.4
Lithuania	3,110	94.1	83.4	88.1	4.3	11.6	63.0[a]	75.0[a]	13.9	18.2	7.1
Albania	999	85.0[a]	na	90.1[b]	5.6[a]	19.2[a]	69.3[d]	75.4[d]	33.2[a]	44.1[c]	2.2[d]
Belarus	6,240	93.5	84.2	90.8	4.1	10.7	63.5	74.3	13.2	16.2	6.6
Bulgaria	4,100	97.1	65.0	93.3	7.5	9.4	67.2	74.8	16.3	20.9	4.6
Moldova	2,870	77.0	74.0	90.0	6.1	14.3	64.3[a]	71.1[a]	22.6	28.5	6.9
Rumania	2,800	99.4	75.5	93.9[a]	10.9[a]	10.9	66.6[b]	73.2[b]	23.9	30.3[a]	5.2[a]
Russia	5,050	94.2[a]	71.7	89.6	6.3	9.4	58.2	71.4	18.7	25.0	9.1
Ukraine	4,450	82.7	46.9	93.5	na	10.0	66.0[c]	74.0[b]	14.3	19.9[a]	6.5[a]
Armenia	2,040	na	na	87.7	7.4[a]	13.6	67.9[a]	74.4[a]	15.1	24.2[a]	4.2[a]
Azerbaijan	2,190	na	76.0	61.0[b]	5.4[a]	21.4	65.2[a]	73.9[a]	26.9	45.2	5.7
Georgia	1,750	86.6[a]	75.9[a]	30.5[a]	5.8[a]	10.7	68.7[d]	76.1[d]	23.2	17.4[b]	4.1[d]
Low income[3]	1,370	89.5[10,b]	41.0[11]	88.6[9]	11.3[10]	28.0	61.0	63.0	64.0	103.0	na
Without China & India	1,347	58.0[10,b]	na	na	21.4[10]	40.0	54.0	57.0	89.0	144.0	na
China	2,330	96.0[b]	53.0[11]	94.0[9]	6.0[c]	19.0	68.0	71.0	30.0	54.0	na
Low-middle income[8]	3,891	68.9[10,b]	53.0[11]	79.9[9]	11.0[10]	23.0	64.0	70.0	40.0	63.0	na

Table 7.1 Continued

Upper-middle income[8]	8,318	91.0[10,b]	53.0[11]	78.1[9]	10.6[10]	24.0	66.0	72.0	36.0	43.0	na
High-income[8]	18,682	97.0[10,b]	92.0[11]	86.3[9]	6.5[10]	13.0	74.0	80.0	7.0	9.0	na

Notes:

The data, except column 1 and the last 4 rows, were compiled by UNICEF-ICDC and reported, for a subgroup of countries, in *Central and Eastern Europe in Transition, Regional Monitoring Report 3*, 1995. Unless otherwise indicated, the figures refer to 1994. The symbols indicate the following years: [a] 1993, [b] 1992, [c] 1991 and [d] 1990. When available figures were rounded, we have put a zero after the decimal point. The country groupings within table follow the pattern that is set out on page 24.

1 PPP stands for purchasing power parity. The estimates quoted here are taken from *World Development Report 1995* (World Bank), except for Albania and Slovenia. Estimates for the latter come from *** (June 1995). To compute these estimates, each country's nominal GNP per capita was divided by the 'purchasing power parity', defined as the number of units of the country's currency required to buy the same amount of goods and services in the domestic market as one US dollar would buy in the United States. Given the difficulties of measurement, particularly where many statistical offices and price mechanisms were in a state of flux, the PPP-GNP figures should be treated with some circumspection.

2 Figures refer to the unweighted average of immunisation rates for diphtheria and measles.

3 Defined as the percentage of live births weighing less than 2,500 grams.

4 Figures refer to net enrolment rates, defined as the percentage of the relevant age group enrolled in primary and secondary school education.

5 Defined as the number of live and still births in a year per 1,000 population.

6 Defined as the expected number of years for a newborn, assuming the prevailing mortality rates remained unchanged.

7 Calculated as the unweighted average of mortality rates for the age groups 20–39 and 40–59. [8] The figures shown in these rows are weighted averages of available observations for low, lower-middle, upper-middle and high income countries as defined according to the World Bank's classification. The exception is column 1, which refers to unweighted averages. Countries are categorised based on the following ranges for the *World Bank Atlas (1994)* estimates *** lower-middle income US$6969,785; upper-midle income US$2,706–8,625; and high income US$8,626 or more. Unless otherwise indicated, the data refer to 1993. Among the countries of the table Albania, Armenia and Georgia are 'low' on this definition; Belarus, Estonia, Hungary and Slovenia are 'upper-middle'; and the remaining 11 are 'high'.

9 Refers to the most recent estimates of the indicator provided in *Social indicators of Development 1995* (World Bank).

10 The group averages should be interpreted with care since data are available only for a subset of countries. Comparability across countries may be limited by variation in data collection, definitions and statistical methods.

11 Figures refer to gross enrolment rates, defined as the number of pupils enrolled in primary and secondary school education as a percentage of the population in the relevant age group.

12 The values for China and India are 94 and 88, respectively.

13 The values for China and India are 53 and 44, respectively.

Source: Transition Report 1995 Investment and Enterprise Development.

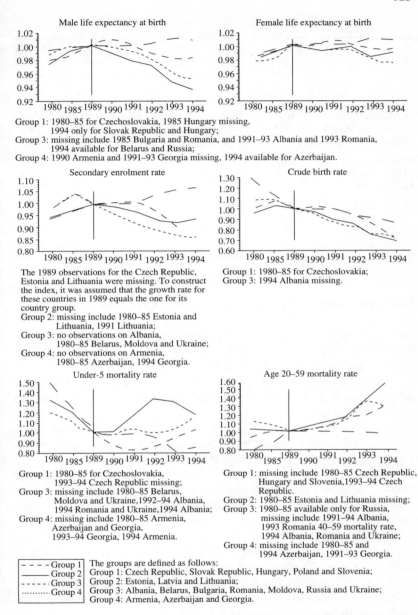

Male life expectancy at birth

Female life expectancy at birth

Group 1: 1980–85 for Czechoslovakia, 1985 Hungary missing,
          1994 only for Slovak Republic and Hungary;
Group 3: missing include 1985 Bulgaria and Romania, and 1991–93 Albania and 1993 Romania,
          1994 available for Belarus and Russia;
Group 4: 1990 Armenia and 1991–93 Georgia missing, 1994 available for Azerbaijan.

Secondary enrolment rate

Crude birth rate

The 1989 observations for the Czech Republic,
Estonia and Lithuania were missing. To construct
the index, it was assumed that the growth rate for
these countries in 1989 equals the one for its
country group.
Group 2: missing include 1980–85 Estonia and
          Lithuania, 1991 Lithuania;
Group 3: no observations on Albania,
          1980–85 Belarus, Moldova and Ukraine;
Group 4: no observations on Armenia,
          1980–85 Azerbaijan, 1994 Georgia.

Group 1: 1980–85 for Czechoslovakia;
Group 3: 1994 Albania missing.

Under-5 mortality rate

Age 20–59 mortality rate

Group 1: 1980–85 for Czechoslovakia,
          1993–94 Czech Republic missing;
Group 3: missing include 1980–85 Belarus,
          Moldova and Ukraine,1992–94 Albania,
          1994 Romania and Ukraine,1994 Albania;
Group 4: missing include 1980–85 Armenia,
          Azerbaijan and Georgia,
          1993–94 Georgia, 1994 Armenia.

Group 1: missing include 1980–85 Czech Republic,
          Hungary and Slovenia,1993–94 Czech
          Republic.
Group 2: 1980–85 Estonia and Lithuania missing;
Group 3: 1980–85 available only for Russia,
          missing include 1991–94 Albania,
          1993 Romania 40–59 mortality rate,
          1994 Albania, Romania and Ukraine;
Group 4: missing include 1980–85 and
          1994 Azerbaijan, 1991–93 Georgia.

- - - - Group 1
———— Group 2
- - - - Group 3
·········· Group 4

The groups are defined as follows:
Group 1: Czech Republic, Slovak Republic, Hungary, Poland and Slovenia;
Group 2: Estonia, Latvia and Lithuania;
Group 3: Albania, Belarus, Bulgaria, Romania, Moldova, Russia and Ukraine;
Group 4: Armenia, Azerbaijan and Georgia.

Figure 7.1 Change in social indicators in countries of the region, 1960–94

Table 7.2 Percentage share of income or consumption

	Lowest 20 per cent	Second 20 per cent	Third 20 per cent	Fourth 20 per cent	Highest 20 per cent	Highest 10 per cent
Poland (1989)	9.2	13.3	17.9	23.0	36.0	21.6
Hungary (1989)	10.9	14.8	18.0	22.0	34.4	20.8
Yugoslavia (1989)	5.3	10.7	16.2	23.7	44.2	27.4
Bulgaria (1992)	10.4	13.9	17.3	22.2	36.2	21.9
Low-income	2–9	6–13	10–16	19–22	40–60	25–45
Middle-income	2–7	7–12	11–16	19–22	45–60	25–45
High-income	4–8	10–13	16–18	22–25	40–45	20–30
G-7 countries (various years)	6.2	11.7	17.2	24.0	41.1	25.0
South America (various years)	4.1	8.0	12.4	19.7	55.9	40.1

Per Capita Output, Income and Completion since 1990

Table 7.3 shows the path of recorded output in 25 transition economies since 1990, as published in the EBRD's *Transition Report* (October 1995). Half of the economies are shown as resuming growth.

Table 7.4 presents the same data as the cumulative fall, the date of the turning point, the extent of the subsequent recovery, and additionally the unemployment rate.

It is, of course, necessary to enter several caveats about the data reflected in this table. Figures were distorted under the old regime, probably upwards, and downwards under the new regime as coverage ceased to be complete and enterprises saw merit in understating output and incomes. Poland's relatively small decline and large recovery reflect revised figures (earlier ones depicted a much greater decline), however even here unemployment is in the high teens.

Eastern Europe as a whole saw a GDP decline of over 10 per cent and has experienced a smaller recovery since 1993. There is little reason to doubt that the region has experienced a setback to output and a rise in unemployment larger than that experienced in the great slump of the 1930s. UNICEF is not the only agency to make comparisons between the present problem of the region and such earlier episodes.

The CIS has seen an even more serious decline, not yet generally reversed and owing little, in total, to the devastations of war or civil war.

Table 7.3   Growth in eastern Europe, the Baltics and the CIS, 1990–4,[a]
Percentage change (1989 = 100)

	Real GDP					1995 (Projection)	Projected level of real GDP in 1995
	1990	1991	1992	1993	1994		
Individual countries							
Albania	−10	−28	−10	11	7	6	75
Armenia	−7	−11	−52	−15	5	5	37
Azerbaijan	−12	−1	−23	−23	−22	−15	35
Belarus	−3	−1	−10	−12	−22	−10	54
Bulgaria	−9	−12	−7	−2	1	3	75
Croatia	9	−14	−9	−3	1	2	84
Czech Republic	0	−14	−6	−1	3	4	85
Estonia	−8	−11	−14	−7	6	6	74
FYR Macedonia	−10	−12	−14	−14	−7	−3	53
Georgia	−12	−14	−40	−39	−35	−5	17
Hungary	4	−12	−3	−1	2	3	86
Kazakstan	0	−13	−13	−12	−25	−12	14
Kyrgyzstan	3	−5	−25	−16	−27	−5	43
Latvia	3	−8	−35	−15	2	1	54
Lithuania	−5	−13	−38	−24	2	5	42
Moldova	−2	−12	−29	−9	−22	−5	42
Poland	−12	−8	3	4	5	6	97
Romania	−6	−13	−10	1	3	4	81
Russia	−4	−13	−19	−12	−15	−3	49
Slovak Republic	0	−15	−7	−4	5	5	84
Slovenia	−5	−8	−5	1	6	6	94
Tajikistan	−2	−7	−29	−11	−21	−12	40
Turkmenistan	2	−5	−5	−10	−20	−5	63
Ukraine	−3	−12	−17	−17	−23	−5	43
Uzbekistan	2	−1	−11	−2	−3	−4	82
Aggregates							
Eastern Europe and the Baltics[b]	−8	−10	−3	1	4	5	88
The Commonwealth of Independent States[c]	−4	−12	−18	−13	−17	−4	48

Notes:

[a] Data for 1990–4 represent the most recent official estimates of outturns as reflected in publications from the national authorities, the IMF, the World Bank, the OECD, the UNECE PlanEcon and the Institute of International Finance.

Data for 1995 reflect EBRD evaluations, partly based on information from the aforementioned sources about developments in the first half of the year. See the caveats in the initial paragraphs of this Annex.

[b] Estimates for real GDP represent weighted average for Albania, Bulgaria, The Czech Republic, Estonia, FYR Macedonia, Hungary, Latvia, Lithuania, Poland, Romania, the Slovak Republic and Slovenia. The weights used were national GDP estimates for 1992 converted into common currency at the average official exchange rate for 1992.

[c] Here taken to include all countries of the former Soviet Union, except Estonia, Latvia and Lithuania. Estimates for real GDP represent weighted averages, using the nominal levels of WMP in each country in 1991 as weights.

Table 7.4   Universal output declines and partial energy as of 1995

Country	Cumulative fall per cent	Turning point	Recovery per cent	1994 per cent unemployment
Albania	35	1992/3	25	9.3
Armenia	65	1994	neg	26 (1993)
Azerbaijan	55 so far	not yet	na	..
Belarus	45 so far	not yet	na	2.5
Bulgaria	20	1994	4	12.5
Croatia	25	1994	3	18
Czech. Rep.	20	1993	8	3
Estonia	25	1993/4	11	3.5 (1995)
FYR Macedonia	40	1995	na	19
Georgia	80 so far	not yet	na	8.4 (1993)
Hungary	17	1993/94	5	10
Kazakhstan	65 so far	not yet	na	2
Kyrgyzstan	45	1995	na	..
Latvia	45	1994	3	7
Lithuania	55	1994	8	7 (1995)
Moldova	55	1995	na	..
Poland	8	1992	20	16
Romania	25	1993	8	11
Russia	50 so far	not yet	na	3.5 (1995)
Slovak Rep.	25	1993/4	11	15
Slovenia	13	1993	14	13 (1995)
Tajikistan	70 so far	not yet	na	..
Turkmenistan	40 so far	not yet	na	..
Ukraine	50	1995	na	0.5
Uzbekistan	20 so far	not yet	na	..
EE	14	1993	8	11
CIS	50	not yet	na	3.5

Notes:
neg = Negligible.
na = Not applicable.
.. = Not available.

Output was projected to decline a further 4 per cent in 1995. Remarkably however, only Armenia reported a remotely commensurate level of unemployment. Before turning to that subject, however, I address the distributional issue. Data on distribution year by year is hard to obtain in most of the countries.

Income Distribution and Transfers

In Russia, the ratio of the income of the top decile to that of the bottom decile nearly doubled between the end of 1991 and the end of 1993 and rose further in 1994 (to 14 from 5.4 in 1991, *Financial Times*, 19 April 1995) while according to *Russian Economic Trends*, the Gini coefficient of personal incomes in Russia rose from 0.28 in late 1991 to over 0.4 in late 1994. According to the *Economist* (29 April 1995) in Britain it rose from 0.23 in 1977 to 0.34 in 1991 and in the United States from 0.35 in 1969 to 0.4 in 1992. Thus a trend to greater inequality is not restricted to transition economies, but the Russian experience is of a different order – doing in three years what took 15 years of radical policy changes in the United Kingdom and twice as much as occurred more spontaneously in nearly 25 years in the United States.

Income distribution in Russia has thus deteriorated unprecedently to be less equal than most G-7 countries from having been more equal in 1990 – and this relative decline among the poorer coincided with an apparently almost catastrophic 50 per cent decline in the mean, implying a dramatic deterioration of conditions for the poor. As shown in Table 7.5 where proverty is defined in terms of a percentage of 1989 wages, on this criterion its incidence has quadrupled in Bulgaria, the Czech Republic, Slovakia and Russia but increased by 50 per cent or less in Hungary, Poland and Romania. Extreme poverty increased five–ten fold in the former and 2–3 times in the latter.

Figure 7.2 shows that the Gini coefficient has risen in all transition economies except Belarus and Slovakia, and that there is a weak relationship with cumulative GDP declines aggravating the implication of either change for the poor. On this data, there is little to choose between the CIS and the Eastern European economies as far as relevant impoverishment is concerned.

Unemployment

Rising unemployment will have contributed to inequality in income and consumption, but is not considered here only for that reason but as a socio-economic indicator in its own right. Unemployment, traditionally reported as negligible throughout the region, has risen everywhere. As Table 7.4 shows it has reached double digits in Armenia, (26 per cent) and Eastern Europe (11 per cent), but remains in single digits or lower in the CIS and the Czech Republic. Clearly, recorded output falls account for little of the

Table 7.5 Incidence of poverty and extreme poverty among households, persons, children, adults and elderly in Eastern Europe, 1989–93

A Estimates of poverty and extreme poverty (Percentage of relevant population)

	Poverty					Extreme Poverty				
	1989	1990	1991	1992	1993	1989	1990	1991	1992	1993
Bulgaria (poverty line = 45% 1989 average wage)										
Households	–	13.6	49.0	53.1	54.7	–	2.1	11.3	23.3	23.9
Children	–	17.7	61.7	59.9	64.4	–	2.0	16.8	26.6	32.2
Adults	–	11.0	49.2	48.7	53.7	–	1.3	12.0	20.1	24.9
Elderly	–	18.3	50.0	59.7	58.6	–	3.8	10.6	27.6	24.6
Population	–	13.3	52.1	53.6	57.0	–	2.0	12.7	23.4	26.2
Czech Rep. (poverty line = 35% 1989 average wage)										
Households	4.6	7.6	23.3	18.2	–	0.3	0.3	0.3	1.6	–
Children	4.2	12.5	43.2	38.3	–	0.3	0.3	0.2	1.1	–
Adults	4.4	7.6	26.3	22.5	–	0.2	0.1	0.5	1.3	–
Elderly	5.7	3.2	12.9	9.6	–	0.4	0.1	0.3	0.4	–
Population	4.2	8.6	29.3	25.3	–	0.2	0.2	0.2	1.3	–
Hungary (poverty line = 40% 1989 average wage)										
Households	12.3	–	13.9	–	–	0.5	–	1.5	–	–
Children	20.6	–	27.0	–	–	1.1	–	3.7	–	–
Adults	12.3	–	18.5	–	–	0.7	–	2.4	–	–
Elderly	11.3	–	10.6	–	–	0.3	–	0.4	–	–
Population	14.5	–	19.4	–	–	0.7	–	2.5	–	–

Table 7.5 Continued

	Poverty					Extreme Poverty				
	1989	1990	1991	1992	1993	1989	1990	1991	1992	1993
Poland (poverty line = 40% 1989 average wage)										
Households	22.9	38.3	33.9	35.7	—	5.1	11.3	8.1	10.4	—
Children	32.3	60.2	58.7	61.3	—	8.3	23.6	21.3	25.9	—
Adults	19.7	37.9	37.0	40.1	—	4.8	13.0	10.3	13.4	—
Elderly	29.5	39.5	29.2	29.5	—	5.2	7.5	3.8	5.2	—
Population	24.7	43.1	41.2	43.7	—	5.5	15.0	12.3	15.1	—
Romania (poverty line = 45% 1989 average wage)										
Households	29.9	17.6	25.1	44.3	—	7.7	2.4	6.8	15.2	—
Children	41.2	28.6	38.1	62.3	—	10.8	3.4	11.6	26.1	—
Adults	29.5	18.2	25.7	47.2	—	7.1	2.4	6.9	16.4	—
Elderly	43.9	21.0	32.1	45.9	—	14.4	3.6	8.4	15.3	—
Population	33.9	21.4	29.7	51.5	—	8.6	2.8	8.4	19.1	—
Slovakia (poverty line = 40% 1989 average wage)										
Households	5.7	6.2	24.9	30.3	34.5	0.2	0.2	2.4	2.9	—
Children	8.8	10.0	42.4	51.1	—	0.2	0.3	6.0	8.1	—
Adults	4.2	4.5	21.2	27.0	—	0.1	0.1	2.1	2.8	—
Elderly	6.2	6.7	25.4	29.0	—	0.2	0.2	2.5	2.4	—
Population	5.8	6.4	27.7	34.1	—	0.1	0.2	3.2	3.9	—

Table 7.5 Continued

	Poverty					Extreme Poverty				
	1989	1990	1991	1992	1993	1989	1990	1991	1992	1993
Russia (poverty line = 40% 1989 average wage)										
Households	–	–	–	–	–	–	–	–	–	–
Children	–	–	–	–	–	–	–	–	–	–
Adults	–	–	–	–	–	–	–	–	–	–
Elderly	–	–	–	–	–	–	–	–	–	–
Population	15.8	14.0	15.5	61.3	–	2.5	2.7	2.5	23.2	–
B Estimates of the 'poverty gap' (in percentage of the relevant poverty line)										
Bulgaria	–	21.9	27.2	36.4	36.6	–	21.7	18.8	25.9	26.6
Czech Rep.	8.3	2.7	14.5	16.5	–	18.1	16.4	16.1	13.6	–
Hungary	16.3	–	16.9	–	–	14.8	–	20.0	–	–
Poland	25.9	30.4	27.9	30.5	–	22.3	25.5	25.3	27.1	–
Romania	28.1	21.3	28.7	33.1	–	24.9	17.9	25.4	26.9	–
Slovakia	12.4	13.2	16.5	19.3	–	11.3	17.9	17.4	17.7	–

Figure 7.2   As GDP of transition economies declines, inequality increases
(percentage changes, 1987–93)

variation of recorded unemployment rates either across or between groups.
More important are the roles of enterprises in income support and welfare
provision and the level and control of benefit distributions.

Nominal benefit rates have been reduced in a number of cases; they
were often much more generous under the old regime than would be
thought wise in the West. Transition has put budgets under strain for
several reasons and transfers have come under corresponding scrutiny,
sometimes resulting in delayed indexation and sometimes in explicit
nominal adjustment.

Health

Table 7.6 reports the change in many indicators of health and welfare
between 1989 and 1993 for nine countries, seven in Eastern Europe, together with Russia and the Ukraine.

The picture is generally, but not uniformly, gloomy. It is particularly
bad for Russia, the Ukraine and Bulgaria and relatively good for Poland,
the Czech Republic and Hungary. Not only has the crude birth rate fallen
everywhere, but the incidence of low birthweight has risen everywhere
except in Albania and Hungary, while life expectancy has also declined
except in Poland and the Czech Republic. Education indicators, mainly
enrolment, have declined except in Hungary.

Table 7.7, gives more detailed health sector figures for Russia in
1990–3, which is almost uniformly bleak with dramatic increases in the incidence of diptheria (up 400 per cent), measles (up 150 per cent) and
syphilis (up 400 per cent).

Table 7.6 Summary of welfare changes in nine Eastern European countries 1989–93

Indicator	Unit	Albania	Bulgaria	Czech B.	Slovakia	Hungary	Holand	Romania	Russia	Ukraine	Number of cases				Bank	Average change in indicator
											decrease	increase	no case	% deteriorations		
(a) Income and consumption-based indicators																
Real income per capita	%	–	–39.2	–17.8	–30.3	–12.8	–38.3	–20.7	–38.3	–3.7	8	–	1	100	1	–22.3
Poverty rate	% points	–	43.2	22.1	29.4	4.2	19.0	17.5	36.0	–	7	–	2	100	1	24.5
Food share	% points	–	4.1	0.1	1.0	0.3	–6.9	5.9	12.3	6.6	7	1	1	88	10	2.9
Calorie consumption per capita	%	–	–18.0	–	–3.3	–5.7	–5.1	–9.2	–2.0	–18.7	7	–	2	100	1	–8.9
(b) Demographic indicators																
Crude marriage rate	%	–4.5	–33.8	–18.4	–19.1	–18.0	–19.8	–7.8	–27.3	–13.7	9	–	–	100	1	–19.8
Remarriage rate	%	–	–49.1	–9.9	–38.5	–28.3	–29.2	–13.3	–	–	6	–	3	100	1	–28.1
Crude divorce rate	%	–16.9	–22.0	–3.2	1.7	–13.5	–13.7	–17.1	11.1	11.6	3	6	–	33	27	–10.2
Crude birth rate	%	–22.3	–21.4	–5.9	–9.8	–3.6	–14.5	–31.7	–34.2	–20.0	9	–	–	100	1	–18.2
(c) Mortality indicators																
Life expectancy males	years	–	–0.9	–0.4	–0.1	–0.9	0.6	–	–5.2	–2.0	5	2	2	71	17	–1.0
Life expectancy females	years	–	–0.7	0.7	–0.1	–0.1	0.5	–	–1.8	–1.0	5	2	2	71	17	–0.3
Infant mortality rate	%	7.7	7.3	–14.8	–21.2	–15.5	–16.9	–13.4	12.9	15.6	4	5	–	44	26	–4.2
1–4 mortality rate	%	–	–5.2	0.0	–12.5	–27.3	–18.3	–29.1	–3.8	–4.9	–	8	1	0	29	–12.6
5–19 mortality rate	%	–	0.7	8.0	1.3	–1.5	–12.4	–14.6	19.2	6.9	5	3	1	63	19	1.0

Table 7.6 Continued

Indicator	Unit	Albania	Bulgaria	Czech R.	Slovakia	Hungary	Holland	Romania	Russia	Ukraine	Number of cases — decrease	increase	no case	% deteriorations	Bank	Average change in indicator
20–39 mortality rate	%	–	10.0	5.2	3.7	10.6	-8.1	-3.1	65.8	28.0	6	2	1	75	13	14.0
40–59 mortality rate	%	–	4.1	-2.1	-9.2	8.7	-9.2	12.2	50.2	27.3	5	3	1	63	19	10.3
60+ mortality rate	%	–	-0.7	-4.5	-7.7	1.6	-1.3	1.5	17.0	16.6	4	4	1	50	24	28
Maternal mortality rate	%	-16.9%	-24.1	-9.7	-74.0	-36.0	10.3	-64.4	3.7	-20.1	2	7	–	22	28	-29.0
(d) Health indicators																
Abortion rate	%	60.1	7.7	-26.1	-8.3	-12.0	-84.5	488.7	10.3	0.8	5	4	–	56	23	48.5
Low birth weight rate	%	-3.2	33.7	13.9	13.6	-5.7	3.9	48.8	7.1	–	6	2	1	75	13	14.0
New tuberculosis cases	%	–	45.2	4.3	35.2	14.9	4.0	59.0	14.1	9.7	8	–	1	100	1	23.3
(e) Social cohesion and protection indicators																
% of births to mothers < 20	% points	–	4.0	1.9	2.4	0.2	1.0	2.2	5.5	4.8	8	–	1	100	1	2.4
No. of adoptions	%	–	-12.5	-15.8	33.2	-6.0	-21.9	–	13.1	14.7	4	3	2	57	22	0.7
Crime rate	%	–	194.6	87.0	50.4	82.9	53.6	87.3	67.9	24.6	5	–	1	100	1	81.1
Youths sentenced	%	–	-68.3	-20.1	24.4	6.7	123.6	58.3	45.8	10.0	6	2	1	75	13	22.5
Homecare rate	%	–	80.3	22.1	42.9	46.3	12.4	-51.5	141.1	–	6	1	2	86	12	–

Table 7.6 Continued

Indicator	Unit	Albania	Bulgaria	Czech B.	Slovakia	Hungary	Poland	Romania	Russia	Ukraine	Number of cases				Bank	Average change in indicator
											decrease	increase	no case	% deteriorations		
(f) Child education indicators																
Creche/parental leave coverage	% points	–	-2.1	-11.6	-3.5	4.3	-18.2	0.4	-10.4	-9.5	6	2	1	75	13	-6.3
Pre-primary enrolment rate	% points	–	-13.0	-16.0	-13.4	0.9	-6.0	-9.7	-12.7	-3.7	7	1	1	88	10	-9.2
Primary enrolment rate	% points	-4.0	-6.6	1.2	1.6	0.1	-0.9	-3.4	-0.6	–	4	4	1	50	24	-1.6
Secondary enrolment rate	% points	-12.0	-7.5	-0.1	0.3	3.3	1.7	-19.8	-4.8	–	5	3	1	63	19	-5.6
Total number of observations		9	29	28	29	29	29	26	28	23	165	65	31	71.7	–	–
– number of deteriorations		6	24	17	20	18	17	18	25	20	–	–	–	–	–	–
– number of improvements		3	5	11	9	11	12	8	3	3	–	–	–	–	–	–
Percentage of deteriorations		67	83	61	69	62	59	69	89	87	–	–	–	–	–	–

Table 7.7   The health sector in the Russian Federation, 1990–93 (revised 9/11/93) (table for C. Davis RFE/RL article with detailed source notes)

Indicator	Year 1990	1991	1992	First half of 1993
Birth rate	13.4	12.1	10.8	9.6
Salmonellosis	70.4	74.2	80.1	82.0
Diphtheria	0.8	1.3	3.1	4.6
Whooping cough	16.9	20.8	25.0	29.0
Measles	12.4	13.8	15.2	30.0
Cancer	264.5	266.0	267.56	269.2
Tuberculosis	34.2	34.0	35.8	43.0
Syphillis	5.3	5.8	13.4	26.8
Hospital beds	137.5	134.7	130.9	124.3
Doctors	46.9	44.3	44.0	42.7
Invalids from childhood	43.1	61.6	62.0	62.0
Infant mortality	17.4	17.8	18.0	18.8
Maternal mortality	47.4	52.4	50.8	52.0
Male mortality (40–44 years)	7.6	8.0	8.8	10.9
Crude death rate	11.2	11.4	12.1	14.4
Life expectancy	69.2	69.0	68.6	67.2

Pressure on Budgets and Inflation

Four issues are relevant here.

1. The old regime was undermined by intensifying repressed inflation as growing fiscal deficits were monetized and the natural consequences restrained by price controls.
2. Liberalization therefore not only involved a once-for-all price jump, but continuing inflation if deficits were not curtailed (inflation performance is shown in Table 7.8).
3. The diversion of resources into the shadow economy involved a narrowing of the tax base, as did recession and the loss of revenue at a time when explicit taxation replaced proprietorial accrual of nearly all non-labour income to the state.
4. Remaining state enterprises had their profitability squeezed by competition from more enterprising and less fiscally compliant private enterprises, further eroding the tax base, indeed calling in many cases for cash or credit subventions.

Table 7.8 Inflation in eastern Europe, the Baltics and the CIS, 1991–5

	Retail/consumer prices (end-year)				
	1991	1992	1993	1994	1995 Projection
	(Percentage change)				
Albania	104	237	31	16	5
Armenia	25	1341	10,996	1885	45
Azerbaijan	126	1395	1294	1788	100
Belarus	93	1558	1994	1875	260
Bulgaria	339	79	64	122	50
Croatia	149	937	1150	–3	3
Czech Republic	52	13	18	10	10
Estonia	304	954	36	42	22
FYR Macedonia	115	1935	230	55	10
Georgia	131	1463	7492	7380	25
Hungary	32	22	21	21	28
Kazakstan	150	2567	2169	1160	60
Kyrgyzstan	170	1771	1366	87	25
Latvia	262	958	35	26	23
Luthuania	345	1175	189	45	30
Moldova	162	2198	837	98	20
Poland	60	44	38	30	23
Romania	223	199	296	62	30
Russia	144	2318	841	203	145
Slovak Republic	58	9	25	12	10
Slovenia	247	93	23	18	10
Tajikistan	204	1364	7344	5	240
Turkmenistan	155	644	9750	1100	2500
Ukraine	161	2000	10,155	401	150
Uzbekistan	169	910	885	423	155

These many pressures impinged upon transfer payments as well as product subsidies and social expenditures, as illustrated for health expenditure in Table 7.9.

3 POLICY ISSUES

Policies Relating to Output and Employment

There has been an enormous amount of discussion of the causes of the fall in output in transition economies. Is (or was) it due to restrictive stabiliz-ation policies, or the breakdown of the old coordination (planning) mechan-

Table 7.9   Index of real public health expenditure in Eastern Europe, 1990–93
(1989 =100)

	1990	1991	1992	1993
A Computed using the overall GDP deflator				
Albania	100.0	115.9	142.5	85.7
Bulgaria	111.1	100.0	120.0	102.1
Czech Republic	104.1	91.2	154.1	–
Slovakia	109.6	104.9	96.9	81.1
Hungary	107.7	108.5	106.1	96.0
Poland	144.7	116.7	124.3	–
Romania	107.6	96.7	77.3	–
Russia	124.1	69.7	60.0	67.4
Ukraine	108.0	110.7	118.2	–
B Computed using the medical services and health expenditure deflator				
Albania	–	–	–	–
Bulgaria	93.4	70.2	68.9	52.5
Czech Republic	94.8	81.1	122.9	–
Slovakia	68.1	70.5	72.0	70.0
Hungary	115.6	115.5	101.4	82.7
Poland	106.3	75.2	73.6	–
Romania	104.8	93.4	86.7	–
Russia	120.8	94.6	63.2	33.6
Ukraine	–	–	–	–

ism without its replacement by the organic network of contacts crucial to a market economy? Was destocking important, or the collapse in trade with former CMEA partners? Was that collapse inevitable or the result of partial uncoordinated reforms? Did liberalization of trade and prices lead to asymmetrical responses by winners and losers? Did the losers contract more rapidly than the winners could, or would, expand? Do the statistics impute high values to reduced activities which subtract value at world prices?

There is an element of truth in all the suggested hypotheses, but few of them call for reconsideration of policy. Stabilization and liberalization could, and should, not be avoided. Their speed may, however, be up to a point a choice variable. Stabilization is best done quickly, and so is liberalization in the sense of decriminalizing trading activities and abolishing the monopoly of state trading organizations.

Prices also should almost certainly be freed from administrative control. It would, however, even then be possible to intervene to affect the path of liberalized prices. This could most easily be done either by offering a transitional employment subsidy or transitional protection. The argument for an employment subsidy is that with specific capital goods, liberalization of a very distorted economy will typically lead to a sharp fall in the market-clearing real wage even if labour is shifted out of value-subtracting activities into ones where it can make a modest positive contribution so that real output at world prices actually rises. The market-clearing real wage falls because labour shed by value-subtracting activities drives down the marginal physical product elsewhere very rapidly given the fixed stock (in the short run), of specific (putty-clay) capital (see Flemming, 1993).

The fall in the real wage would challenge political sustainability even if the market cleared. In practice, political, social and benefit-induced constraints, (such as minimum wages or unemployment compensation) tend to convert in incipient fall in real wages into actual unemployment. If this is much above the 10 per cent norm of Western Europe since 1980, and we have seen that it is in many cases, the shadow wage probably falls considerably below the market wage. An employment subsidy might not, in a competive labour market, raise real wages but enable (low) value-adding enterprises to pay the conventional wage. If the subsidy is less than the benefit due to the unemployed it is quite possible for output, consumption, investment and the net fiscal position all to improve.

The alternative procedure, involving fewer risks with the budget, is to convert all the inherited distortions, (except those requiring more than 100 per cent effective protection), into transparent border taxes and to announce from the start that they will be phased out over, say, 10 years (as advocated in a different context by, for instance, Little, Scitovsky and Scott, 1970). Neither measure, if credible, should distort the allocation of either capital or labour. Investment in a sector should be more sensitive to future, undistorted, prices than to current prices. Workers in enterprises kept going by the policies are on notice to raise efficiency or to get out. Even if their true current value-added is low, it is higher than in the more realistic short-term alternative of unemployment.

How can the temporary nature of this transparent distortion be guaranteed and made credible? The first point to make is that a policy of free trade is not credible if it generates unemployment and a political backlash. Indeed, protective distortions have increased since 1991, in most of Eastern Europe (see EBRD, *Transition Report* 1994, p. 114). A less provocative initial stance might have been easier to sustain.

The EC–EU might also have imposed declining ceilings on Eastern European tariffs in the Europe Agreements even if they did not initially bind. A group of reforming countries eliminating similar distortions at the same time could lend each other credibility in a customs union which would reduce the misallocation cost of the policy for small open economies. As it is, protectionist lobbies may believe that they have liberal governments on the run and that they will be able to extract ever-greater concessions.

It is important not to respond to rising unemployment by offering a more generous safety net for job losers. In this analysis such a measure not only has an immediate budgetary cost but almost certainly pushes up the reservation real wage, increasing unemployment.

Policies Relating to Liberalization, Quasi-rents and Rent-seeking

The recommended procedure, most obviously in the case of a protective structure mimicking the old distortions, effectively takes away large positive quasi-rents in previously controlled sectors and converts negative to positive quasi-rents in some other cases. As we have seen this should not reduce total profits (rents) and resources for investment because it raises total resource utilization. Unrestrained quasi-rents in disequilibrium would otherwise attract protection racketeers and contribute to income inequality, corruption and criminality (see the homicide figures in Table 7.6). Such racketeers would not plough back their profits – to do so would erode the quasi-rents. They also thrive in a world of less transparent support to unprofitable but value-adding enterprises through partial control, direction of credit, discretionary granting of exemptions, etc.

Again, the distinction needs to be made between the urgency of dismantling administrative controls and the decade over which convergence on world prices is best achieved. These can be reconciled by market-conforming interventions, such as protective duties, although their enforcement in the CIS would not be easy. If such measures reduced the proportion of loss-making enterprises to a low enough level, they would facilitate the more rapid application of bankruptcy laws and the implementation of privatization policies which are delayed in many cases by policy compromises.

Policies Relating to the (Re-)integration of the Shadow Economy

The budgetary problems discussed above (p. 137), are linked, as explained there, to the narrowing of the effective tax base relative even to diminished GDP. In the Ukraine, for instance, a figure of 40 per cent was widely quoted in 1994 for the share of GDP contributed by the shadow economy. Under these circumstances the (re) integration of the shadow economy into the regular economy is vital. One approach is to send in shock troops in jackboots to enforce the letter of still-extant anti-enterprise regulations and taxes. This would be disastrous. It would lead to the closure of many valuable activities and would set back private enterprise for a decade. It is also unnecessary as a 40 per cent increase in income is more than is needed.

Clearly if one believed the base-broadening operations would be successful, one could afford a 25 per cent reduction in nominal tax rates. Suppose they amount to 60 per cent (see EBRD, 1993, p. 49) then 60 per cent of 60 per cent of GDP yields 36 per cent. The tax rate could be cut to 40 per cent, and if all liabilities were enforced revenue would rise. The challenge is to come up with a credible enforcement programme to allow the tax rates to be cut before enforcement begins so as to ensure the survival of the egg-laying geese.

As important as explicit taxes in this context is the array of regulations with which the survival of private enterprises in particular can be challenged. Typically, those operating in the shadows do not get away scot-free but pay protection money and payoffs to induce officials to turn a blind eye. This means that a credible liberal regime would be attractive to them, even with a significant explicit tax rate. It would, however, have to provide adequate assurances that unofficial depredation would cease. Moreover, if the corrupt officials rely on the payments of the shadow economy to provide them with a living wage, it may be necessary to provide for enhanced salaries out of the additional revenue, diminishing the scale of tax cuts that can be considered.

Ukrainian experience suggests that there is scope for a package of reforms along these lines that would deregulate the economy, reduce regulatory and fiscal burdens on enterprises, and provide enhanced revenue. The trick by which it should be achieved involves, however, elements of confidence which are not easy to construct. Several of the transition economies, especially in the CIS, present a tougher case than did the Israeli case of the 1970s (see Bruno and Habib, 1976).

Policies Relating to Social Safety Nets and the Delivery of Social Services

One reason for the low recorded unemployment in much of the CIS is that redundant workers are retained on enterprise payrolls. This in turn is due to several factors:

(a) The excess wage tax makes it attractive to reduce average wages by retaining or even hiring people at the statutory minimum wage which, partly because of inflation, is even lower relative to the average wage than unemployment compensation would typically be in the West.

(b) Blanchard, Commander *et al.* suggest that boosting nominal employ-
     ment may improve access to bank credit and that this explains contin-
     ued hiring, despite the 50 per cent fall in output across many sectors.
     The rise in unemployment is smaller than would have occurred if
     many new entrants to the labour force had failed to find jobs

(c) While these two factors might account for a supply of low-paid jobs the
     supply of people to fill them requires that benefits elsewhere be very
     modest. Not only is this true of cash benefits – which may also be avail-
     able only in relatively few places – but also of many other benefits.

The survey (see Table 7.10) identified 19 benefits, which can be grouped
under headings such as housing benefits, child benefits, food aid, health
and recreation, etc. Although the inference is not strictly valid and the
samples are small, it would appear that virtually every enterprise offers

Table 7.10 Enterprise-provided social benefits in Russia – type and availability,
by firm size, November 1992, percentages

Firm size	80–350	351–700	701–900	901–
Sample size	10	11	10	10
Housing (permanent)	20	50	80	50
Housing (temporary)	10	30	40	30
Kindergarten	40	50	80	80
Land for dachas	30	70	70	90
Canteen (subsidized)	40	60	80	90
Polyclinics (access)	20	20	50	70
Community house	0	10	30	30
Fitness facilities	0	0	10	20
Sanatorium	0	60	40	50
Food store with subsidized prices	80	80	70	80
Sick pay	0	0	30	30
Housing rents assistance	0	0	0	10
Other forms of housing help	0	60	40	40
Transport allowance	30	30	10	50
Maternity allowance	100	100	100	90
Child care allowance	100	100	90	100
Paid vacation	40	70	70	30
Pre-dismissal allowance	80	90	80	90
Sanatorium vouchers	80	90	90	90

Source: World Bank Survey.

assistance to employees under every major heading. This underlines the extent to which social support has been enterprise-based and the reluctance of people to allow enterprise links to lapse, especially if substantial cash income from a private enterprise is not available.

The enterprise basis of social provision is unacceptable in the medium term for three reasons:

1   It may be doubted whether those normally employed but on minimum wages perform the economic role of the unemployed in a market economy. Do they effectively restrain nominal wage increases? Do they constitute a pool of labour from which new enterprises can recruit? The excess wage tax probably serves to undermine the first role while the insecurity of much full-time private employment would make even such people reluctant to accept private sector jobs while their attachment to old enterprises might reduce their search activity.

2.   Existing enterprise-based systems are probably not spreading to new businesses whose ex-employees will be uncovered.

3.   Privatization and subsidy reduction will make it increasingly difficult for old enterprises to offer uniform or equitable benefits.

Thus a high priority should be attached to transferring responsibility for social provision from enterprises to some organ of the state such as the municipalities. This is not simply to propose the transfer of a liability from one to the other. A suitable payroll tax would, in aggregate, replace enterprises' in-kind liabilities and finance the new state supply of a reduced list of standardized market-conforming benefits.

In practise such a programme faces three difficulties:

(a)   Organizing state provision in replacement of provision sometimes integrated with enterprise operations.

(b)   Synchronizing the transfer over a suitable area so that the tax can be introduced and the transfer made on an essentially revenue and expenditure neutral basis.

(c)   Dealing with the inter-enterprise distributional consequences of a uniform pay roll tax (for example) in replacement of provision whose value in relation to the payroll will have varied with many factors, especially demographic ones. This is particularly true of China where SOEs have a liability for pensions which does not feature in the World Bank survey.

4 CONCLUSION

The data surveyed in this chapter suggest that there is a serious welfare problem in transition. Depending on how quickly the transition economies can catch up with richer market economies, some degree of increased inequality was implicit in their transition and thus inevitable. However the decline in output, speed of adverse redistribution and decline in social provision and associated welfare indicators was not inevitable and has contributed to political trends inimical to the sustenance of the reform programme, particularly in CIS countries.

The proposals for more coherent and radical reform programmes reintegrating the 'grey economy', and transferring social provision from enterprises to government are broadly conventional. Any originality in this discussion lies in an urging of caution in the advocacy of a bigger and better social safety net to compensate any 'victims' of transition. This is because their number is largely due to the decline in recorded output and consequent fiscal problems would almost certainly be aggravated by such a programme of expenditure which would raise effective reservation wages. A programme of transitory protection or employment subsidy, particularly the former, would not strain the budget, would reduce demands on the safety net, and by increasing the proportion of enterprises viable financially would reduce their need for 'soft credits', facilitating the hardening of budget constraints and early orderly privatization.

Notes

*   I am indebted to my colleague C. M. Davies of Wolfson College, Oxford, for directing me to much of the data presented in this chapter.

1.   And one confronting reform in China (Goodhart and Cheng, An Xu, 1996)

References

Balcerowicz, Leszek (1995) *Socialism, Capitalism, Transformation* (Budapest: Central European University Press and Oxford University Press), chapter 9.
Blanchard, O. and S. Commander *et al.* (1995) *Unemployment, Restructuring and the Labour Market in Eastern Europe* (Washington, DC: IBRD).
Bruno, M. and J. Habib (1976) 'Taxes, Family Grants and Redistribution', *Journal of Public Economics*, vol. 5 (1 & 2) Jan/Feb.
EBRD (1993) *Annual Economic Outlook.*
EBRD (1994) *Transition Report: European Transition in Eastern Europe and the Former Soviet Union*, European Bank for Reconstruction and Development (October)

Flemming, J. S. (1993) 'Public Finance, Unemployment and Economies in Transition' in D. Bös (ed.) *Economics in a Changing World* (London: Macmillan).

Goodhart, C. A. E. and Xu, Cheng An (1996) 'The Rise of China as an Economic Power', *National Institute Economic Review*, February.

Layard, R. and A. Richter, A. (1995) 'Labour Market Adjustment: The Russian Way', in A. Åslund (ed.) *Russian Economic Reform at Risk* (London).

Little, I. M. D., T. Scitovsky and M. F. G. Scott (1970) *Industry and Trade in Some Developing Countries* (Oxford: Oxford University Press).

Pudney, S. E. (1995) 'Income Distribution and the Reform of Public Housing in Hungary', *Economics of Transition*, vol. 3, no. 1.

Rose, Richard *et al.* (1994) *Studies in Public Policy* (Glasgow Centre for the Study of Public Policy, University of Strathclyde).

8 What Can We Learn from China's Economic Reform?*

Justin Yifu Lin

PEKING UNIVERSITY, CHINA,
HONG KONG UNIVERSITY OF SCIENCE AND TECHNOLOGY,
AUSTRALIAN NATIONAL UNIVERSITY,
CANBERRA, AUSTRALIA

1 INTRODUCTION

China is the first among the socialist countries to engage in wide-range economic reforms and so far the most successful one. China's reforms started at the end of 1978. Since then, China has joined the rank of East Asian NIEs and achieved an average annual growth rate of 9.6 per cent, while the price level has been relatively stable (see Figure 8.1). In the

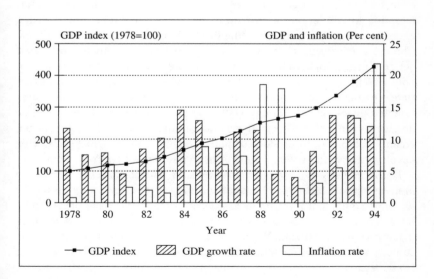

Source: State Statistical Bureau (1995, pp. 4, 8, 45).

Figure 8.1 Economic growth and inflation in China, 1978–94

17 years between 1978 and 1995, the size of China's GNP increased about five times. As a consequence, the living standard of people improved significantly. It is no exaggeration to say that such a rapid rate of economic growth in such a large country for such a long period of time has never occurred elsewhere in human history. This achievement is especially extraordinary when the Chinese experience is compared with the economic collapse and stagnation in Eastern European countries and the Former Soviet Union (FSU) during their reform process.

In this chapter, I would like to provide an explanation for why it is possible for China to achieve such a remarkable performance and to draw some lessons for other countries in the process of reform. The organization of the chapter is as follows: Section 2 analyzes the roots and problems in Chinese economy before the reforms in 1979. Section 3 provides an analytical review of China's approach and process of reforms. Some lessons of China's economic reforms are summarized in section 4.

2 MAJOR PRE-REFORM PROBLEMS IN THE CHINESE ECONOMY

The major pre-reform problems in Chinese economy were the suppression of incentives and misallocation of resources which were the result of attempting to accelerate the growth of heavy industry in a capital-scarce agrarian economy. At the founding of the People's Republic in 1949, the Chinese government inherited a war-torn agrarian economy in which 89.4 per cent of the population resided in rural areas and industry consisted of only 12.6 per cent of the national income. Inspired by the successful experience of the Soviet Union Chinese leaders adopted an heavy industry-oriented development strategy (HIODS) after recovering from war-time destruction in 1953. The goal was, as rapidly as possible, to build the country's capacity to produce capital goods and military materials. This development strategy was shaped through a series of Five-Year Plans.[1]

Heavy industry is a capital-intensive sector. The construction of a heavy industry project has three characteristics: (1) it requires a long gestation; (2) most equipment for a project, at least in the initial stage, needs to be imported from more advanced economies; and (3) each project requires a lump-sum investment. When the Chinese government initiated this strategy in the early 1950s, the Chinese economy had three characteristics: (1) the available capital was limited and, consequently, the market interest rate was high; (2) foreign exchange was scarce and expensive because exportable goods were limited and primarily consisted of low-priced agricultural products; and (3) the economic surplus was small and scattered due to the nature of a poor agrarian economy. Because these characteristics of the Chinese economy were mismatched with the three characteristics of a heavy industry project, spontaneous development of capital-intensive industry in the economy was impossible. Therefore, a set of distorted macro-policies was required for the development of heavy industry. At the beginning of the first Five-Year Plan in 1953, the government instituted a policy of low interest rates and overvalued exchange rates to reduce both the costs of interest payments and of importing equipment. Meanwhile, in order to secure enough funds for industrial expansion, a policy of low-input prices, including nominal wage rates for workers and prices for raw materials, energy and transportation, evolved alongside the adoption of this development strategy. The assumption was that low prices would enable enterprises to create profits large enough to repay the loans or to accumulate enough funds for re-investment. If the enterprises were privately owned, the state could not be sure that the private entrepreneurs would re-invest the policy-created profits on the intended projects. Therefore, private enterprises were soon nationalized and new key enterprises owned by the state to secure the state's control over profits for heavy industry projects. Meanwhile, to make the low nominal-wage policy feasible, the government had to provide urban residents with inexpensive food and other necessities, including housing, medical care and clothing. The low interest rates, overvalued exchange rates, low nominal wage rates and low prices for raw materials and living necessities constituted the basic macro-policy environment of the HIODS.

The above macro-policies induced a total imbalance in the supply and demand for credit, foreign exchange, raw materials and other living necessities. Because non-priority sectors would be competing with the priority sectors for low-priced resources, plans and administrative controls replaced markets as the mechanism for allocating scarce credit, foreign reserves, raw materials and living necessities, ensuring that limited resources would be used for the targeted projects. Moreover, the State monopolized banks, foreign trade- and material distribution systems.[2]

In this way competition was suppressed, and profits ceased to be the measure of an enterprise's efficiency.[3] Because of the lack of market discipline, managerial discretion was potentially a serious problem. Managers of state enterprises were deprived of autonomy to mitigate this problem.[4] The production of state enterprises was dictated by mandatory plans and furnished with most of their material inputs through an administrative allocation system. The prices of their products were determined by the pricing authorities. Government agencies controlled the circulation of their products. The wages and salaries of workers and managers were determined not by their performance but by their education, age, position and other criteria according to a national wage scale. Investment and working capital were mostly financed by appropriations from the state budget or loans from the banking system according to state plans. The state enterprises remitted all their profits, if any, to the state and the state budget would also cover all losses incurred by the enterprises. In short, the state enterprises were like puppets: they did not have any autonomy over the employment of workers, the use of profits, the plan of production, the supplies of inputs and the marketing of their products.

The development strategy and the resulting policy environment and allocation system also shaped the evolution of farming institutions in China. In order to secure cheap supplies of grain and other agricultural products for urban low-price rationing, a compulsory procurement policy was imposed in the rural areas in 1953. This policy obliged peasants to sell set quantities of their produce, including grain, cotton, and edible oils to the state at government-set prices.

In addition to providing cheap food for industrialization, agriculture was also the main foreign-exchange earner. In the 1950s, agricultural products alone made up over 40 per cent of all exports. If processed agricultural products are also counted, agriculture contributed to more than 60 per cent of China's foreign exchange earnings up to the 1970s. Because foreign exchange was as important as capital for the heavy industry-oriented strategy, the country's capacity to import capital goods for industrialization in the early stage of development clearly depended on agriculture's performance.

Agricultural development required resources and investment as much as industrial development. The government, however, was reluctant to divert scarce resources and funds from industry to agriculture. Therefore, alongside the HIODS, the government adopted a new agricultural development strategy that would not compete for resources with industrial expansion. The core of this strategy involved the mass mobilization of rural labour to work on labour-intensive investment projects, such as irrigation, flood control and land reclamation, and to raise unit yields in agriculture through traditional methods and inputs, such as closer planting, more careful weeding and the use of more organic fertilizer. The government believed that collectivization of agriculture would ensure these functions. The government also viewed collectivization as a convenient vehicle for effecting the state's low-priced procurement programme of grain and other agricultural products (Luo, 1985). Income distribution in the collectives was based on each collective member's contribution to agricultural production. However, monitoring a member's effort is extremely difficult in agricultural production due to dimensions of time and space. The remuneration system in the collectives was basically egalitarian (Lin, 1989).

The distorted macro-policy environment, planned allocation system, and micro-management institutions outlined above all made the maximum mobilization of resources for the development of heavy industry possible in a capital-scarce economy. As a result, the gross output value of heavy industry in the combined total output value of agriculture and industry grew from 15 per cent in 1952 to about 40 per cent in the 1970s.

Judging from China's sector composition, the trinity of the traditional economic structure – a distorted macro-policy environment, a planned allocation system, and a puppet-like micro-management institution – reached its intended goal of accelerating the development of heavy industry in China. However, China paid a high price for such an achievement. The economy was very inefficient, for two reasons:

(1) *Misallocation of resources*   The comparative advantage of Chinese economy is in an abundant labour endowment. If investments had been guided by market forces, profit incentives would have induced entrepreneurs to adopt capital-saving and labour-using technologies and to allocate more resources to labour-intensive industries. However, for the development of heavy industry, the state monopolized the allocation system and used administrative measures to direct the allocation of resources to the uncompetitive heavy industries, resulting in a deviation of the industrial structure from the pattern dictated by the comparative advantages of the economy.

(2) *Low incentives*   Because profits ceased to be a measure of efficiency and the planned allocation system often failed to distribute materials in time, managers were forced to keep large reserves and had no incentive for utilizing resources economically. Overstaffing, underutilization of capital resources, and overstocking of inventories are all characteristics of puppet-like state enterprises. Moreover, managers had no authority over workers' wage rates and bonuses. A worker's payment was not related to his or her effort in the enterprise nor to the enterprise's profits. The remuneration system hence invited low work incentives. Similarly, in the agricultural collectives, the farm worker's incentive to work was low because the link between reward and effort was weak.[5]

Because of the above two factors, the Chinese economy was very inefficient. The most important indicator that reflected this inefficiency was the extremely low rate of total factor productivity (TFP) growth in

China. A World Bank study shows that, even calculated on the most favourable assumptions, the growth rate was only 0.5 per cent between 1952 and 1981, only a quarter of the average growth rate of 19 developing countries included in the study (World Bank, 1985a). Moreover, the TFP of China's state enterprises was in a state of stagnation or even negative growth between 1957 and 1982 (World Bank, 1985b).

3   ANALYTICAL REVIEW OF CHINA'S ECONOMIC REFORMS

The main fault of the traditional Chinese economy was low economic efficiency arising from structural imbalance and incentive problems. The government had made several attempts before the late 1970s to address the structural problems by decentralizing the allocative mechanism from central to local government.[6] However, the administrative nature of the allocative mechanism was not changed and the policy environment and managerial system were not altered, and thus the attempts failed to rectify the structural imbalance and improve economic incentives. The goals of the reform in late 1978 were also to rectify the structural imbalance and improve incentives. However, what set the reforms apart from previous attempts were the micro-management system reforms, that made farmers and managers and workers in state enterprises partial residual claimants. This small chink in the trinity of the traditional economic structure led to the gradual dismantling of the traditional system.

The Micro-Management System Reforms

The most important change in the micro-management system was the replacement of collective farming by a household-based system, now known as the 'household responsibility system'. The change in farming institutions had not been intended by the government at the beginning of the reforms. Although it had been recognized in 1978 that solving managerial problems within the collective system was the key to improving farmers' incentives, the official position at that time was still that the collective was to remain the basic unit of agricultural production. Nevertheless, a small number of collectives, first secretly and later with the blessing of local authorities, began to try out a system of leasing a collective's land and dividing the obligatory procurement quotas to individual households in the collective. A year later these collectives brought out yields far larger than those of other teams. The central authorities later conceded to the existence of this new form of farming, but required that it be restricted to poor agricultural regions, mainly to hilly or mountainous areas, and to poor collectives in which people had lost confidence in the collective system. However, this restriction was ignored in most regions. Production performance was improved after a collective adopted the new system, regardless of its relative wealth or poverty. Full official recognition of the household responsibility system as a nationally acceptable farming institution was eventually given in late 1981, exactly two years after the initial price increases. By that time, 45 per cent of the collectives in China had already dismantled and instituted the household responsibility system. By the end of 1983, 98 per cent of agricultural collectives in China had adopted it. When the household responsibility system first appeared, the land lease was only 1–3 years. However, the short lease reduced farmers' incentives for land-improvement investment, and the lease contract was allowed to be extended up to 15 years in 1984. In 1993, the government allowed the lease contract to be extended for another 30 years after the expiration of the first contract.

Unlike the spontaneous nature of farming institution reform, the reform in the micro-management system of the state enterprises was initiated by the government. These reforms have undergone four stages. The first stage (1979–83) emphasized several important experimental initiatives that were intended to enlarge enterprise autonomy and expand the role of financial incentives within the traditional economic structure. These measures included the introduction of profit retention and performance-related bonuses and permitted the state enterprises to produce outside the mandatory state plan. The enterprises involved in exports were also allowed to retain part of their foreign exchange earnings for use at their own discretion. In the second stage (1984–6) the emphasis shifted to a formalization of the financial obligations of the state enterprises to the government. Profit remittances were replaced by a profit tax. In 1984, the government allowed state enterprises to sell output in excess of quotas at negotiated prices and to plan their output accordingly, thus establishing a dual-track price system. During the third stage (1987–92), the contract responsibility system, which attempted to clarify the authority and responsibilities of enterprise managers, was formalized and widely adopted. The last stage (1993-present) attempted to introduce the modern corporate system to the state enterprises. In each stage of the reform, the government's intervention was reduced further and the state enterprises gained more autonomy.

The reform of the micro-management system has achieved its intended goal of improving technical efficiency. Empirical estimates show that almost half of the 42.2 per cent growth of output in the cropping sector in the years 1978–84 was driven by productivity change brought about by the reforms. Furthermore, almost all of the above productivity growth was attributable to the changes resulting from the introduction of the household responsibility system (Fan, 1991; Huang and Rozelle, 1994; Lin 1992; McMillan *et al.*, 1989; Wen, 1993). Production function estimates in several studies find that for industry the increase in enterprise autonomy increased productivity in the state enterprises (Chen *et al.*, 1988; Gordon and Li 1991; Dollar, 1990; Jefferson *et al.*, 1992; Groves *et al.*, 1992). Therefore, the reforms in the micro-management system in both agriculture and industry have created a flow of new resources, an important feature of China's reforms.

The increase in enterprise autonomy under a distorted macro-policy environment, however, also invited managers' and workers' discretionary behaviour. Despite an improvement in productivity, the profitability of the state enterprises declined and the government's subsidies increased due to a faster increase in wages, fringe benefits and other unauthorized expenditures (Fan and Schaffer, 1991) and the competition from the autonomous township-and-village enterprises (TVEs) (Jefferson and Rawski, 1995).[7] However, once the enterprises has tasted autonomy, it would have been politically too costly to revoke it. The decline in the profits of state enterprises and the competition from TVEs forced the government to try other measures that further increased the autonomy of state enterprises in the hope that the new measures would make the enterprises financially independent.

Resource Allocation System Reform

The increase in enterprise autonomy put pressure on the planned distribution system. Because the state enterprises were allowed to produce outside the mandatory plans, the enterprises needed to obtain additional inputs and to sell the extra outputs outside the planned distribution system. Under pressure from the enterprises, material supplies were progressively delinked from the plan, and retail commerce was gradually deregulated. At the beginning, certain key inputs remained controlled. However, the controlled items were increasingly reduced. Centralized credit rationing was also delegated to local banks at the end of 1984.

An unexpected effect of the relaxation of the resources allocation system was the rapid growth of the non-state enterprises, especially the TVEs.[8] Rural industry already existed under the traditional system as a result of the government's decision to mechanize agriculture and to develop rural processing industries to finance the mechanization in 1971. In 1978 the output of TVEs consisted of 7.2 per cent of the total value of industrial output in China. Before the reforms, the growth of TVEs was severely constrained by access to credits, raw materials and markets. The reforms created two favourable conditions for the rapid expansion of TVEs.

(1)   A new stream of surpluses brought out by the household responsibility reform provided a resource base for new investment activities.
(2)   The relaxation of rigidity in the traditional planned allocation system provided access to key raw materials and markets. In the period 1981–91, the number of TVEs, employment and the total output value grew at an average annual rate of 26.6 per cent, 11.2 per cent, and 29.6 per cent, respectively. TVEs' annual growth rate in total output value was three times that of the state firms in the same period. In 1993, TVEs' output accounted for 38.1 per cent of the total industrial output in China. The share of industrial output from nonstate enterprises increased from 22 per cent in 1978 to 56.9 per cent in 1993 (State Statistical Bureau, 1995, p. 73).

The rapid entry of TVEs and other type of non-state enterprises produced two unexpected effects on the reforms. First, non-state enterprises were the product of markets. Being outsiders to the traditional economic structure, non-state enterprises had to obtain energy and raw materials from competitive markets, and their products could be sold only to markets. They had budget constraints and they would not survive if their management was poor. Their employees did not have an 'iron rice bowl', and could be fired. As a result, the non-state enterprises were more productive than the state enterprises. As a result the non-state enterprises were mine productive than the state Enterprises. The dynamism of non-state enterprises exerted a pressure on the state enterprises and triggered the state's policy of transplanting the micro-management system of the non-state enterprises to the state enterprises and of delegating the latter more autonomy. Reform measures for improving the micro-management system of state enterprises – such as replacement of profit remittance by a profit tax, the establishment of the contract responsibility system, and the introduction of the modern corporate system in state enterprises – were responses to competitive pressure from TVEs and other non-state enterprises (Jefferson and Rawski, 1995). Secondly, the development of non-state enterprises significantly rectified the misallocation of resources. In most cases, non-state enterprises had to pay market prices for their inputs, and their products were sold at market prices. The price signals induced non-state enterprises to adopt more labour-intensive technology and to concentrate on more labour-intensive small industries than on state enterprises. Therefore, the technological structure of non-state enterprises was more consistent with the comparative advantages of China's endowments. The entry of TVEs mitigated the structural imbalance caused by the HIODS.

Macro-Policy Environmental Reform

Among the trinity of the traditional economic structure, the distorted macro-policy environment was linked most closely to the development strategy, and its effects on allocative and technical efficiency were indirect. The reforms on macro-policies were thus the most sluggish. We will argue later that most economic problems that appeared during the reforms – for example, the cyclic pattern of growth and the rampant rent-seeking – could be attributed to the inconsistency between the distorted policy environment and the liberalized allocation and enterprise system. The Chinese government therefore, constantly faced a dilemma: to make the macro-policy environment consistent with the liberalized micro-management and resource allocation system or to re-centralize the micro-management and resource allocation system for maintaining the internal consistency of the traditional economic structure. The deprivation of enterprise autonomy would definitely face the resistance of employees of state enterprises. A return to the traditional economic structure would also mean the re-appearance of economic stagnation. Therefore, no matter how reluctant the government might be, the only sustainable choice was to reform the macro-policy environment and make macro-policies consistent with the liberalized allocation and micro-management system.

Changes in the macro-policy environment started in the commodity price system. After the introduction of profit retention, the enterprises were allowed to produce outside the mandatory plan. The enterprises first used an informal barter system to obtain the outside-plan inputs and to sell the outside-plan products at premium prices. In 1984, the government introduced the dual-track price system, which allowed the state enterprises to sell their output in excess of quotas at market prices and to plan their output accordingly. The aim of the dual-track price system was to reduce the marginal price distortion in the state enterprises' production decisions while leaving the state a measure of control over material allocation. By 1988 only 30 per cent of retail sales were made at plan prices, and the state enterprises obtained 60 per cent of their inputs and sold 60 per cent of their outputs at market prices (Zou, 1992).

The second major change in the macro-policy environment occurred in foreign exchange rate policy. In the years 1979–80, the official exchange rate was roughly 1.5 yuan per US$. The rate could not cover the costs of exports, as the average cost of earning 1 US$ was around 2.8 yuan. A dual rate system was adopted at the beginning of 1981. Commodity trade was settled at the internal rate of 2.8 yuan per US$; the official rate of 1.53 yuan per US$ continued to apply to non-commodity transactions. After 1985, the yuan was gradually devalued. Moreover, the proportion of retained foreign exchange, which was introduced in 1979, was gradually raised, and enterprises were allowed to swap their foreign exchange entitlement with other enterprises through the Bank of China at rates higher than the official exchange rate. Restrictions on trading foreign exchanges were further relaxed with the establishment of a 'foreign exchange adjustment centre' in Shenzhen in 1985, in which enterprises could trade foreign exchanges at negotiated rates. By the late 1980s, such centres were established in most provinces in China and more than 80 per cent of foreign exchange earnings was swapped there (Sung, 1994). The climax of foreign exchange rate policy reform was the establishment of a managed floating system and unification of the dual rate system on 1 January 1994.

Interest rate policy is the least affected area of the traditional macro-policy environment. Under the HIODS, the interest rate was kept artificially low to facilitate the expansion of capital-intensive industries. After the reforms started in 1979, the government was forced to raise both loan rates and savings rates several times.[9] However, the rates were maintained at levels far below the market-clearing rates throughout the reform process. In late 1993, the government announced a plan to establish a development bank with the function of financing long-term projects at subsidized rates and to turn the existing banks into commercial banks. The completion of this reform was expected to take 3–5 years. Moreover, it is unclear whether after the reform the interest rate will be regulated or will be determined by the markets. The mentality of the HIODS is deeply rooted in the mind of China's political leaders; to accelerate the development of capital-intensive industry in a capital-scarce economy, a distorted macro-policy environment – at the very least in the form of a low interest rate policy – is essential. It is likely that administrative interventions in the financial market will linger for an extended period.

Because the reforms in macro-policies, especially those regarding the interest rate, lagged behind the reforms in the allocation system and micro-management institutions, there were several economic consequences. The first one was the recurrence of a growth cycle. The interest rate was maintained at an artifically low level. The enterprises had incentives to obtain more credits than the supply permitted. Before the reforms, the excess demands for credit were suppressed by restrictive central rationing. The delegation of credit approval authority to local banks in the autumn of 1984 resulted in a rapid expansion of credits and an investment thrust. As a result, the money supply increased 49.7 per cent in 1984 compared to its level in 1983. This caused the inflation rate to jump from less than 3 per cent to 8.8 per cent in 1985 (see Figure 8.1). In 1988 the government's attempt to liberalize price controls caused a high inflation expectation. The interest rate for savings was not adjusted. Therefore, panic buying and a mini-bank run occurred. Loans, however, were maintained at the previously set level. As a consequence, the money supply increased by 47 per cent in 1988. The inflation rate in 1988 reached 18 per cent (see Figure 8.1). During the periods of high inflation, the economy overheated. A bottleneck in transportation, energy and the supply of construction materials appeared. Because the government was reluctant to increase the interest rate as a way to check the investment thrust, it had to resort to centralized rationing of credits and direct control of investment projects – a return to the planned system. The rationing and controls gave the state sectors a priority position; the pressure of inflation was reduced, but a slower growth followed.

As mentioned earlier, although the reforms in the micro-management system improved the productivity of the state sector, its deficits increased due to the discretionary behaviour of the managers and workers in the state enterprises. Fiscal income therefore increasingly depended on the non-state sectors. During the period of tightening state control, the growth rates of the non-state sectors declined because their access to credits and raw materials were restricted. Such a slowdown in the growth rate became fiscally unbearable; the state was forced to liberalize the administrative controls in order to give some room for the growth of the non-state sectors. A period of faster growth followed. Nevertheless, conflicts between the distorted macro-policy environment and the liberalized allocation and micro-management system arose again.

A second consequence of the inconsistency between the distorted policy environment and the liberalized allocation system and micro-management institutions was a rampant rent-seeking phenomenon. After the reforms market prices existed, legally or illegally, along with planned prices for almost every kind of input and commodity that the state controlled. The difference between the market price and the planned price was an economic rent. It is estimated that the economic rent from the controlled commodity price, the interest rate and the exchange rate was at least 200 billion yuan, about 21.5 per cent of national income in 1988. In 1992, the economic rent from bank loans alone reached 220 billion yuan (Hu, 1994).[10] The non-state enterprises as well as the autonomous state enterprises certainly had incentives to engage in rent-seeking activities through bribes and other measures to obtain underpriced resources from the state allocation agencies. It is reported that under competitive pressure, the state enterprises in the heavy industries, which were given priorities in obtaining state-controlled resources, also needed to give certain side-payments to the banks and other allocation agencies in order to secure the earmarked loans and materials, or to obtain them promptly.

Because of the rent-seeking activities of other types of enterprises, State enterprises were often unable to obtain the credits and materials indicated in the plans. The rent-seeking activities also caused widespread public resentment and became a source of social instability. To guarantee the survival of the state enterprises and to check social resentment, the government attempted to re-institute tight controls on the allocation system in the austerity programmes of 1986 and 1988. However, the controls were later relaxed to allow the growth of the non-state sectors. Except for the interest rate, administrative controls on the prices of most materials and commodities have been removed.

4   CONCLUDING REMARKS

Even though China's leaders did not have a detailed blueprint in mind when reforms started, the reforms have followed a path that can be explained by the theory of induced institutional innovation (Lin, 1989b; North, 1990). The traditional economic structure was itself a product of institutional innovation induced by the government's attempt to pursue a HIODS in a capital-scarce economy. The traditional system made the mobilization of resources for building up the strategy-determined priority sectors possible. However, its economic efficiency was low. Therefore, once the integrity of the traditional economic system was breached by the introduction of enterprise autonomy, institutional changes occurred in a way that was self-propelling toward the replacement of the traditional system with a more efficient market system. In the process, the efficiency of the state enterprises was improved through greater autonomy and by having to meet competition from the non-state sectors. However, the dynamism of the economy came mainly from the swift entry of new, small, non-state enterprises. The old planned allocation system and distorted macro-policy environment gradually became unsustainable, and were discarded. During the reform process, the state, the enterprises and the people had sufficient time to make adjustments to the new market system. The reforms benefited the majority of people as the economy maintained a strong growth throughout the whole process.

So far, most elements in China's reforms were induced rather than designed. However, the experience of China's reforms may provide a useful

lesson for designing reform policies in other economies where the heavy industry-oriented strategy or other similar development strategies are adopted
under capital-scarce conditions.[11] Certainly, stages of development, endowment structures, political systems and cultural heritage are different from
one economy to another. To be effective, a reform should take the
economy's initial conditions into consideration and exploit all favourable
factors within and without the economy.[12] The specific design and sequence
of reforms in an economy should therefore be 'induced' rather than
'imposed'. However, in addition to the general advice of maintaining economic and political stability and moving the reforms in a path-dependent
manner, the following lessons may be useful for a government attempting
reforms in an economic system similar to that of pre-reform China:

(1) Grant autonomy to the micro-management unit so as to improve the
     incentive structure and create a new stream of resources by improv-
     ing productivity
(2) Allow the new stream of resources to be allocated by the
     autonomous enterprises outside the plan and at market price to the
     suppressed sectors while maintaining the survival of the old priority
     sectors with the resources still under the state's plan control
(3) Liberalize the distorted policy environment and planned allocation
     system to make them consistent with the autonomous micro-manage-
     ment system when the new stream of resources allocated under
     market outweighs the stream of resources allocated under the plan.

Notes

*   This chapter draws heavily on Lin, Cai and Li (1997).

1.   The Five-Year Plan was disrupted from 1963 to 1965, the period immedi-
       ately after the agricultural crisis of 1959–62. The first to the seventh Five-
       Year Plans covered, respectively, the periods 1952–7, 1958–62, 1966–70,
       1971–5, 1975–80, 1981–5, and 1986–90.
2.   In the literature in China and other socialist countries, many authors pre-
       sumed that the distorted policy environment and the administrative controls
       were shaped by socialist doctrines. The socialist ideology might play a role
       in the formation of these policies; however, the existence of these policies
       and controls also had an economic rationale. They facilitated the implemen-
       tation of a HIODS in a capital-scarce economy. This explains why non-
       socialist developing economies, such as India, also had a similar policy en-
       vironment and administrative controls when they adopted the same develop-
       ment strategy.

3. An enterprise is bound to be loss-making if its outputs happen to be inputs to the other sectors – for example, energy and transportation – because the prices of its outputs are suppressed. An enterprise is bound to be profit-making if its outputs are at the low end of the industrial chain, because the enterprise can enjoy low input prices and high output prices at the same time.

4. The state enterprises were granted some autonomy after the reforms in the late 1970s. One of the results of this reform was a rapid increase in wages, bonuses and fringe benefits at the expense of the enterprise's profits.

5. Lin (1992) estimates that losses due to low incentives in the agricultural collectives were as much as 20 per cent of TFP. For a theoretical model of the monitoring problems regarding incentives in a collective farm, see Lin (1989a).

6. The first attempt was made in 1958–60, the second in 1961–5, and the third in 1966–76 (Wu and Zhang, 1993, pp. 65–7).

7. We discuss the emergence of TVEs and its impacts on the reform of State enterprises in the following sub-section.

8. The non-state enterprises include the TVEs, the private enterprises, and joint-venture enterprises, overseas Chinese enterprises and foreign enterprises. Among them, the TVEs are the most important in terms of output share and number of enterprises. It is noteworthy that TVEs, although different in many aspects from state enterprises, are public enterprises that are funded, owned and supervised by the township or village governments.

9. To stop bank runs, savings rates were indexed to inflation rates in October 1988. But the policy was revoked in 1991. In May 1993, the interest rate for a 1-year time deposit was 9.18 per cent, and for a 1–3 year basic investment loan it was 10.80 per cent (*China Statistics Yearbook*, 1993, pp. 670–1). However, the market rate for a commercial loan was between 15 and 25 per cent.

10. The total credit of the state banks was 2161.6 billion yuan (US$ 248.5 billion at the swap market exchange rate). The difference between the official interest rate and the market rate was about 10 per cent. The rents from bank loans alone were as high as 216 billion yuan.

11. In essence, the HIODS is a forging-ahead strategy in which the government distorts the macro-policy environment in order to facilitate the development of some industries which exceed the stage of development dictated by the comparative advantages of the economy's endowment structure. The import-substitution (15) strategy widely adopted in Latin America is another example.

12. The presence of overseas Chinese, the existence of a large stock of industrial resources in the rural sector prior to the start of reform. the continuation of substantial marketing activity throughout the agricultural sector during the entire socialist period, and so on are important initial conditions that have contributed unequivocally to the success of China's reforms.

References

Chen, K., H. Wang, Y. Zheng, G. Jefferson and T. Rawski, T. (1988) 'Productivity Change in Chinese Industry: 1953–1985', *Journal of Comparative Economics*, vol. 12, no. 4 (December), pp. 570–91.

Dollar, D. (1990) 'Economic Reform and Allocative Efficiency in China's State-Owned Industry', *Economic Development and Cultural Change*, vol. 39, no. 1 (October), pp. 89–105.

Fan, Q. and M. E. Schaffer (1991) 'Enterprise Reforms in Chinese and Polish State-Owned Industries', Research Paper Series, no. 11 (Washington, DC: Socialist Economies Reform Unit, World Bank).

Fan, Shenggen (1991) 'Effects of Technological Change and Institutional Reform on Production Growth in Chinese Agriculture', *American Journal of Agricultural Economics*, vol. 73, no. 2 (May), pp. 265–75.

Gordon, R., and Wei Li (1991) 'Chinese Enterprise Behavior Under the Reforms', *American Economic Review: Papers and Proceedings*, vol. 81, no. 2 (May), pp. 202–6.

Groves, T., Y. Hong, J. McMillan and B. Naughton (1992) 'Autonomy and Incentives in Chinese State Enterprises', (San Diego: University of California, Graduate School of International Relations and Pacific Studies), mimeo.

Hu, Shuli (1994) '1994: Reforms Have No Romantic Melody,' *Gaige* (Reform), no. 1 (January).

Huang, J. and S. Rozelle (1994) 'Technological Change: The Re-Discovery of the Engine of Productivity Growth in China's Rural Economy,' *Journal of Development Economics*, vol. 49, pp. 337–69.

Jefferson, G. and T. Rawski, (1995) 'How Industrial Reform Worked in China: The Role of Innovation, Competition, and Property Rights,' *Proceedings of the World Bank Annual Conference on Development Economics 1994* (Washington, DC: World Bank), pp. 129–56.

Jefferson, G., T. Rawski, and Y. Zheng (1992) 'Growth, Efficiency and Convergence in China's State and Collective Industry,' *Economic Development and Cultural Change*, vol 40, no. 2 (January), pp. 239–66.

Lin, Justin Yifu, (1989a) 'The Household Responsibility System Reform in China's Agricultural Reform: A Theoretical and Empirical Study,' *Economic Development and Cultural Change*, vol. 36, no. 3, Supplement (April), pp. S199–S224.

———— (1989b) 'An Economic Theory of Institutional Change: Induced and Imposed Change,' *Cato Journal*, vol. 9, no. 1 (Spring–Summer), pp. 1–33.

———— (1992) 'Rural Reforms and Agricultural Growth in China,' *American Economic Review*, vol. 82, no. 1 (March), pp. 34–51.

Justin Yifu Lin, Fang Cai and Zhou Li (1994) *The China Miracle: Economic Development Strategy and Economic Reform* (Hong Kong: Chinese University Press and Shanghai: Shanghai People's Publishing House).

———— (1997) 'The Lessons of China's Transition to a Market Economy', *Cato Journal*, vol. 16, no. 2, pp. 201–31.

Luo Hanxian (1985) *Economic Changes in Rural China* (Beijing: New World Press).

McMillan, J. J. Whalley and L. Zhu (1989) 'The Impact of China's Economic Reforms on Agricultural Productivity Growth,' *Journal of Political Economy*, vol. 97, no. 4 (August), pp. 781–807.

North, Douglass C. (1990) *Institutions, Institutional Change, and Economic Performance* (Cambridge, Mass.: Cambridge University Press).

State Statistical Bureau *Zhongguo Tongji Nianjian 1993* (China Statistical Yearbook, 1993, 1994) (Beijing: Zhongguo Tongji Chubanshe).

————— (1995) *Zhongguo Tongji Zaiyao, 1995* (A Statistical Survey of China, 1995) (Beijing: Zhongguo Tongji Chubanshe).

Sung, Yun-wing, (1994) 'An Appraisal of China's Foreign Trade Policy, 1950–1992,' in T.N. Srinivasan (ed), *The Comparative Experience of Agricultural and Trade Reforms in China and India* (San Francisco: International ICS Press), pp. 109–53.

Wen, Guanzhong James (1993) 'Total Factor Productivity Change in China's Farming Sector: 1952–1989,' *Economic Development and Cultural Change*, vol. 42, no. 1 (October), pp. 1–41.

World Bank (1985a) *China: Economic Structure in International Perspective, Annex to China: Long Term Issues and Options* (Washington, DC: the World Bank).

World Bank (1985b) *China: Long-term Issues and Options* (Oxford: Oxford University Press, for the World Bank).

Wu, Jinglian and Zhuoyuan Zhang (eds) (1993) *Zhongguo Jingji Jianshe Baikequanshu* (The Encyclopedia of China's Economic Construction) (Beijing: Beijing Gongye Daxue Chubanshe).

Zou, Gang (1992) 'Enterprise Behavior under the Two-Tier Plan/Market System,' *Mimeo* (Los Angeles, CA: IBEAR/SBA, University of Southern California, mimeo.

9 The Roles of Chinese Economists in the Economic Reform*

Fang Cai

POPULATION INSTITUTE, CHINESE ACADEMY OF
SOCIAL SCIENCES, BEIJING, CHINA

Section 1 of this chapter discusses the change of roles and professional capacity building of Chinese economists in response to the challenges of economic reform. Section 2, through a brief account China's economic reform process, describes how economists can influence the decision-making process of reform. Some comment is also made on their actual roles. Section 3 looks at Chinese economists' special roles in promoting a pro-reform social consciousness, and section 4 provides an analytical review on institutional constraints and historical background to the limited roles that Chinese economists have played in economic reform in an international perspective.

1 THE HISTORICAL EVOLUTION OF THE ROLE OF ECONOMISTS

Before the economic reform, economists had rarely played any important roles in the decision-making processes of China's economy. For example, both China and the former Soviet Union (FSU) had adopted the heavy industry-oriented development strategy at the start of forming the traditional socialist system (Lin *et al.*, 1994; see also chapter 8 in this volume). Nevertheless in the FSU, a heated debate occurred among economists over the choice of development model. In China, the heavy industry-oriented development strategy was initiated and adopted by Chinese politicians in the 1950s and a corresponding economic system was selected in the same manner. No dissenting voice was heard from Chinese economists, and few of them raised any economic objections from the perspective of policy cost. Similarly, every erroneous decision affecting China's economic development, such as 'the Great Leap Forward' in 1958 and 'Stop the production for the sake of revolution' during the Cultural Revelation in 1966 was implemented in the form of political campaigns with no intervention from economists. When the consequences, in the form of economic crisis, occurred it was once again the politicians themselves who stepped in to correct their own mistakes.

During the period between the inception of the Chinese planned economy and the beginning of the economic reform, economists inside and outside of government organizations mainly fulfilled two types of responsibilities. The main responsibility of economists in the government was to distribute resources according to the plan. Because the prices of products and production factors were kept artificially low, products and resources were in short supply. The resources and the intermediate products demanded by enterprises had to be allocated by the planning departments. Consequently, economists in the major government departments (the State Planning Commission, the State bank, the Ministry of Finance) had to decide on how to allocate the limited resources to each industrial sector by processing and analyzing the information collected from all the sectors in the context of their positions in the overall plan; ministries in change of industrial sectors (Ministry of Agriculture, Ministry of Light Industry) and local government tend to obtain as much of scarce resources as possible. The economists employed by these ministries mainly shouldered the responsibility for turning the argument to the benefit of their own sectors and local areas based on the special data they obtained on their sectors and their regions so as to support their leaders in bargaining for resource allocation from central government.

Economists outside the government were mainly engaged in defending China's socialist economic system. Based on the conclusions of Marxist economics, they supported theoretical issues by quoting authoritative works. A small number of economists criticized the traditional economic system and made proposals for reform (Sun, 1979; Zhuo 1981). The most outstanding figure was Sun Yefang. He called for putting the plan and statistics in the context of a law of value based on his understanding of Marxist economics and with reference to the contradictions of the economic system. Some of his specific critiques did occasionally influence decision-making. But he was severely criticized for his theoretic arguments and advocacy of the law of value, of raising a profit indicator in economic management and granting more autonomy to enterprises. It was believed that these ideas ran counter to socialist theory and would damage the internal integrity[2] of the traditional economic system.

Since the economic reform in China in the late 1970s, great changes have taken place concerning economists' roles. The channel linking economists with policy-makers was opened up. Economic reform, aimed at introducing the market mechanism to the planned economic pattern was unprecedented in the history of China. Decision-makers were badly in need of economists to advise then in the process of reform. Thus the central government established and strengthened economic advisory institutions and filled them with a group of young and talented economists. In addition, in order to deepen economic research, the government encouraged the development of a number of non-governmental economic research institutes. A group of economic research institutes outside the government was thus established.

Second, the research orientation of economists tended to be more applied and diversified. After the reform, the economists ruthlessly criticized the traditional economic system, expounding the necessity of reform. Encouraged by the effects of the reforms, they began to introduce alternative systems, helping design and formulate reform programmes; further, they helped expand and extend the reform process by formulating experience and lessons. They supported the new-born interest groups coming into being, and the ideological barriers to further marketization were gradually overcome.

Third, economists' analytical methodologies and techniques were improved. The Chinese economic heritage was mainly drawn from the analysis of capitalist economies by classical Marxist writers and the Soviet theory of the socialist economy. Since the start of economic reforms Chinese economists concentrated on empirical research on the defects of the traditional economic system and the problems arising from the on-going reform. They put forward their comments and advice (e.g. Development Institute, 1988). Meanwhile, a number of economists began to systematically introduce to China relevant theories and anecdotes drawn from the experience of other countries. They started by introducing theories on the socialist economic system in Eastern European countries and how such systems had been reformed. Later, institutional and policy models in the developed market economies as well as western economic theories finally found their way into China. In this 'change-over' period, more and more people came to understand the market mechanisms in the developed economies, their understanding of western economics deepened.

Scholars gradually moved towards making comparative approaches and studying the different types of market economies (such as the United States, Japan and Germany). Using western economics for reference, economists began to compare and select among Keynesianism, Neo-Classicism and Institutional Economics (see Liu, 1988; Li, 1987; Wu *et al.* 1993). The purpose was to build up their own model of China's economic system reform and to identify the concrete measures needed to deal with the problems which had surfaced in the value of reforms.

Economists were thus led into providing decision-makers with a series of competitive policy options in order to avoid the mistakes made elsewhere (Lee, 1992). The opening of China's economy to the outside world offered a broad information base for decision-making, some economists began to apply the standard analytical approaches of modern economics to study the issues of reform. Studying the transition of China's economic system, for example, economists began to provide decision-makers and society at large with information on the cost and benefits of reform (Sheng, 1994).

Finally, economists deepened their research on the changes which were afoot, shedding light on the essence of China's economic reform. The low efficiency of the micro-management mechanism and the inadequate incentives which resulted were the immediate cause of China's economic reform in the late 1970s. Success came through implementing the household responsibility system in rural areas and the 'transferring power and profits to the enterprises' policy. Economists concentrated on reform at the micro-level, suggesting a series of reform proposals (Li, 1987). Reform at the micro-level gradually led to reform of the traditional resource allocation and price systems. Economists further saw the need of a development strategy reform. They realized the economic management system was subordinate to the development strategy, and the two were interactive; they saw China's economic reform as the transition between two models (development model and system model) and raised a series of a deeper-level strategic transition issues (Liu, 1986, Liu and Zhao, 1989; Wu and Ding, 1987; Lin *et al.*, 1994).

2   ECONOMISTS AND THE DECISION-MAKING PROCESS OF ECONOMIC REFORM

China's traditional economic system had been formed to respond to the development of heavy industry. It had three components: (1) a micro-management mechanism with no autonomy; (2) a planned resources allocation system which rejected the market mechanism, and (3) a macro-policy environment which distorted the price of products and factors (Lin *et al.*, 1994). The reform of the late 1970s started by transferring power and profits to the micro-management system. The newly added resources created by improved productivity were re-invested in the market by its producers who initiated the marketization of resource allocation and pricing. The macro-policy environment which distorted price was the basic institutional arrangement which supported the heavy industry-oriented development strategy. Its gradual slackening pushed the development strategy toward change. The economic reforms that China then experienced resulted in a series of specific reforms. According to the characteristics of the Chinese economic reform process, we can divide the key reforms into three categories,[3] and we can observe the role of economists in the decision-making process within each category.

Bottom-up Reform

The first type of reform was the bottom-up reform which was initiated by the economic agents with the approval of decision-makers. The most typical example of this type was the rural reform started by the household responsibility system and later joined by the development of township-and-village enterprises (TVEs) and the private economy. In the early years of the people's commune, the farmers took the initiative in creating the agricultural management system of contracting production to the household. But it was repeatedly banned by the government as being inconsistent with the traditional economic structure. It was not until the late 1970s when China put an end to the Cultural Revolution that the government took a more realistic attitude towards a form of management which, despite being contrary to traditional ideology, was enthusiastically supported by labourers. The government gave encouragement and support to the farmers who introduced this system; by the end of 1984, 100 per cent of production teams and 97.9 per cent of households practised the household responsibility system in the country as a whole.

Once it became the main form of agricultural management the household responsibility system led to profound changes in the rural economic system. The fundamental functions of the People's Communes and the production teams were to collectively organize agricultural production and to manage and coordinate agricultural production factors. When the production-related contract system eased the conflicts between implementing the state's programme to procure grain and other agricultural products and having freedom to allocate the factors of production and to arrange production, the value-system of the People's Communes collapsed. The Communes were dissolved and replaced by township-and-village community autonomous organizations. The household responsibility system allowed households the right to allocate production factors and profits. Collective assets would no longer be the only legal basis of rural property. The private economy was thus born of the mobility of the factors of production and their reallocation. In order to develop, the township-village autonomous organizations also needed to rely on community strength to develop and increase collective assets, which had provided the initial motivation for their development. When the agricultural production process was determined by the farmers themselves, the increase in surplus of goods broke down the monopoly distribution system of agricultural products; this promoted the formation and development of rural markets. We can observe the spontaneous creation of direct agents – farmers and rural community cadres. But no economists' input could be seen at all. The role of economists was mainly to spread information on the reform process, to help decision-makers understand the effects of the reform, and society to develop a common understanding of the process.

Agreement Reform

The second type of reform is the 'agreement reform' which was achieved through negotiation between direct agents and responsible governmental departments. Typical of this type was a series of reforms focused on transferring power and profits to state enterprises. Although this type of reform could only be carried out at the initiative of government, government had to consul the enterprises, and the reform of state enterprises started in the late 1970s and the early 1980s. As this experiment was gradually extended, the enterprises' responsibility system was continuously improved. It later developed into a contract responsibility system commonly conducted in the enterprises. A series of further reforms were then implemented to perfect the enterprises' contract system. By 1987, 90 per cent of industrial enterprises in the budget had adopted the contract responsibility system.

Once the state enterprises were allowed to sell products in excess of plan quotas at a market price and have the autonomy to plan part of their production accordingly, they would demand a market supply of the products and the factors of production, hence the promotion of an allocative system reform. A dual-track system served as the transitional form for the reform of traditional macro-policy environment. Meanwhile, several reforms of enterprises management other than the enterprise contract responsibility system were being experimented with, such as joint stock systems in the profitable enterprises and lease systems in small enterprises. Until very recently, decision-makers have identified the target model of the reform for the state enterprises – the modern enterprise system, the public corporation, and private corporation being the basic forms (Editorial Committee, 1994, pp. 1–12).

In reviewing the process of state enterprise reform, we can see an increasing economists' role. In the initial reform of transferring power and profits to enterprises, the government gave up certain powers to the enterprises themselves, to counter low efficiency and lack of incentives. The actual practice turned out to be the outcome of one-to-one negotiation between government departments and enterprises under their control. Such practice has remained throughout the whole process. As a consequence, the economists played only a minor role in the form, execution and decision-making of the contract system. But in the case of problems and challenges that this system faced, economists could advise on possible improvements.

Some economists even designed alternative programmes (He *et al.*, 1987). No matter how these ideas were appreciated by decision-makers, compromise between the enterprises and the responsible departments was still reached through negotiation. However, the debate over the choice of forms and system of enterprise management among economists was very lively, which helped decision-makers avoid taking a one-sided view of the problems of state-owned enterprises, and the final selection of a modern enterprise management system as the goal of the reform was undoubtedly aided by such widespread and prolonged debate and discussion. Economists have been directly involved in the design of the forms that the modern enterprise system should take. But in its implementation, the conflict of interests and compromises among the different parties will unavoidably deform the programmes from their original designs.

Top-Down Reform

The third type of reform was the top-down reform initiated and guided by central government, and implemented by local governments. The most typical was the Special Economic Zone (SEZ) policy and the development strategy of the coastal areas. In 1979, Deng Xiaoping set up Special Economic Zones to attract overseas Chinese investment and foreign investment; direct investment and joint-venture factories were encouraged. In 1980, the policies for the Special Economic Zones was finalized by the Communist Party Central Committee and the areas expanded to 14 coastal cities. In early 1988, the it was decided to adopt the economic development strategy in the coastal areas and extend the special policies to more areas in China.

As the development strategy in the coastal area tookshape, economists gradually strengthened their role. When the Special Economic Zones were first established, the government mainly focused its attention on their self-development and use as a 'window of opportunity'. The development strategy of the coastal areas later took into account the government's overall economic development strategy, such as the transfer of rural labour forces and the reform of traditional industrial structure. Decision-makers in this case paid special attention to economists' input – in conversations between economists and top-level decision-makers, opinions and ideas were exchanged the development strategy of the coastal areas formulated. The establishment of the Special Economic Zones and the coastal areas provided economists a good laboratory where economic system reform could be tested and replicated. Both Shenzhen and Hainan Special Economic Zones invited economists from Beijing to conduct investigations, advising on local economic and social development strategy. In the dialogue between local government and economists, the economists' notion of 'small government and large society' was directly applied in Hainan (Deng, 1991); the Shenzhen Special Zone, and Shanghai and other coastal cities also took the lead in setting up stock markets. Because their economic reform and development were ahead of their time, the coastal and interior areas differ greatly in development pattern. Some national macro-adjustment and control measures imposed by the central government found themselves in conflict with the interests of the coastal areas; economists could appear as the spokespersons for the interests of the coastal areas and use their influence to criticize central policy, at the very least exercising some checks and balances and offering alternative ways of thinking.

This brief description of the three types of economic reforms and a review of economists' roles have left us with two impressions. The roles the economists played in the economic reform got stronger as time went on. The more the reforms were driven by top-down forces or by government behaviour, the greater the economists' roles became.

3   EVOLUTION OF REFORM CONSCIOUSNESS

China's gradual and incremental process of reform has been carried out under the leadership of the Communist Party of China. Thus, the success of the reforms will largely depend on the state's ideology moving from a belief in the working of the planned economy to an understanding and recognition of the value of market economy principles.

Even before the economic reform, economists had theoretically begun to argue that the plan and market were complementary to each other.

However, they did not believe that the plan and the market were equivalent in their roles and positions and maintained that central planning should retain a key role in the economy to be supplemented by certain market rules. They also believed that they were the result of socialism and capitalism, respectively, and that it would therefore be impossible to integrate them. It was on the basis of official ideology and of mainstream economic views that the economic reform of the late 1970s was initiated.[4]

As economic reforms proceeded the economists' continuous exploration of the relationship between planning and the market finally received a response from the leadership (Wu *et al.*, 1993, pp. 136–7). This was reflected in 'The Chinese Communist Party Central Committee's Decision on the Reform of the Economic System' approved at The Third Plenary Session of the Twelfth Central Committee of the Communist Party held in 1984. This document marked a big step forward in the understanding of relations between plan and market, affirming for the first time that the socialist economy was a planned commodity economy. However the document still emphasized that the planned economy was the predominant form and that market mechanisms should be confined to some secondary economic sectors, whose role should be a subsidiary one.

As the reform proceeded, economists deepened their understanding of the theoretical and practical relationship between plan and market. When reform began to affect the management behaviour of state enterprises, the price of products and production factors, people's understanding of the relationship between plan and market began to evolve. The economists did not believe that plan and market were mutually exclusive. Instead they believed that they could infiltrate each other. This latest theoretical development was reflected in a report adopted at the 13th National Congress of the Communist Party in October 1987. The document summarized the official view that 'the state regulates the market while the market guides enterprises'. This marked a breakthrough compared to the old belief which rejected the role of market. But how to manage the national economy by using both planning and market tools remained a dilemma at the operational level. The theoretical understanding of the relationship between the plan and the market endorsed by the authorities was akin to Utopian wishful thinking. To be of practical use, the government either had to go further or move one step back.

China's economic reforms entered a new era in the 1990s. The coastal free zone areas underwent a thorough reform against traditional micro-management and resource allocation systems and also rectified the distorted price system by reforming the macro-policy environment. The market mechanism played an ever-important regulatory role in distributing products and production factors. This reform was rewarded by high economic growth which displayed the superiority of the market mechanism as a means of allocating resource and regulating the economy. Theory followed practice.

It was also through the efforts of economists,[5] after Deng Xiaoping's inspection of the southern cities of China, that' creating a socialist market economy in China was explicitly adopted at the 14th Session of the CPC National Congress held in August 1992. This Congress also agreed that the market should play a basic role in allocating resources under the macro control of the socialist state – economic activities had to be regulated by supply and demand in the market while resources would be allocated according to price and competition mechanisms.

It should be noted that it was not only through academic discussion that China's economists played such a new role in the change of ideology. In the later 1970s, after the Cultural Revolution, the Communist Party of China and the government gradually shifted their priorities to the economic sector. They involved themselves in economic reforms, relying on economists to help design and prove the value of the reform programme and to guide the general direction of the reform within society. Since the 1980s economists have participated in the formulation and drafting of all the important documents and regulations concerning economic reform issued by the Party and the government. It was through direct participation or through dialogue with the decision-makers that economists made their most important contribution to the evolution of a social consciousness of reform.

4   CONSTRAINTS ON ECONOMISTS' ROLE IN THE REFORM

The core of the economic reform in China is a transition from a centrally-planned system to a market economy. Three basic tasks must be fulfilled in order to realize this transition. The first is to abandon the ideology of a traditional system of planned economy; the second is to identify the target model of a market economy; the third is to realize the actual transition from the planned to the market system. As stated above, well before the initiation of economic reform economists had begun to criticize the traditional system of the planned economy. Throughout the years of the economic reform, reflection on and criticism of the traditional system had become even more profound. Economists persistently argued that establishing a market economic system, which would help the whole society was both necessary and inevitable.

However, we can see the role that China's economists played in the transition process was limited. Reforms were not originally conceptualized by economists. Moreover it was often the case that reform programmes formulated by economists were regarded as purely academic endeavours and the ideas they suggested were often distorted when applied in practice. To better understand this phenomenon, we must first understand the specific characteristics of the Chinese transition. China's traditional system of planned economy has characteristics different from those of Eastern Europe and the FSU. Although China chose a similar heavy industry-oriented development strategy and followed a traditional planned economic system (Lin *et al.*, 1994), the system had undergone many adjustments from its inception making it more flexible than its Soviet equivalent, and price distortions were less serious (Perkins, 1992). On the other hand, the target model of China's reform was unique. China's economic reform was less radical and took place under the leadership of the Communist Party. China's traditional culture offered many features which were compatible with a market economy. Nor will the system of Chinese market economy be a replica of Japanese or American models. So China's transition from the planned system to the market system itself was naturally an unprecedented and unique process. So far China's reform differs substantially from that of East European countries and Russia (Lin *et al.*, 1994).

First, western decision-makers tend to raise a lot of questions for economists, expecting their input on a number of issues, such as appropriate monetary and financial means and the correct approach to high employment and low inflation (Lee, 1992). Western economists have accumulated a large amount of knowledge on applied macroeconomic theory and policy, but the macroeconomics developed from the mature market economy does not have the capacity to solve macroeconomic problems in the transitional period.

Second, traditional socialist economic theory was mainly established to serve a centrally-planned economy. It is of little help to understand and explain the issues which will appear during the transition of one economic system to another. Socialist economics had produced criticisms of traditional socialist systems and offered a theoretical framework for an alternative socialist system (for example, Kornai, 1980). Nevertheless, most of these theories were produced well in advance of real transition and their assumption proved to be naive when faced with the real problem of transition. There existed a historically important school in the history of Marxist economic theory whose immediate mission was to study the transition of systems (Preobrazhensky, 1926) even though their conclusions were exactly opposite to what happened after real transition took place.

Third, in order to rectify the neo-classical tradition in Western economic thought which sees institutions as a fixed factors, the Neo-

Institutional Economics studied the issue of institutional equilibrium, the innovation and change within an institution and other related theoretical issues. It regarded the institution as an endogenous element, explaining and reviewing a series of institutional arrangements and innovations at different moments in history (see Davis and North, 1979). To study the transition from a planned to a market system should be a part of the tasks of Institutional Economics, although it is a narrow field (Sheng, 1994, p. 2). Analysis of Institutional Economics provides useful tools to study the problem of economic transition. However, since the practice of transition from the planned economy to the market economy only began a decade or so ago, the academic response of economics to it is rather preliminary, and the knowledge it has accumulated is limited. Transition economics is still a very young discipline, unable to provide economists with mature and ready-made analytical tools. Despite the demand created by the advent of the reform period, the number of economists is limited and thus theoretic research and analytical methodology are inadequate. Chinese economists are therefore learning while doing, and their role as advisers to decision-makers is inevitably limited.

Market-oriented reforms are being carried out in all the former planned economies. The unique feature of China's transitional process makes it impossible to find a blueprint or a pre-existing implementation procedure. The truth is that China has adopted a gradualist approach to its reform. This approach focuses on the country's specific environment and the special issues faced at the time. For example, when the micro-management system was reformed in 1979, the environment in rural areas was quite different from that prevailing in urban areas. Although the ruling ideology did not support reform with a view to privatization, the household responsibility system in agriculture went further than parallel attempts to reform property rights. In carrying out the household responsibility system, the first step was to improve incentive mechanisms to save the rural economy from collapse. At that time this reform was a makeshift policy. Only when this change proved to be effective and convincing to society, were the terms of the contract prolonged. Thereafter, the household responsibility system won complete recognition in society. Only after this was the policy extended with a 30-year maturity, which helped encourage long-term agricultural investment. Every step of the reforms was the result of negotiations between peasants, consumers and government. Any one of those agents cannot alone decide the direction and intensity of the reform.

Economists thus played a limited role in decision-making in the early stage of reform. As direction of the reforms became clearer, ideological restrictions lessened. As social consciousness became greater, the economists' advisory role increased. Increased democratization and better democratic procedures in decision-making will widen the channel which allows economists to influence decisions. Improvement in the number and quality of economists will broaden the value of applied economics and allow economists to gain greater independence. We thus expect that Chinese economists will in future further extend their roles.

Notes

*   While writing this chapter, the author had several discussions with Justin Lin and got much useful comment and advice from him. I would like to take this opportunity to express my gratitude to him, but the author is of course solely responsible for any errors or omissions.

1.   Under the circumstance prevailing in the management of state-owned enterprises, the interests of managers and staff are often in conflict with the state's interest. State enterprises try their best to decrease the profit turned over to the state by expanding the cost and reporting less output. Due to information asymmetry, the cost of monitoring the enterprises is very high for the state; whereas when macro-policy distorted price and eliminated competition, management of the enterprises could not be reflected in the market. In order to prevent the enterprises from appropriating state-owned assets and profits, the state cannot give state enterprises managerial autonomy. Therefore, the state has to control the supply of means of production, buy their products and distribute them according to the plan. The state also controls the finance and budget of enterprises. The management system of the state-owned enterprises is endogenous, and shares the inherent institutional adaptability with the traditional economic development strategy and the environment of macro-policy (Lin *et al.* 1994).

2.   This classification does not mean that all the reform stages have their own explanation. Some reforms (for example, fiscal reform) can fall into different categories at the same time.

3.   Although some influential economists began to criticize the 'plate theory' about the plan and the market, and put forward the 'infiltration theory' instead to suggest the plan and the market should be complementary (e.g. Liu and Zhao, 1979), their arguments were not the mainstream view and were frequently and repeatedly criticized (Hsu, 1991, pp. 33–9).

4.   The debate lasted for a long time and continues even today. So far, the economists have not be able to reach a uniform opinion about the market.

References

Davis, L. and North, D. (1979) 'Institutional Change and American Economic Growth: A First Step toward a Theory of Institutional Innovation', *Journal of Economic History*, vol. 30.

Deng, Y. (1991) 'Characteristics, Problems and Treatments of Hainan Model', in World Bank Loan Office in Hainan Province (ed.), *Characteristics, Problems and Perspective of Hainan Model* (Beijing: Time Press).

Development Institute (1988) *The Reform Faces Institutional Innovation* (Shanghai: Shanghai Sanlian Publishing House).

Domar, E. D. (1957) *Essays in the Theory of Economic Growth* (New York and Oxford: University Press).

Editorial Committee (ed.) (1994) 'The Important Policies and Regulations for New System of Market Economy', Printed by *Journal of China Administration Management*.

Gu, H. (1994) 'The Responsibility, Rights of Economists and the Discussion around Zuo's Paper among the Chinese Economists', *Journal of Reform* no. 4.

He, J. *et al.* (1987) 'An Analysis of Experiment Outcomes of the Asset Management Responsibility System', *Economic Daily* (2 May).

Hsu, R. C. (1991) *Economic Theories in China (1979–1988)*, Cambridge: Cambridge University Press), pp. 33–9.

Jones, H. (1976) *An Introduction to Modern Theories of Economic Growth* (New York: McGraw-Hill).

Kornai, J. (1980) *Economics of Shortage* (Amsterdam: North-Holland).

Lee, H. H. (1992) 'Economists as Public Policy Advisers', *Journal of Economic Perspective*, vol. 6, no. 3, pp. 61–4.

Li, Y. (1987) *Study of Economic System Reform* (Beijing: People's Daily Publishing House).

Lin, Y., F. Cai and Li, Z. (1994) *China's Miracle: Development Strategy and Economic Reform* (Shanghai: Shanghai People's Publishing House).

Liu, G. (1985) 'On Two Pattern's Transformations', *Newspaper of World Economy* (26 August).

————— (1986) 'The Issues of Economic Development Strategy in China', in *Selection of Liu's Economic Essays* (Taiynan: Shanxi People's Publishing House).

Liu, G. (ed) (1988) *Study on China's Model of Economic System Reform* (Beijing: Chinese Social Sciences Publishing House).

Liu, G. and R. Zhao (1979) 'Several Issues about the Relationship between Plan and Market', *Journal of Hongqi*, no. 9.

Perkins, D. H. (1992) 'China's Gradual Approach to Market Reforms', paper Presented at a Conference on Comparative Experiences of Economic Reform and Post-Socialist Transformation (6–8 July) (El Escorial, Spain).

Preobrazhensky, E. (1926) *New Economics: An Attempt at Theoretical Analysis of the Soviet Economy* (Moscow: Communist Academy Press).

Sheng, H. (ed) (1994) *Transitional Economics in China* (Shanghai: Shanghai People's Publishing House).

Sun, Y. (1979) *Several Issues of Socialist Economy* (Beijing: People's Publishing House).

Wu, J., Li, J. and Ding N. (1987) 'China's Economic Development Stage and Basic Contradictions', *Journal of Management World*, no. 1.

Wu, J. *et al.* (1993) *The Reform of Large and Middle-Size Enterprises: Creation of a Modern Enterprise System* (Tianjin: Tianjin People's Publishing House).

Zhuo, J. (1981) *On a Socialist Commodity Economy* (Guangzhou: Guangdong People's Publishing House).

10 Economic Reforms in Latin America: The Decade of Hope

Vittorio Corbo

PONTIFICIA UNIVERSIDAD CATÓLICA DE CHILE, SANTIAGO, CHILE

1 INTRODUCTION

After pursuing for many decades economic policies which disregarded macroeconomic fundamentals and were based on heavy government intervention and isolation from foreign trade, the last decade has witnessed a major overhaul of economic policies in Latin America. These changes were started in Chile in the middle of the 1970s and then extended to most countries in the region. This revolution resulted in a frontal attack on public sector deficits and in a drastic change of the traditional import substitution-cum-government intervention model that had emerged following the great depression and the end of the Second World War.[1]

Many factors lie behind this drastic change in the development model, but one can single out a few more important ones. (1) The very poor performance of most of Latin American countries in the post-1970 period. In some countries it was the disorder associated with open hyperinflation (Bolivia, 1985; Peru, 1989; Argentina, 1987–9), in others a string of economic crises (Brazil, 1985–93), while in others it was the clear desire to remove obstacles to sustainable growth (Colombia, 1990; El Salvador, 1990; Venezuela, 1989). (2) The observation of the stellar performance of the East Asian countries. (3) The successful transformation of the Chilean economy initiated by the Pinochet regime and continued under the democratic governments that followed it. This example was important as it illustrated a successful transformation of a country in the region. (4) The influence of the international financial institutions (World Bank, IMF and IDB) through its economic dialogue and lending in support for structural reforms (Corbo and Fischer, 1995). (5) The collapse of the socialist model in East and Central Europe and the former Soviet Union.

The new model emphasizes macroeconomic stability, integration to the world economy (outward orientation), deregulation and competitive

178

market structures, and a government sector responsible for putting in place the institutions necessary for the functioning of a market economy together with the provision of public goods and improving the access to social services for the poorest groups in the population.[2]

In the new model, to achieve macroeconomic stability public finances have to be put in order and monetary and exchange rate policy has to be designed with the main objective of achieving a credible and sustainable reduction in inflation and a sustainable balance of payments situation. The creation of an independent Central Bank has been part of the institution-building effort to facilitate macroeconomic stability. In this new model the role of the public sector has changed drastically. Now the government is entrusted with the responsibility of delivering macroeconomic stability – in the form of a sustainable current account deficit and a low and predictable rate of inflation – and of creating the conditions for the development of an open and competitive private economy. For the latter purpose, the state is supposed to gradually dismantle trade protection, deregulate labour and financial markets, and get out of the production and distribution of private goods. Furthermore, it has to create an appropriate regulatory framework to promote competition and private ownership in public utility services and develop a safe and sound financial system. But this is not all; the state also has to concentrate its efforts on the development of a system where property rights are clearly defined and enforced and where the poorest groups in the population have proper access to basic health and education. Some of these policy actions where included in the Washington consensus of Williamson (1989) but as the recent experience of Argentina and Mexico indicates, Latin America has gone much further than the Washington consensus in carrying out a complete overhaul of its economies.

The new winds of reforms led CEPAL – the UN Economic Commission for Latin America and the Caribbean – which was the intellectual home and strongest supporter of the import substitution (IS) model – to also endorse the new development strategy. Thus CEPAL(1992) proposes a new development model based on restoring and maintaining macroeconomic balances, increasing the outward orientation, increasing the role of market forces, and the introduction of social programmes targeted on the poorest groups of the population.

The rest of the chapter is divided in four sections. In section 2 we present the main developments that led to the current view on development policies. Section 3 analyzes the Chilean reform model, section 4 discusses reforms in other countries of the region and section 5, by way of conclusion, presents the unfinished reform agenda of the main countries in the region.

2   THE ROAD TO REFORM

From the 1960s dissenting views started to emerge on the appropriateness
of the economic policies that had been followed in the region. One of the
early critics was Roberto Campos (1961) in Brazil, who questioned the
emphasis in favour of industry and against agriculture, the confidence
shown in the theory that by substituting public initiative for private initiative, new resources would be created, and the assumption that inflation
could be used to increase capital formation in a sustainable way. In particular, Campos stated that economic incentives are one of the main factors
accounting for the economic performance of Latin America. Nevertheless,
it was ECLAC's thoughts on the role of the state in providing protectionism and undertaking a developmental role that reigned supreme up to the
early 1960s. With inflation a major problem in the region, rationalization
of the protection system did not seem as pressing as stabilization.

Still, in the context of the stabilization programmes, overvalued exchange rates were adjusted and the multiple exchange rate system eliminated or improved as ways to reduce part of the anti-export bias. However,
as public sector deficits were not reduced, the overvalued exchange rate returned fairly quickly, and the anti-export bias remained. There were,
however, a few more substantial departures from excessive IS policy, stimulated in part by the exposure of a new generation of economists to alternative schools of economic thought. In the late 1950s, and especially in the
1960s, there was a substantial increase in the number of Latin Americans
pursuing graduate studies in economics abroad, both in the United States
and Europe. On returning to their countries, most of these newly trained
economists contributed to a marked improvement in the level of economic
debate. In particular, they called into question stabilization policies, trade
policies – and the selection of public investment projects (Díaz, 1966;
Universidad de Chile, 1963; Ffrench-Davis, 1971). The first major depar-
ture was initiated by Brazil in 1964, some 16 years after Viner had first
questioned this type of policy. This and subsequent policy initiatives in the
direction of greater liberalization are discussed in the next section.

Early Liberalization Attempts

As noted, while the rest of Latin America was still struggling to deepen
import substitution, Brazil undertook a set of reforms designed to improve
the functioning of its markets and the profitability of export activities. The
measures included: (1) a more realistic real exchange rate and elimination
of most export taxes; (2) introduction of subsidized credit and tax incentives for export activities; (3) reduction of the public sector deficit and

control of inflation; (4) development of a capital market; and (5) downward adjustment of real wages. Later on, Argentina under Onganía in 1966, Colombia in 1967, Chile in 1964–70 and Mexico in 1976 made some attempts at reducing the extreme anti-export bias of their trade policies.

However, it was in post-Allende Chile where the most frontal attack on the previous development model took place. Indeed, starting in 1975 Chile introduced a major stabilization and structural adjustment programme oriented towards re-establishing the basic macro-balances and creating the conditions for sustainable growth. Similar attempts, but without much success, were also made in Argentina starting in 1976 and in Uruguay in 1974. Although the Chilean reform effort encountered major problems in the early 1980s, the model survived these problems and it was strengthened thereafter.

However, it was not until the need to adjust to the second oil shock, especially when the easy option of foreign borrowing all but disappeared, that the demand for reforms was extended to the rest of the region. In these years a major re-examination of economic policies was undertaken all over Latin America. After 1982, one by one the countries in Latin America had to adjust their policies as they could not continue to finance the large current account deficits of the pre-crisis period. They also started to recognize, one by one, the need for major policy reforms to enable them to achieve a sustainable current account deficit reduction with a higher level of output than otherwise, while creating the conditions for sustainable growth. Key among these reforms has been a comprehensive programme of structural adjustment that addresses concurrently stabilization, efficiency and growth objectives. These are two principal components to the reform programmes being undertaken. One involves restoration of macroeconomic balances, with the emphasis on bringing the level of demand and its composition (tradeables relative to non-tradeables) into line with the level of output and the level of external financing that can be mobilized on a recurring basis. In addition, the high rates of inflation and the external deficit must be reduced, objectives that usually require a credible and sustainable reduction in the public sector deficit. The other component aims at increasing efficiency and restoring growth, with the focus on creating more appropriate incentives, removing the constraints on factor mobility and utilization and increasing saving and investment.

A major component of these structural reforms has been a redefinition of the role of the state. This redefinition includes its role as producer, regulator and distributive agent. Thus, the restructuring of public enterprises and privatization of most of them have become key areas of reform.

One could ask why these reforms had to wait for a crisis to be introduced. There are two parts to the answer. First, the intensity of the crisis increased the demand for reform. Second, the intensity of the crisis decreased the political power of the rent-seeking groups that had previously resisted this type of reform.

Post-Debt Crisis Reforms

In the post 1982 period drastic reform programmes were implemented, in Mexico starting in 1983 but increasingly so after 1985, in Uruguay starting in 1984, in Bolivia in 1985, in Venezuela in 1989 and in Costa Rica in 1985. Chile, a country that had made the most progress on structural reform before its own severe crisis of 1982–3, concentrated starting in 1984 on creating a stable macroeconomic situation as a way of providing a framework for a sustainable expansion in tradeable activities. In the 1990s Peru and Argentina undertook the most radical reform programmes in the region, while Brazil since early 1994 has made much progress in reducing its inflation and is initiating profound reforms of its overall economic system. El Salvador and Honduras have also initiated major reform efforts while Nicaragua eliminated its hyperinflation and has also been reforming its economy. Venezuela, however, has become the major exception to the rule, returning to the discredited economic policies of the 1950s and 1960s.

In the implementation of these reforms, political resistance has been the greatest to the reform of the public sector, trade regime and labour and domestic markets. Reforms of the public sector and of the trade regime have faced strong opposition from rent-seekers that have traditionally benefited from a larger public sector, suppliers of the public sector and the trade unions (Brazil and Venezuela are good examples here), and the producers and employees of highly protected industries. Major progress has been achieved in controlling inflation in Argentina, Bolivia, Peru, Costa Rica and Chile. Chile first and then Mexico, Costa Rica, Bolivia, Venezuela (and more recently El Salvador and Honduras) have also made major inroads in liberalising foreign trade. Good progress in restructuring the public sector and reducing the role of the public sector in the production and distribution of private goods has been made in Argentina, Chile, Peru, Bolivia and Mexico. However, achieving sustainable high growth in income *per capita* has been very difficult in most of the region.

However, in spite of the difficulties encountered, there is an increasing acceptance in Latin America that a major overhaul of policies and institutions must be carried out to create the basis to achieve efficient and sustainable growth. The eventual recovery of growth needs not only less distortionary policies (Easterly and Wetzel, 1989) but also higher investment and saving rates. The eventual recovery of investment requires a stable and predictable macroeconomic situation where long-term commitments can be made (Serven and Solimano, 1992). On the other hand, a higher saving rate to finance the higher investment requires a major fiscal effort in the early years (Summers, 1985; Corbo and Schmidt-Hebbel, 1990).

The reforms undertaken in Latin America have drawn on the rich experience of the East Asian countries and of the Chilean economy. The interest in learning from the Chilean model is based not only on its success but also because it is considered a model much closer to home and therefore easiest to imitate. Furthermore, part of the crisis in Latin America was a crisis of the state and this gave an additional attraction to the Chilean model as it relies much less on the state than the East Asian model.

3   THE CHILEAN REFORM MODEL[3]

In this section we provide a summary of the Chilean reforms. As stated above the Chilean development model has had substantial influence in the rest of the region.

One of the main objectives of the military government that took power in September 1973 was to eliminate the severe and pressing macroeconomic disequilibria that it inherited and to re-establish a market economy. The reduction of inflation required a deep structural reform of the public sector to reduce the size of the public sector deficit. To restore the role of the market as the main instrument to guide economic decisions and the private sector as the most important agent of economic development it was necessary to deeply reverse public sector responsibilities, reduce drastically the size of this sector and its role in economic activities, and deregulate commodity, financial and labour markets.

Towards this end, reforms were initiated in eight main areas: (1) a stabilization programme to reduce inflation that was reaching a rate of 1000 per cent per year; (2) public sector reforms to achieve macroeconomic stability and improve the efficiency of the public sector and of the economy as a whole; (3) trade reforms to provide appropriate incentives to export-oriented and import-competing activities; (4) a social security reform to change a bankrupt pay-as-you go pension system into one based on individual capitalization; (5) financial sector reform to improve the efficiency of financial intermediation; (6) labour market reform to facilitate industrial restructuring and the drastic reallocation of labour that had to take place from the highly protected import-competing sectors towards export-oriented activities; (7) a comprehensive privatization programme to get the state out of activities that the private sector could undertake and to expand activities where the public sector has a central role to play – provision of basic health, education and nutrition for the poorest groups in the population; and (8) social sector reforms to improve the incentive system in the production and provision of social services and to target the provision of social programmes to the poorest groups in the population.

The Stabilization Programme

Chile has had a long history of inflation. In the 1960s, inflation reached a compounded annual rate of 21.1 per cent. In the early 1970s, under the populist policies of the Allende government, inflation accelerated, reaching an annual rate close to 1000 per cent in August 1973, the month before the fall of Allende. The monetization of a public sector deficit close to 30 per cent of GDP was behind the acceleration of inflation of this period.

In the initial years of the military government inflation was attacked by a drastic reduction in the public sector deficit accompanied by severe monetary discipline; however, in a heavily indexed economy (where most key prices were indexed to the Consumer Price Index or CPI) there was a very strong inertia in the evolution of inflation. Not surprising, inflation stayed at the three-digit annual level well into early 1977. This was in spite of a large reduction in the public sector deficit that reached close to 21 percentage points of GDP between 1973 and 1974. Disappointed with the inflation figures, the government decided to re-examine the whole mechanism behind the slow pace of inflation reduction. One group of economists within the government started to develop a view that the Chilean economy was increasingly integrated to trade in goods and services. For this group, the tradeable component of domestic inflation was the sum of international inflation and the rate of devaluation.[4] As this view became more widespread in government circles, an important shift in stabilization policy started to take place around 1976 and especially in early 1978. The exchange rate began to be used to shape inflation expectations and through import competition to influence directly the evolution of tradeable goods (import competing and exportable goods) prices. In February 1978 the government instituted a system of pre-announced rates of devaluation of the peso that culminated in June 1979 in a fixed exchange rate of 39 pesos per dollar, a rate that was maintained until June 1982.

Every economic system requires an anchor for the price level. The two typical candidates are the money supply and the exchange rate. However, the use of either of these two anchors has to be consistent with other characteristics of the economy. A system of full wage indexation, instituted by law and in existence in the late 1970s, that linked nominal wage adjustments to the increase of the CPI in the previous year was, in the context of declining inflation with a fixed exchange rate, bound to result in a very slow pace of inflation reduction and therefore an appreciation of the real exchange rate. This was indeed the case, and a balance of payments crisis was postponed only thanks to the easy access to foreign borrowing that the Chilean private sector had at the time. When in 1982 external financing was drastically reduced, the contractionary monetary policy that was followed raised real interest rates and reduced expenditures. As the fixed exchange rate and the indexed wage system impeded a real devaluation, a large recession resulted. The sharp external shocks initiated the process but the rigidities that had been built in made the adjustment just too costly.

As the government had to intervene to rescue the financial system, to support financially distressed firms and households, and to support the unemployed, the claim on public resources increased, resulting in a large increase in the public sector deficit.

Following the crisis of the early 1980s, stabilization problems took the form of an unsustainable current account deficit. The adjustment required a sharp reduction in absorption and a real devaluation. A large fiscal adjustment – that included reduction in government expenditures and an increase in taxation – and a flexible exchange rate (at the time, wage indexation had been suspended) were at the centre of the post-1984 adjustment. On the other hand, the successful microeconomic reforms of the 1970s and the substantial open unemployment of the time had created the conditions for a large supply response to the real devaluation. The ensuing expansion in the import competing and exportable sectors pulled the dramatic recovery of the Chilean economy.[5]

Public Sector Reforms[6]

Public sector reforms included a tax reform, a sharp reduction in public subsidies and a policy of returning enterprises illegally seized to the previous owners. This was followed by a privatization programme focusing on commercial banks and firms in the manufacturing sector. The privatization programme is discussed on p. 190 below. A major tax reform was introduced in 1974. that aimed at increasing tax revenues in order to reduce the fiscal deficit. A value-added tax was introduced to replace the sales tax that suffered from the cascade effect of adding tax burden at each transaction stage. This tax became the main source of fiscal financing in the years to come.

The tax reform also sought to improve the incentives to work by reducing marginal income tax rates. On the expenditure side, public employ-

ment and public investment were drastically reduced. The fiscal adjustment was dramatic – the fiscal deficit was reduced from 24.7 per cent of
GDP in 1973 to 3.5 per cent of GDP in 1974. In 1975 Chile suffered a
severe terms of trade shock from a combination of a sharp drop in the price
of copper – then Chile's main export – and a sharp increase in the price of
oil. As Chile had its access to external financing severely curtailed, the
lack of external funding forced a drastic reduction of expenditures to deal
with the emerging trade deficit. This second fiscal adjustment was as
severe as the first. A further 26 per cent cut in real public expenditures, in
the middle of a severe contraction, reduced the fiscal deficit from 3.5 per
cent of GDP in 1974 to a mere 0.9 per cent of GDP in 1975. The restitution
to the owners of enterprises that had been seized by the workers during the
Allende government also contributed to the fiscal adjustment (these enterprises were receiving large transfers from the fiscal budget to keep them in
operation). The public sector deficit was also reduced by improving the
efficiency of public enterprises and the privatization of some of them.

The recession of 1975 did not slow down the retrenchment of the public
sector. In 1976 the non-financial public sector reached a surplus of 0.6 per
cent of GDP, and inflation was 174.3 per cent. Current expenditures, in
real terms, stayed at their 1975 value but revenues started to recover. From
then on, the non-financial public sector surplus lasted until the eve of the
crisis, reaching a peak of 4.5 per cent of GDP in 1980. The non-financial
public sector accounts deteriorated again during the crisis years with the
deficit reaching 3.5 per cent of GDP in 1982.

Improvements in the tax administration were implemented throughout
the 1970s and a radical reform to the pension system, that in the short run
worsened the fiscal situation, was introduced in 1981. The latter reform is
discussed on the next page.

Trade Reform[7]

The new government that took power in 1973 recognized, from the beginning, that for a small country like Chile to achieve efficient levels of operation, growth had to be based on an export-led growth model. Trade
reforms were required to make production for the external market much
more profitable and at the same time to introduce competition for import-
competing industries. Trade reforms in the period 1974–6 included the
unification of the multiple exchange rate system, the replacement of non-
tariff barriers for tariffs and the reduction of extreme tariffs.

At this stage, the fiscal consequences of trade liberalization were
minimal, as the higher tariffs were generally redundant – no trade took

place in those commodities – and the replacement of non-tariff barriers by tariffs provided additional revenues. A large devaluation at the time of the unification of the exchange rate, together with the drastic fiscal adjustment, helped to achieve a large real devaluation. Later on, the rate of devaluation was synchronized with the slowdown of inflation and the change in the fundamental determinants of the real exchange rate (i.e., terms of trade changes, differences in productivity between tradeable and non-tradeable activities, the sustainable level of the trade balance). Within this framework, early in 1975 – following the first oil shock and a 45 per cent reduction in real copper prices – a large nominal devaluation was introduced to go with the sharp fiscal adjustment used to reduce the trade balance deficit. As further progress was made in the reduction of inflation, the trade reform proceeded in parallel with other reforms.

At the beginning of the trade liberalization, in the period 1974–6, there was no clear view with respect to the speed and depth of the reforms. However, as a liberal economic team strengthened its position within the government the speed and depth of the reforms was increased. By 1979, the trade reform was completed when a uniform tariff rate of 10 per cent was established, with just one exception for the car industry.

Social Security Reform

The old Social Security system existed from 1920 up to the reform of 1980. At that time it covered 60 per cent of the labour force and was formed by several coexisting institutions. The type of benefits were similar across institutions but the prerequisites to obtain them and the amounts were quite different among institutions. It was a scheme based on a pay-as-you-go system, meaning that retirement pensions were financed with contributions paid by active affiliates and, therefore, the survival of the system was subordinated to the prevailing active – passive ratio of the population at all times. In this type of system, the pensions received by the participants had no relation to the contributions made to the system during the active working period.

Starting in 1974, the government carried out numerous modifications to this scheme, oriented towards simplifying, unifying and making the system more equitable. Furthermore, the rate of employees' and employers' contributions were reduced substantially; the system of family allowances and of unemployment compensation were simplified. The criteria for adjustment of pensions, retirement age and years of contributions were all unified, and a minimum pension for the non-contributing poor was created. By 1979 all these reforms had been implemented and special treatment for some groups eliminated. The reforms permitted an important reduction in the rates of contribution, which went from 33 per cent to 20 per cent of wage payments.

The reforms to the social security system culminated with the introduction of a capitalization system.[8] The new pensions system was created on 13 November 1980, and is based on three basic principles: (1) solidarity with the poor: there exists a (low) guaranteed minimum pension for every Chilean citizen, irrespective of his or her contributions to the system; (2) individual capitalization: the benefits obtained by the affiliates are directly related to the amount of their contributions during their working life; and (3) private and competitive administration of the pension funds in order to promote efficiency in fund management. In this capitalization scheme, the contributions made by the affiliate are deposited into an individual, non-transferable account, with a minimum of rentability and security guaranteed by the state (administrators have to have a minimum amount of capital and a minimum rentability), thus generating a pension fund.

The pension funds grow with the affiliate contributions and the return of the flow of investment during the contributing period of the affiliated (net of administrative commissions) and decrease with pension payments and other permitted outflows. State supervision is executed by an autonomous entity that supervises and controls the pension administrators. The approval, modification and rejection of the classification of different financial instruments in which the administrators can invest, is done by a risk classification commission. The affiliate also has the right to transfer its funds from one administrator to another searching for a better service and rentability. The amount of the pension can be adjusted by increasing or decreasing the voluntary contribution. The amount of the contribution is tax-deductible at the time that it is made, but the income from pensions is taxable.

The process of transferring from the old to the new system was facilitated by the creation of a public debt instrument called recognition bond (*bono de reconocimiento*) that documented the total contributions made to the old pay-as-you-go system with a non-tradeable bond. This bond is indexed to the evolution of the CPI and yields a 4 per cent real interest rate up to the time of retirement. The government then pays this bond adding it to the affiliate's accumulated pension fund.

Financial Sector Reform[9]

In 1974 the process of privatization of financial institutions began, as nominal interest rates were gradually liberalized. However, the lack of appropriate regulation and supervision was later to create major difficulties in this sector.

In 1977, a mid-size bank, that had been privatized, and which belonged to a financial conglomerate, entered into bankruptcy, and was taken over by the regulators. This action signalled to depositors and banks' owners that there existed *de facto* deposit insurance and the stage was set for the exacerbation of unsound banking practices. For the financial conglomerates this action provided an incentive to take further risk, as risk was not properly supervised and the existence of *de facto* deposit insurance discouraged the incentive of holders of bank liabilities to carefully evaluate bank risks. In this framework, the financial conglomerates could lend, almost without limit, to their own enterprises as the higher risk due to the concentration of its portfolio in their own enterprises was not being considered by the regulators when assessing the risks of banks' portfolios. The existence of *de facto* deposit insurance without the required prudential regulation and banking supervision also encouraged the banks to take undue currency risk. The latter created a major distortion in the pricing of credit in different currencies. The stage was set for a large financial crisis when severe external shocks hit the country in 1982.

Labour Market Reform

By 1973, the labour code was very restrictive, giving a high degree of rigidity to labour market operations. Rigidities took the form of labour immobility, unlimited compensation for labour dismissal, minimum wages, etc. In the initial years of the reforms, individual work legislation in Chile (as in the rest of the world), was geared towards the protection of the worker. Nevertheless, with the passing of time it turned into a mechanism to grant benefits to pressure groups within the workforce, to the detriment of unorganized labour and the overall efficiency of the economy. Many trade unions enjoyed special working and salary conditions, as did organized labour in the copper, petroleum, railroad, steel, electricity and communication sectors. All privileges and licences were eliminated starting in 1974, and this process ended with the law No. 18 018 of 1982, which revoked some privileges that still persisted. Reforms of labour regulations can be grouped into three categories: wage policy, layoff and severance payments regulations, and trade unions and the right to strike.

Wage Policy

Wage policy was also changed starting in 1973. In the early years up to 1979, collective bargaining was suspended and with the exception of the minimum wage and public sector wages, the government did not intervene much in the determination of private sector wages. However, as public sector wages were periodically adjusted for the inflation of the previous period, this policy was usually extended also to private wages. In 1979 the New Labour Code was enacted. This introduced collective negotiations at the firm level. However, surprisingly enough the law also established that the minimum wage offer had to be equal to the previous level of wages adjusted by the CPI inflation since the last contract.

Layoffs and Severance Payments

Layoffs were severely restricted in Chile. The structural transformation undertaken in the 1970s required a relaxation of layoff practices to permit the restructuring of the economy. Layoffs were restricted by setting a set of preconditions, and by imposing high severance payments. During the 1970s preconditions were made less restrictive, including the right to terminate a contract when economic reasons required an adjustment, but the employer had to pay a compensation equivalent to 1 month's wage for each year of continuous service, with a maximum of 5 months. However, the labour law of 1981 again restricted the conditions for layoffs.

Trade Unions and the Right to Strike

During the 1973–9 period the activities of trade unions were severely restricted. They could not elect their leaders and could not hold meetings without permission. With the Labour Code of 1979, the activities of trade unions were much liberalized. The new Labour Code sanctioned four types of unions: (1) unions at the enterprise level, (2) inter-enterprise unions, (3) unions of independent workers and (4) unions of temporary workers. Trade union affiliation is voluntary, and a worker's contribution to a union can only be deducted from the payroll with the written authorization of the worker or when the absolute majority of the trade union agree . The right to strike was restricted in the 1973–9 period. The Labour Code of 1979 established a maximum limit of 60 days for the duration of a strike. Beyond that period, workers were considered as having resigned, losing their rights to severance payment.

Privatization[10]

In the period 1974–82 Chile initiated a privatization process. During this period, almost all the enterprises taken over during the Allende government were restored to their legitimate owners, and all non-traditional state enterprises that were producing goods and services that traditionally are produced by private enterprises were privatized, with the exception of the big copper companies, the large steel companies, ENAP (Petroleum National Company), the railroads and public utilities – electricity, telephone, water and sewerage.

The Privatization effort was undertaken in two stages:

(1) The first was in 1974, when the administration of those enterprises that had been illegally taken over during the Allende years was given back to then owners. In this stage, 325 enterprises were returned under the condition of refraining from initiating lawsuits against the state. In some special cases additional conditions were imposed in order to secure the maintenance of employment levels, the competition between related industries and a certain level of new investment to be undertaken by the original owners.

(2) The second consisted mainly in the transfer to the private sector of approximately US$ 1200 million in assets corresponding to 207 enterprises. These included financial institutions, manufacturing enterprises and other corporations that had been taken over by the public sector throughout the years.

As a result of the privatization process undertaken in this period employment in the state enterprises sector was drastically reduced from 5.6 per cent to 3.2 per cent of the labour force. Nevertheless, only part of this decrease can be attributed to the privatization process, the rest is due to government efforts in trying to increase public sector efficiency.

Privatization was carried out using a variety of methods. These included:

- *Liquidation* – due to operational losses, which could not be reduced through efficiency improvements, many firms had to close down and their assets auctioned.
- *Open bidding* – the government Development Corporation (CORFO) introduced an auction system to sell the enterprises. CORFO had the right to reject the offers, as well as to negotiate better prices and/or conditions with those who bid the highest offer. The bidding's main objective was to maximize the sale price of the public assets. For this purpose, blocks of shares providing a controlling interest were usually sold. The concentration of the property of financial institutions and some key manufacturing enterprises in the same hands was later on to create some difficulties in the financial system.
- *Direct sale* – this procedure was applied to smaller firms, where the cost of organizing a bidding process was considered larger than the expected sale price of the firm.

On the other hand, from the total of agricultural land that had been expropriated by the Agrarian Reform Corporation (CORA), 28 per cent of the irregularly expropriated total was returned to its legitimate owners; 52 per cent was divided into 52 603 farms which then were sold, on very favourable terms, to the previous workers of the expropriated lands; and the rest was sold in public auctions. It is estimated that the privatization of farms that had been taken over by CORA amounted to US$ 800 million dollars in assets.

Social Sector Reform

The reforms carried out in the 1970s also included reforms to the social sectors such as education, health nutrition and housing. These reforms were intended to improve efficiency in the production and distribution of social services, as well as to target subsidies in these sectors to the poorest groups in the population.

Educational Reforms

The purpose of the educational reforms initiated in 1980 was to increase public education efficiency and expand opportunities. In particular, opportunities were created for private sector participation in the production of educational services. The old system, where public funds were given directly to schools and universities, was replaced by one where resources were distributed in proportion to the number of students enrolled.

Up until 1980 the supply of educational services was almost completely centralized in the Ministry of Education. This bureaucratic system was very inefficient and it had few incentives to attract and keep students. Not surprisingly, the quality of education was poor. No major reforms were taken between 1973 and 1980. In order to correct these problems, the government carried out an important curricular, administrative and financial reform of the education system in the period 1980–1. The curricular reform modified the educational plans, trying to give more flexibility and facilitating its adaptation to local needs.

Among the administrative and financial reforms, the most important ones were: (1) The transference of public schools (pre-school, primary and secondary) to the municipalities and the vocational secondary schools to non-profit private organizations, with the purpose of improving their administration, increasing the number of students and raising the quality of education. (2) The participation of the private sector in the production of free education, promoted by a subsidy system. This subsidy, that consisted of a payment for each student enrolled, was received by the private subsidized schools as well as the schools transferred to the municipalities.

Unfortunately, the amount of subsidies was later reduced in real terms, with a negative effect on the quality of the education.

Major reforms were also introduced in higher education. Up until 1980, the higher education system consisted of two public and six private universities. All of them, including the private ones, relied mainly on public funding, with approximately the same proportion of their expenses financed by the state. In that year, universities received more than 30 per cent of the total public expenditures in education. On the other hand, it was understood that the marginal rate of return was the highest for primary education, followed by secondary and finally higher education.

The existing higher education system faced many problems since vacancies were limited and the decision of the government to concentrate resources in primary and secondary education threatened its possibilities of expansion. The first step taken was to eliminate the prohibition to the entrance of the private sector to produce higher education. The allocation of the state subsidy was also in need of adjustment. Further steps taken in this area consisted of the decentralization of large national universities, to give a formal rank of higher education to non-university alternatives and to change the funding of universities from general grants to a payment per student and the introduction of a student loan programme.

Reform in Health and Nutrition

In the early years of the Pinochet government, reforms in this sector were concentrated in improving the access to health of the poorest groups in the population. Later on, a major restructuring took place with the purpose of improving efficiency and of targeting the subsides to the poorest groups. To accomplish these objectives a two-tier system was been created. Middle-income and upper-income groups had access to privately produced health services; public resources were concentrated on the provision of health services to the groups that could not afford the private system. The development of private health plans was permitted.

Institutional and financial reforms taken to improve the efficiency of the public health and nutrition systems include the separation of production from distribution of health services with the creation of a financial institution for the funding of health services for the groups in the population that could not afford private health services; the decentralization of the National Health Service; and the reinforcement of the role of the Ministry of Health as a supervisory and evaluating entity instead of a producer of health services. In 1981 the transfer of primary services and their infrastructure to the municipalities was started, and the possibility of choosing between public and private health insurance plans was introduced.

To target health and nutrition expenses on the poorest groups in the population, the services of preventive and primary health care were focused on the most vulnerable groups among the poor (i.e. mothers and small children). These services were extended and improved. More emphasis was given to primary health attention. Nutrition subsidies were gradually channelled toward the most need, basically by three means. The distribution of nourishing supplements only through health establishments; the creation of rehabilitation centres with pre-school programmes for undernourished children; and the implementation of nutrition programmes in schools.

Although the financing of these programmes amounted only to around 0.6 per cent of GDP, it is accepted internationally that they have accomplished much in improving the social welfare of the poorest groups in the population.

Housing Reform

From 1975 on, there was a change in the subsidy policy toward the poorest sectors of the population that were not home owners, creating programmes more tailored to their needs and their economic capacity. Starting in 1974, housing policies were governed by two general principles, on the one hand to direct subsidies only to those who could afford an adequate place to live; on the other hand to give direct and transparent subsidies.

Subject to the accumulation of a minimum amount of savings, a direct subsidy for the downpayment was introduced, replacing the former indirect subsidy consisted in low interest rates or a lower house price. The role of the public sector in construction, financing and urbanization was reduced to providing and selecting the beneficiaries of the direct subsidy. With the new reforms the private sector is in charge of urbanization, supply of basic services, construction and financial intermediation.

One can say that the Chilean reforms anticipated by around a full decade the major shift in development policies that took place towards a market-friendly and outward-orientated development strategy and away from excessive state intervention.[11] This strategy underscores the importance of macroeconomic stability and efficiency-enhancing reforms in policies and institutions as the basis for sustainable growth.

4   REFORM IN OTHER COUNTRIES

There is one main difference between the Chilean reforms described in the previous section and the reforms implemented later on in other countries of the region. The Chilean reforms were implemented under a military regime; all the others by democratic governments, and while the Chilean reforms were implemented one by one, the most recent reforms have been implemented in bundles. The fact that democratic governments have been implementing radical market oriented reforms is an indication also of the maturity of the political leadership in the region as well as of the effects of globalization where good economic policies find their way in neighbouring countries. The fact that the new generation of reforms has been much more broad than the ones that Chile undertook in the 1970s and 1980s could be due to the fact that Chilean policy-makers were innovating in areas were there was not much experience on how to proceed.

If one examines different areas of reforms, one can observe that much progress has been achieved in achieving fiscal consolidation and restoring macroeconomic stability in Argentina, Bolivia, Mexico and Peru. All these countries share a common history of previous policies that created hyperinflation that in turn facilitated the introduction of all-encompassing reforms by newly inaugurated democratic governments. Stabilization required a drastic fiscal adjustment, bringing public sector deficits to a level compatible with a drastic reduction of inflation. In most countries, fiscal reforms have included a drastic reduction in government subsidies, adjustment in the prices of government-controlled public utilities, reduction of government expenditures, the introduction of a VAT, and the simplification and upgrading of tax administration.

Colombia – a country with a long tradition of macro-stability but chronic inflation – introduced two tax reforms to finance an orderly increase in public expenditures and to decentralize government expenditures.

Brazil is still struggling to reduce its fiscal deficit through a radical fiscal reform that will have to tackle the large cash and actuarial deficits of its social security system. Although the central American countries have made progress on tax administration and tax reform they have been much less successful in adjusting expenditures. Improvements in tax administration have been hard to achieve and this is an area where much still has to be done. A weak tax administration encourages the development of a parallel economy, discriminating between legal and illegal activities and usually resulting in higher tax rates than otherwise in the formal economy, increasing the distortionary costs of taxation.

In some countries the sustainability of the stabilization effort has been assisted by the creation of an independent central bank with a clear mandate to achieve a gradual and sustainable reduction of inflation (Argentina, Chile, Colombia, Peru and, most recently, Bolivia).

It is on the trade front that the most radical change in policies has taken place. In this area important reforms have been introduced in Argentina, Bolivia, Brazil, Colombia, Costa Rica, Ecuador, Guatemala, Honduras, Jamaica, Mexico, Nicaragua, Paraguay, Peru, Trinidad and Tobago, Uruguay and Venezuela. Most of these trade reforms had in common the dismantling of quantitative restrictions (QRs) to trade and a reduction in the tariff range and average tariff level; maximum tariff levels were reduced to values below 25 per cent in all the above countries with the exception of Jamaica, Paraguay, Trinidad and Tobago and Venezuela (Alam and Rajapatirana, 1993). Usually QRs were reduced before the reduction in tariffs. The more recent trade reforms have also been much faster and all-encompassing than the early reforms.

In most cases, the unification of the exchange rate system has proceeded in parallel with the reduction of tariffs levels. Furthermore, a common objective and practice have been to accompany the reduction in tariffs with a combination of macroeconomic policies aimed at achieving and maintaining a real depreciation.

The reforms of the trade regime have been carried out within the Central American Common Market (CARICOM) for the Central American countries and within the CARICOM agreement for the Caribbean countries. In many cases in Central American the common market has followed the lead of a member country, as was the case with Costa Rica in the second half of the 1980s and with El Salvador today.

Among the large countries Argentina has liberalized its trade substantially, reduced import tariffs to a range of 0–22, unified its exchange rate system, eliminated export taxes and reduced drastically QRs. Colombia implemented a radical trade reform during the Gaviria administration (1990–4) that brought the average tariff rate from 85 per cent in 1985 to only 7 per cent in 1992 and the tariff range from 0–220 to 5–20. Mexico also carried out a major trade liberalization, reducing significantly the coverage of QRs, reducing the tariff range from 0–100 in 1985 to 0–20 in 1990 and the average tariff from 24 per cent in 1985 to 13 per cent in 1990. A further trade liberalization took place with its signing of NAFTA as the United States is its main import source. Peru has also made much progress in liberalizing its trade. The tariff range has been reduced from 0–120 in 1988 to 0–15 today, most QRs to import have been eliminated and export taxes have been abolished. Venezuela made progress in 1991 towards the reduction of import restrictions and the range of tariffs was reduced from 0–135 in 1989 to 0–50 in 1991 and today is in the 0–25 range. The average tariff level has been reduced from 37 per cent in 1989 to 19 per cent in 1991 (Alam and Rajapatirana, 1993).

Brazil has made some progress in liberalizing its trade, but still has a long way to go. The tariff range was reduced from 0–105 in 1987 to 0–65 in 1992, while the average tariff was reduced during the same period from 51 per cent to 21 per cent.

Another important area of reform has been the privatization and sometimes restructuring of public enterprises. In this area, Argentina, Mexico and Peru have gone the furthest, and recently Bolivia and Brazil have initiated a privatization process. An area that has proven to be the most difficult has been the liberalization of labour markets, although Argentina, Colombia and Peru, especially the latter, have made progress.

The prominent role of financial sector reform is a result of both the perception that an efficient financial sector is essential to growth, the generally poor performance of development banks and the widespread failures of financial institutions during the debt crisis.[12] This is an area where research finds many possibilities of market failure (Villanueva and Mirakhor, 1990; McKinnon, 1991; Stiglitz, 1993), and where some proponents of the East Asian model of development advocate the directed allocation of credit.

Initial conditions play a central role in the design and implementation of financial reforms. If a large proportion of assets of financial institutions are held at below market rates, or are not performing, then financial reforms will create difficulties for existing institutions. In particular, if deposit and lending rates are deregulated simultaneously, and free entry is permitted into the banking system, then existing banks will be forced to pay market interest rates. They will then suffer substantial losses, jeopardizing the banking system's solvency and macroeconomic stability. It may be necessary in such cases to allow for a transition phase, in which lending rates are deregulated first, with deposit rates following only gradually (World Bank, 1989). In other cases, most banks may already be insolvent before the financial reforms are implemented. The banks have then to be closed down or recapitalized before deregulation. Otherwise, as the banks have already lost their capital, moral hazard problems will be exacerbated, and the future collapse of many financial institutions could be very costly.

Financial sector reforms are especially difficult because the running of such institutions requires a great deal of specific business knowledge and experience. They are also difficult to evaluate, in particular because undercapitalized institutions can run for some time without problems becoming evident. It is also necessary before liberalizing to have in place an appropriate regulatory and supervisory capacity in an independent Superintendency of Banks, or similar organization (Villanueva and Mirakhor, 1990; Stiglitz, 1993). Reforms in the financial sector recognize the complexities of the credit markets by emphasizing the need for prudential supervision and regulation of financial institutions. In moderate and high inflation countries, controlled interest rates are typically well below the inflation rate, and reform programmes typically seek to raise real interest rates to positive levels.

Not surprisingly, this is an area where there have been major differences about the content and the extension of the reforms across countries. In general, credit allocation has been reduced when controlled nominal interest rates have been adjusted to obtain positive real rates for borrowers. In some cases interest rates have been left free (among the large countries Argentina, Colombia, Mexico and Peru). In general financial liberalization has been held back by weak regulation and supervision and severe macroeconomic imbalances that make financial liberalization a risky option.

Another case is where there has been much innovation in social security reforms. One by one major countries in the region have been shifting from the traditional pay-as-you-go system to an individual capitalization system where the retirement benefits are based upon the rentability of the funds invested in individual accounts. The individual accounts are administered by private companies that specialize in this activity. This type of reform was initiated in Chile and has been introduced in Argentina, Colombia and Peru, and Mexico has just unveiled a programme in this direction.

The effect of this reform on the national saving rate depends on the fiscal adjustment to the loss of current government revenues associated with the implementation of the reform. If the pension of the retirees of the old system are suspended or financed out of an increase in taxes or a reduction in public expenditures, rather than through an increase in public debt, the total national saving rate would also increase. The national saving rate would increase also if due to myopia or liquidity constraints the introduction of the private pension system reduces private consumption.

The largest benefits from this type of reforms are on the institutional side. Once an individual capitalization system is created, the pressures for a more transparent, less regulated and better supervised financial system would increase as the holders of individual pension accounts demanded less risk and more return from their investments. The latter effect through rates of return and lower risk could also affect the saving rate.

5 THE UNFINISHED AGENDA

Although much progress has been made in stabilizing their economies and in introducing radical efficiency and growth-enhancing reforms there are still some areas where further progress is required. In particular, the quality of fiscal adjustment needs to be addressed through a major reform of the state. With the reforms implemented in recent years one needs now a state that sets the rules of the game and concentrates on social services in general and to services geared towards the poorest groups in the population in particular. But in many countries the institutions which support the old interventionist model are still there.

Another area where much progress needs to be made is in the areas of health and education and in creating a policy framework much more attractive for the adaptation and the production of new technologies.

But even in the traditional area of reforms there is some unfinished business in the main countries of the region. Argentina is struggling in its adjustment to the drastic reduction in private capital inflows that followed the recent Mexican crisis. Successful adjustment requires a further liberalization of labour markets, to continue their opening to trade and to complete the fiscal adjustment of the provinces.

In the case of Brazil, now that the economy has slowed down, the fiscal deficit is close to 4 per cent of GDP, reduction of which will require a serious fiscal adjustment. The fiscal adjustment will encounter political problems as the reduction of some of the generous benefits of the social security system will have to be reduced. On the trade side, Brazil still has a long way to go in the reduction of tariffs as well as subsidies to exports. Brazil needs to follow through also with the privatization of a host of enterprises that are producing private goods, as well as public utilities. For the latter case, it will need first to put in place a regulatory framework capable of promoting a competitive solution for these sectors.

Colombia has to control the fiscal deterioration of recent years and make a space in the budget for pressing needs in the social sectors. Until now there has been much agreement on where to increase spending but not much on where to reduce them or where to increase taxes.

Mexico has to rebuild its financial system which was practically destroyed during the debt crisis. A privatization of the banking system without proper regulation and supervision must take some of the blame here besides the macroeconomic character of the crisis.

As part of the fiscal adjustment required to restore the basic macroeconomic balances, infrastructure has in most countries not advanced in parallel with the demand for it. Aware of the substantial amount of resources required to satisfy the needs in this area (World Bank, 1994) and taking into consideration the vast resources that are required also to satisfy the needs of the population in the social sectors, some progress has been made in recent years in introducing the Build, Operate and Transfer (BTO) system in basic infrastructure. Here rules of the games and property rights definitions and enforcement have to be upgraded to be able to mobilize the resources required.

An area where there is still much to be done is in improving the access of the poorest groups in the population to education, health and the water and sewerage system. Progress here is required to improve equity, which is a development objective in itself, and to increase support for the reforms. But, as the new literature on endogenous growth underlines, progress in improving the human capital base also can make an important contribution to long-term growth. Here the needs are tremendous and the problem is not only of devoting enough resources but of introducing innovative systems in the production of these services to improve their efficiency. Here some countries have been innovating, providing subsidies to the demand for services and having the private sector as the main producer of them. This is an area where there is much to be learned from some of the Chilean reform initiatives.

Notes

1. For a review of economic policies in Latin America in a historical perspective see Corbo (1988) and Diaz-Alejandro (1983)
2. For an assessment of the consensus on policy reforms, see Williamson (1990), Corbo and Fischer (1992, 1995) and Edwards (1995).
3. On the reforms of the Pinochet regime see Corbo (1985), Edwards and Edwards (1987), Harberger (1985), Meller (1990), and Wisecarver (1992).
4. An extreme version of this view was the one that given the equilibrium real exchange rate, domestic inflation – the denominator of the real exchange rate – was equal to the inflation of tradeables. For this group the evolution of the nominal exchange rate was important not only in the determination of the evolution of the price of tradeables but also for the dynamic of the overall price level. A very influential paper at the time that presented this view was later published as Sjaastad (1984).
5. On the stabilization programme of this period see Corbo and Solimano (1991), Fontaine (1989) and Corbo and Fischer (1994).
6. On public sector reforms see Corbo (1990) and Larraín (1991).
7. See De la Cuadra and Hachette (1992).
8. On the new pension system see Cheyre (1988) and Diamond and Valdés (1994).
9. This is an area of reform that became central to interpreting the developments that followed. On this topic see also McKinnon (1988) and Valdés (1992).
10. On this topic see Hachette and Luders (1993) and Bitr'n and Saez (1995).
11. See World Bank (1991) and Corbo and Fischer (1995).

12. See The World Bank's (1989) study of the financial system for the remarkably long list of countries in which the banking system was essentially bankrupt.

References

Alam, A and S. Rajapatirana, (1993) 'Trade Policy Reform in Latin America and the Caribbean in the 1980s', *Working Paper*, no. 1104 (Washington, DC: The World Bank).

Bitr'n, E. and R. Saez, (1995) 'The Chilean Privatization Process', in B. Bosworth *et al.* (eds), *The Chilean Economy: Policy Lessons and Challenges* (Washington, DC: Brookings Institution).

Campos, R. (1961) 'Two Views on Inflation in Latin America', in A. O. Hirschman (ed.), *Latin American Issues: Essays and Comments* (New York: Twentieth Century Fund).

CEPAL (1992) *Equidad y Transformación Productiva: Un Enfoque Integrado* (Santiago: CEPAL).

Cheyre, H. (1988). *La Previsión en Chile Ayer y Hoy: Impacto de una Reforma* (Santiago: Centro de Estudios Públicos).

Corbo, V. (1985) 'Reforms and Macroeconomic Adjustment in Chile during 1974–84', *World Development*, vol. 13, no. 8.

———— (1988). 'Problems, Development Theory and Strategies of Latin America', in G. Ranis and T. P. Shultz (eds), *The State of Development Economics: Progress and Perspectives* (London: Basil Blackwell).

———— (1990) 'Public Finance, Trade, and Development: The Chilean Experience', in V. Tanzi (ed.), *Fiscal Policy in Open Developing Economies* (Washington, DC: IMF).

Corbo, V. and S. Fischer (1992). 'World Bank Supported Adjustment Programs: Rationale and Main Results', in Corbo V, S. Fischer and S. Webb (eds), *Adjustment Lending Revisited: Policies to Restore Growth* (Washington, DC: World Bank).

———— (1994) 'Lessons from the Chilean Stabilization and Recovery', in B. Bosworth *et al.* (eds), *The Chilean Economy: Policy Lessons and Challenges* (Washington, DC: Brookings Institution).

———— (1995) 'Structural Adjustment, Stabilization and Policy Reform: Domestic and International Finance', in J. Behrman, J. and T. N. Srinivasan (eds), *Handbook of Development Economics*, volume III (New York: Elsevier).

Corbo, V. and K. Schmidt-Hebbel (1990) 'Public Policies and Saving in Developing Countries', *Journal of Development Economics*, vol. 36, pp. 89–115.

Corbo, V. and A. Solimano (1991) 'Chile's Experience with Stabilization Revisited'. in M. Bruno *et al.* (eds), *Lessons of Economic Stabilization and its Aftermath* (Cambridge, Mass: MIT Press).

De la Cuadra, S. and D. Hachette, (1992) *Apertura Commercial: Experiencia Chilena* (Santiago: Chile: Editorial de Economía y Administración, Universidad de Chile).

Diamond, P. and S. Valdés (1994) 'Social Security Reforms', in B. Bosworth *et al.* (eds). *The Chilean Economy: Policy Lessons and Challenges* (Washington, DC: Brookings Institution).

Diáz-Alejandro, C. (1983) 'Stories of the 1930s for the 1980s', in P. Aspe *et al.* (eds). *Financial Policies and the World Capital Market: The Problem of Latin American Countries* (Chicago: University of Chicago Press).

Díz, A. C. (1966) 'Money and Prices in Argentina: 1935–62', PhD dissertation (Chicago: University of Chicago).

Easterly, W. and D. L. Wetzel (1989) 'Policy Determinants of Growth: Survey of the Theory and Evidence', World Bank, *PPR Working Paper*, no. 343.

Edwards, S. (1995) *'Crisis and Reform in Latin America* (Oxford: Oxford University Press).

Edwards, S. and A. C. Edwards (1987) *Monetarism and Liberalization: The Chilean Experiment* (Boston: Ballinger).

Ffrench-Davis R. (1973) *Políticas Económicas en Chile: 1952–1970* (Santiago: Editorial Nueva Universidad).

Fontaine, J. A. (1989) 'The Chilean Economy in the 1980s: Adjustment and Recovery', in S. Edwards and F. Larraín (eds), *Debt, Adjustment, and Recovery* (Oxford: Blackwell).

Hachette, D. and R. Luders (1993) *Privatization in Chile: An Economic Appraisal* (San Francisco: ICS Press).

Harberger, A. C. (1985) 'Observations on the Chilean Economy, 1973–1983', *Economic Development and Cultural Change*, vol. 33 (April).

Larraín, F. (1991) 'Public Sector Behavior in a Highly Indebted Country: The Contrasting Chilean Experience 1970–85', in F. Larraín and M. Selowsky (eds), *The Public Sector Crisis and the Latin American Crisis* (San Francisco: ICS Press).

McKinnon, R. (1988) 'Financial Liberalization and Economic Development', International Center for Economic Growth, *Occasional Paper*, no. 6 (San Francisco).

———— (1991) *The Order of Economic Liberalization: Financial Control in the Transition to a Market Economy* (Baltimore: Md.: Johns Hopkins University Press).

Meller, P. (1990) 'Chile', in J. Williamson (ed.), *Latin American Adjustment* (Washington, DC: Institute for International Economics).

Serven, L. and A. Solimano (1992) 'Private Investment and Macroeconomic Adjustment: A Survey', *The World Bank Research Observer*, vol 7, no. 1.

Sjaastad, L. A. (1984) 'Stabilization and Liberalization Experience in the Southern Cone', in N. A. Barletta *et al.* (eds), *Economic Liberalization and Stabilization Policies in Argentina, Chile and Uruguay: Applications of the Monetary Approach of the Balance of Payments* (Washington, DC: World Bank).

Stiglitz, J. E. (1993) 'The Role of the State in Financial Markets', *World Bank Annual Conference on Development Economics* (Washington, DC: World Bank).

Summers, L. (1985) 'Public Policy and Saving', *NBER Working Paper*.

Universidad de Chile (1963) *La Economía Chilena en el Período 1950–63* (Santiago, Chile: Instituto de Economía).

Valdés, S. (1992) 'Ajuste Estructural en el Mercado de Capitales: La Experiencia Chilena', in D. Wisecarver D (ed.), *El Modelo Económico Chileno* (Santiago de Chile: Catholic University and CINDE).

Villanueva, D. and A. Mirakhor (1990) 'Strategies for Financial Reforms', *IMF Staff Papers*, vol 37, no. 3.

Williamson, J. (1989) *Latin American Adjustment* (Washington, DC: Institute for International Economics).

Wisecarver, D. (ed.) (1992) *El Modelo Económico Chileno* (Santiago de Chile: Catholic University and CINDE).

World Bank (1989) *The World Development Report* (New York: Oxford University Press).

————— (1991) *The World Development Report* (New York: Oxford University Press).

————— (1994) *The World Development Report* (New York: Oxford University Press).

Part III
Economic Integration

11 Growth, the Maghreb and the European Union: Assessing the Impact of the Free Trade Agreements on Tunisia and Morocco[*]

John Page and John Underwood

THE WORLD BANK, WASHINGTON, USA

Morocco and Tunisia both signed comprehensive integration agreements with the European Union in the early 1990s. These agreements consist of two essential elements – increased aid flows and technical assistance in exchange for reductions in trade barriers and other impediments to the flow of goods and investment over a period of 12 years. The EU–Mediterranean initiative, of which these agreements form a major part, is one element of a much broader European strategy to forge trade alliances with countries on Europe's periphery. Agreements with some 10 Eastern European countries in transition were signed in 1991, and the European Union is negotiating with Egypt and Jordan to extend its web of integration agreements to the Mashreq. These European initiatives are intended to promote more rapid convergence of incomes between Europe's transitional and developing economy neighbours and the European Union.

Trade experts have traditionally viewed regional integration schemes as offering few benefits compared with universal trade liberalization. The costs of diversion of trade away from least-cost suppliers may outweigh the potential gains of trade creation among members of the agreement, and even when net trade creation effects are positive, the estimated welfare gains from partial liberalization are frequently small. The failure of numerous integration agreements among developing countries and the success of the East Asian economies without formal regional agreements have added to the scepticism.

Nevertheless, efforts to create regional trading blocs proceed worldwide. In addition to the EU agreements, the NAFTA and, more recently, the ASEAN agreements suggest that policy-makers in both advanced and

207

developing economies remain unpersuaded by static, welfare-based calculations of the limited benefits of regional integration. The potential dynamic benefits of integration agreements – their impact on long-run economic growth – are usually put forward as the rationale for their existence. Broadly, these dynamic benefits fall into two groups – the possibility of increased investment flows and the positive impact of integration agreements on productivity and technological change. Both of these channels can raise growth rates.

Political economy arguments are now routinely brought forward to underpin the impact of integration agreements on investment behaviour. The 'credibility' of the rules affecting domestic and foreign investment is viewed as greater in an integration agreement than from domestically-based rule changes alone, leading to a reduction in perceived political risks of investment (Hoekman, 1995). The opportunities for 'deeper integration', including harmonization of standards, competition policies, taxation and regulations, are also cited as mechanisms by which investor behaviour can be changed (Lawrence, 1991).

The means by which integration agreements can raise productivity growth rates have been less thoroughly explored. One strand of argument emphasizes that some of the deeper integration aspects of the agreements, such as harmonization of standards and improvements in trade facilitation may reduce transactions costs and enhance measured productivity (Rutherford, Rustrom and Tarr, 1995). But the mechanisms by which these cost reductions take place are frequently only sketchily outlined and the resulting estimates of benefits are highly arbitrary. Another emphasizes improvements in learning and productivity change at the plant level, arising from increased export rivalry or import competition. These impacts are of course dependent on the trade creation effects of the integration agreements themselves. Finally, where agreements such as the Euro–Med Initiative, include aid and technical assistance components, technology transfer and productivity enhancement can be explicit aid objectives.

This chapter examines three dimensions of the growth impact of the European Integration agreements on Morocco and Tunisia – gains from trade liberalization, increased foreign investment, and improvements in productivity. Section 1 looks briefly at historical trends in growth, investment, and productivity change in both countries between 1960 and 1994. Section 2 summarizes the results of recent estimates of the welfare effects of trade liberalization under the agreements. Section 3 examines the possible impact of the agreements on investment behaviour, especially on Foreign Direct Investment (FDI), and section 4 reviews possible channels for the acceleration of productivity change.

1   GROWTH, INVESTMENT AND PRODUCTIVITY CHANGE

Morocco and Tunisia are the star performers of the Middle East and North Africa (MENA) region in terms of growth.[1] Between 1960 and 1994, Tunisia grew by slightly more than 5 per cent per year and Morocco by slightly more than 4.5 per cent. As a result, Morocco has been able to more than double *per capita* income in the last 35 years, while Tunisia has tripled its *per capita* income. While these achievements are dramatic and visible, they fall short in comparison with the rapidly growing East Asian economies. If Morocco and Tunisia had grown, in *per capita* terms, as fast as the average for East Asia over the same period, *per capita* income would be $700 higher today in Tunisia and $1300 higher in Morocco.

Using simple growth accounting, we decompose Morocco's and Tunisia's growth into its source elements (Table 11.1). Countries grow by accumulating labour, capital, and human capital and by using these resources more efficiently. There is a substantial recent literature that advances evidence across countries on the relative contribution of these three basic inputs and of efficiency gains – total factor productivity (TFP) – to output growth.[2]

In all countries, labour force growth is a basic source of economic growth. In both Morocco and Tunisia, labour force growth has accounted

Table 11.1   Determinants of long-term growth

	Morocco	Tunisia	E. Asia	Portugal	Spain	France
Per capita income (1994) (US$)[a]	1190	1821	n.a.	7890	13560	22360
GDP growth (1960–94) (per cent)[b]	4.6	5.3	6.1	4.6		
Contribution to growth (percentage points)[b]						
Capital accumulation	2.6	2.3	3	2.4		
Labour force growth	0.9	0.9	0.6	0.2		
Human capital growth	1.8	1.3	1.3	0.6		
TFP[c]	–0.7	0.8	1.2	1.4		

Notes:
[a] 1993 for Portugal, Spain and France.
[b] 1960–87 for Portugal, Spain, and France.
[c] Authors' calculations, using the Nehru and Dhareshwar (1994) data set.

for about 1 percentage point of GDP growth per year on average during the last 35 years. In comparision, labour force growth contributed only about half of 1 per cent to output growth in East Asia, where population growth dropped off earlier and more substantially.

Human capital accumulation, proxied by average educational achievement, has been more important than labour accumulation, especially in Morocco, in contributing to economic growth. Although the level of education of the average Moroccan worker was and is substantially below that of the average Tunisian worker, the rate of accumulation of education was higher in Morocco between 1960 and 1994. In Morocco, human capital accumulation is estimated to have contributed about 2 percentage points annually to growth, more than the roughly $1^1/_4$ percentage point rate in both East Asia and Tunisia. The most important contribution to growth in both Morocco and Tunisia has been the accumulation of physical capital. On average, net new investment added about $2^1/_2$ percentage points per year to growth. In this case, the two Maghreb countries lag the 3 percentage point average for East Asia, where savings rates have been consistently among the highest in the world. (During the last 35 years, investment averaged 20 per cent of GDP in Morocco and 26 per cent in Tunisia.)

Yet, differences in physical capital accumulation are not enough to explain the difference between growth rates in Morocco and Tunisia and East Asia. Estimates of total factor productivity in Morocco and Tunisia show a low or negative average annual contribution to growth since 1960, ranging from 3/4 of 1 percentage point to a significantly negative number. Virtually all of the difference in growth rates between Morocco and Tunisia and East Asia can be explained by lower TFP growth.[3] Morocco and Tunisia have, for the most part, achieved economic growth the hard way – through physical and human capital accumulation. Not only have efficiency gains been lower in Morocco and Tunisia than in East Asia, these gains have also been lower than in Western Europe, where TFP contributed almost $1^3/_4$ percentage points to annual growth between 1960 and 1990.

Morocco and Tunisia have achieved better results in terms of TFP in recent years. Between 1988 and 1994, TFP growth is estimated at about 0.9 per cent per year in Tunisia and 0.4 per cent per year in Morocco. It is likely that these improvements can be linked to structural adjustment, which reduced trade protection substantially in both countries, and to a reduction in the share of public investment in total investment. In both countries, there is evidence that public investment – notably public enterprise investment – has been less productive than private investment (World Bank, 1995a, 1995b). In Morocco, public sector investment fell from 50 per cent of total fixed investment in the early 1980s to about 40 per cent in 1994. In Tunisia, private investment remains a modest one-third of total investment, but has been rising since 1987, when the private share was only one-quarter. However, the recent efficiency gains in Morocco and Tunisia remain insufficient to achieve the high rates of growth required to close the income gap between southern Europe and the Maghreb in a few decades.

2   HOW LARGE ARE THE BENEFITS FROM TRADE LIBERALIZATION?

Traditionally, studies of free trade agreements have focused on the welfare effects of trade liberalization. Recent studies of the possible benefits of the Morocco and Tunisia free trade agreements indicate that the benefits are significant but not enough to imply rapid income convergence (Rutherford, Rustrom and Tarr, 1993, 1995). These results were generated using applied general equilibrium models of the two countries. Using similar policy scenarios, the welfare gains are estimated to be about 1.5 per cent of GDP in Morocco and 1.7 per cent of GDP in Tunisia (Table 11.2). To put these numbers in perspective, the cumulative effect over 10 years of these gains would be an increase of *per capita* income of about $25 per person in Morocco and $40 per person in Tunisia. The gains are, of course, larger if Morocco and Tunisia were to liberalize with respect to the entire world. By doing so, the two countries eliminate the trade diversion effects that reduce the benefits of regional integration agreements. With full liberalization, the welfare benefits to Morocco and Tunisia are between 2 and 2.5 per cent of GDP. (Trade diversion is relatively small because more

Table 11.2   Welfare gains from trade liberalization (percentage of pre-Agreement GDP)

	Morocco	Tunisia
Free Trade Agreement with the European Union	1.5	1.7
Unilateral liberalization with respect to the world	2.5	2.3
Including benefits from harmonization of standards, product quality improvements, and increased trading efficiency, FTA with European Union	n.a.	4.7
Above, with unilateral liberalization with respect to the world	n.a.	5.3

Source: Rutherford, Rustrom and Tarr 1993 (1993, 1995).

Economic Integration

than 50 per cent of Morocco's non-oil imports and more than 70 per cent of Tunisia's already come from Europe.)

The main beneficiaries from the EU free trade agreements are consumers. Currently, Moroccan and Tunisian non-agricultural exports (with a few small exceptions) enter the EU market duty-free. Therefore, the major benefits come from lower traded-goods prices in Morocco and Tunisia. These benefits more than offset the costs of adjusting labour and capital away from uncompetitive activities in traded-goods sectors and a small shift from non-traded to traded-goods production. (In Morocco, adjustment costs were assumed to be zero. Taking these one-time costs into account would reduce, but not eliminate, the estimated gains.)

In essence, the models described above are exercises in comparative statistics. They do not take into account factors that might increase the overall efficiency of production or the level of investment, apart from the reallocation of resources away from some existing activities toward others. In the Tunisia exercise, the authors (who obviously believe that there would be some form of dynamic benefit) enhance the basic model to take into account benefits from harmonization of standards and a reduction in trading costs. They do this by an assumption that harmonization of standards with the European Union will improve export prices by 2 per cent and that improvements in trade-related services would increase export prices by a further 1 per cent and would reduce import prices by 1 per cent. The welfare benefits to Tunisia more than double, to 4.7 per cent of GDP.

It is worth noting that the actual agreements are not identical to the assumed agreements modelled above. The most important difference relates to the timing and sequencing of tariff reductions. Most of the model runs assumed instantaneous reductions in tariffs. However, the actual reductions will be phased in over 12 years, with faster reductions for imported inputs. The impact will be a temporary increase in protection with an implied welfare loss. The only model run close to this scenario, an assumed reduction of tariffs on 40 per cent of the products currently imported from Europe by Tunisia, indicated a small net welfare loss. (Obviously, the analogy is not complete, because tariffs will eventually be completely eliminated between Morocco and Tunisia and the European Union, and welfare gains will predominate.)

3 WILL THE AGREEMENTS INCREASE FOREIGN INVESTMENT?

Experience with other integration schemes suggests that a major potential benefit of the Tunisia and Morocco agreements may come from substantially increased foreign investment. Mexico received some 30 billion dollars of private capital inflow in the run-up to the NAFTA. Portugal and Spain saw private capital inflows increase by 2 per cent of GDP following their integration with the European Union and recently the more aggressive reformers in Eastern Europe have experienced large increases in investment (Dadush, 1995). This section asks whether Morocco and Tunisia can realistically expect a major increase in foreign investment resulting from the recent agreements.

Trends in Foreign Investment

Foreign savings played an important role in Morocco and Tunisia, notably in the 1970s and early 1980s. In the period from 1960 to 1987, the use of foreign savings averaged 6.3 per cent of GDP in Morocco and 6.9 per cent of GDP in Tunisia, 33 and 27 per cent, respectively, of total investment. In recent years, the overall role of foreign savings has declined, averaging 5 per cent of GDP in Morocco and 5.5 per cent of GDP in Tunisia. In both cases, the decline came about in response to balance of payments difficulties in the mid-1980s.

The bulk of foreign savings inflows in both countries has traditionally come in the form of loans from, or guaranteed by, official agencies of industrial country governments, supplemented by several purely private, syndicated loans from commercial banks. Foreign direct and portfolio investment was marginal in both countries, less than 1 per cent of GDP annually, on average through the 1980s. In the Moroccan case, the balance of payments difficulties of the 1980s, combined with the heavy debt component of foreign liabilities, led to the need to reschedule payments on debt service with both official bilateral and private creditors. Recently, the composition of foreign savings inflows has begun to change, notably in Morocco, toward foreign direct investment.

FDI increased substantially in Morocco in the 1990s in line with the rising trend of expanded FDI to developing countries world-wide (Figure 11.1). This is in sharp contrast to largely stagnant FDI flows to MENA countries in general. In 1991 and 1992 FDI flows were in the range of 1.5–2.0 per cent of GDP and reached 3 per cent of GDP in 1994, probably because of transactions related to privatization. In large part Morocco's increase against the trend for the region reflects the fact that by the early 1990s Morocco had implemented all of the formal policies needed to attract FDI, including current account convertibility, full repatriation rights for profits and dividends, no prior approvals, no controls on contracts covering licences, trademarks, management and technical cooperation, and

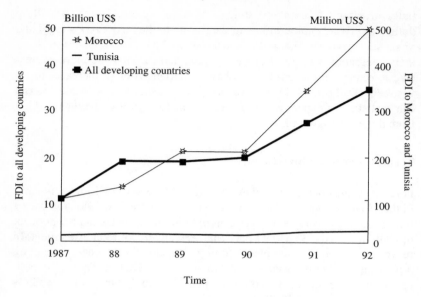

Figure 11.1   Trends in net FDI, 1987–92

no restrictions on foreign ownership except for agricultural land. Even in contrast with high-performing East Asian economies, this was a remarkably liberal foreign investment regime (World Bank, 1995a).

About two-thirds of Morocco's FDI originates in Europe, nearly a quarter from France alone. Middle Eastern investors are an important source of FDI in Morocco, accounting for about 20 per cent of total FDI. The broad geographic patterns have been constant since the mid-1980s, except that the share of FDI originating from other MENA countries has declined and that originating in Spain has increased. The share of foreign investment in manufacturing in Morocco has remained virtually unchanged since the 1980s. Manufacturing accounts for about one quarter of total FDI. Recent trends have resulted in expanding investments in financial services and corresponding declines in tourism and real estate.

Tunisia's FDI flows have also grown in the 1990s, primarily as a result of investments in the energy sector. Investment flows to other activities have been very low and stable since 1990, partly reflecting reservation of investment licensing to the state in such potentially attractive areas as chemicals, cement, mining, electricity and telecommunications. While the Unified Investment Code (1990) lifts restrictions of FDI for all export activities, many service and infrastructure sectors, such as telecommunications, tourism, computer services and information technology, remain subject to prior approval.

One feature of Tunisia's foreign investment regime which differs from that of Morocco is that the bulk of foreign and joint venture investments in manufacturing are concentrated in the so called 'offshore' sector. About 23 per cent of wholly export-oriented offshore enterprises are foreign-owned while another 24 per cent are joint ventures. These firms have few direct links with the domestic Tunisian economy (World Bank, 1994a).

Portfolio Investment and Macroeconomic Management

Integration with the European Union may improve Morocco's and Tunisia's access to portfolio investments. If the agreements enhance Morocco's and Tunisia's perceived macroeconomic management, capital may shift from other locations and/or the debt service costs of existing portfolio flows may decline. Mexico benefited substantially from increased portfolio flows in the run-up to the NAFTA, largely as a consequence of its ability to portray the agreement as enhancing the prospects of sustained good macroeconomic management, but the impact of its failure to adhere to credible macroeconomic rules following the NAFTA is well known. Thus, two key elements for Morocco and Tunisia to enhance access to portfolio investment are first, their historical performance in macroeconomic management and second, the likelihood that good performance will be sustained or improved during the implementation of the agreements.

How credible has macroeconomic management been in Morocco and Tunisia? Figures 11.2–11.4 present three indicators of macroeconomic stability for countries in the Middle East and North Africa. These are the rate of inflation, the budget deficit and movements in the real exchange rate. Morocco and Tunisia rank well in terms of both the rate and volatility of inflation in comparison with other Middle Eastern countries, although the European Union has had marginally superior performance to both economies during the past ten years (Figure 11.2). Both countries' fiscal performance validates their performance on inflation (Figure 11.3). While it is difficult to judge the adequacy of real exchange rate levels in a comparative context, high exchange rate volatility suggests that macroeconomic management is insufficiently flexible to minimise divergences between the equilibrium and observed real exchange rate arising from differential inflation or terms of trade shocks. Morocco and Tunisia have shown a superior ability to manage the real exchange rate (Figure 11.4).

Large external debt burdens tend to have an inhibiting effect on foreign investment (Diwan and Rodrik, 1992). Investors may perceive a debt overhang as indicative of past large macroeconomic imbalances – in particular,

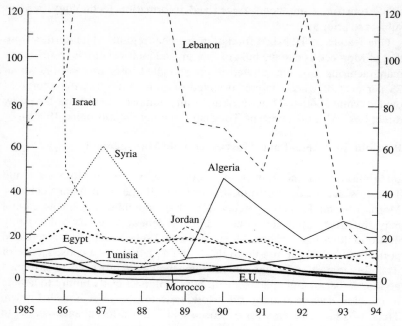

Figure 11.2   Change in consumer price indices, 1985–94

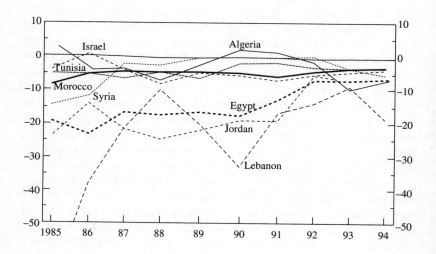

Figure 11.3   Central government balance (per cent of GDP)

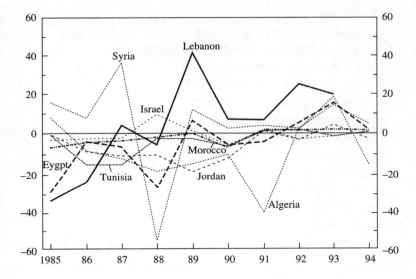

Figure 11.4 Real effective exchange rates (annual rates of change), 1985–94

lack of fiscal discipline – and they may fear that the debt burden will result in future increases in taxation or reimposition of exchange controls. New investors will abstain from funding otherwise good investments out of fear of being 'taxed' by the prior creditors. External debt management in Morocco and Tunisia has been similar to other countries in MENA with debt to GDP ratios of about 60 per cent of GDP (Figure 11.5). This contrasts with lower debt burdens in East Asia and Latin America in general, but is similar to the debt to GDP ratios of such rapidly growing East Asian economies as Indonesia and Malaysia.

In sum, relative to competitors in the region Morocco and Tunisia appear to be well positioned to benefit from their reputation for prudent macro-economic management. Both economies have established long-run credibility in controlling inflation and fiscal deficits and in managing the exchange rate to accommodate external shocks. Debt management has been adequate. The integration agreements will place additional stress on macro-economic management because they are likely to require real depreciations of both currencies (compensating devaluations) as traded goods markets are liberalized and further fiscal prudence as capital markets are liberalized.

Vis-à-vis other MENA countries, the agreements may also enhance investors' perceptions of the creditworthiness of Morocco and Tunisia in the

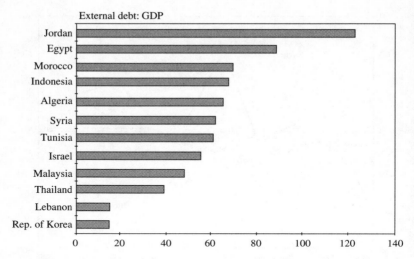

External debt: GDP

Note: The ratios are for debt: GNP instead of debt: GDP for the four East Asian countries. The year for MENA countries is 1994 and for East Asia 1991.

Source: World Bank (1993).

Figure 11.5   International indebtedness, 1990s

future. The substantial aid packages embodied in the Euro–Med initiative can in part be used to facilitate macroeconomic adjustment. But additional effort will be required to shift perceptions of creditworthiness relative to emerging markets within the European Union itself. Figure 11.6 shows credit ratings compiled by the *Institutional Investor* for selected Maghreb and Mediterranean countries. Both Tunisia and Morocco are evaluated by investors as less creditworthy than Spain, Portugal or Greece. Investor attitudes have improved for both economies since 1986, reflecting improvements in macroeconomic management, but neither has recovered its creditworthiness levels of the early 1980s. There has been no sharp upswing in investor evaluation in the past two years, despite the two countries' active negotiations with the European Union. Tunisia leads Morocco in the surveys throughout the entire 15 years, but the gap has narrowed substantially.

Can Financial Markets Absorb Increased Portfolio Flows Efficiently?

Financial markets in Morocco and Tunisia remain relatively undeveloped. Both are bank-based systems where direct instruments of financing –

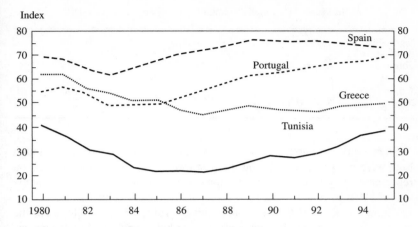

Source: *Institutional Investor Magazine*, various issues.

Figure 11.6   Institutional investors' credit ratings (1980–94)
(selected Mediterranean and European countries)

bonds or share issues – are rarely used by non-government entities. In both countries, the government and public enterprises absorb an inordinate share of the credit available. For example, in Morocco, the Treasury absorbs 35 per cent of domestic credit. Until recently in both countries banks were forced to place a large share of their assets in below-market government paper and to direct credit to state-owned enterprises. In both countries, the banking system has been modernized to a great extent: both have new and reasonably effective capital adequacy requirements and loan provisioning rules, although banks have been given leeway in complying in the short run. Banks are hampered in day-to-day liquidity management by the lack of functioning secondary markets for government securities.

Local currency bond markets, which have been the conduit of portfolio inflows in many countries, including Spain and Portugal, are not deep in Morocco and Tunisia. The markets for government bonds are at an early stage of development and there is no private bond market in the traditional sense. In Tunisia there has been rapid growth in the private bond market, but with a twist. All bond issues by private companies must be guaranteed by banks. In reality, purchasers are only taking on bank risk, just as if they made a long-term deposit in a bank. Banks charge the borrower for the guarantee, meaning that the normal benefit of bond financing, a reduced cost of intermediation, does not occur. No real non-bank private bond market can emerge until this restriction is lifted.

Table 11.3   Stock market capitalization (percentage of GDP)

Morocco	14
Tunisia	16
Jordan	94
Turkey	30
China	100
Thailand (in 1993 – IMF (1995))	105

Stock markets in both countries can best be described as nascent, although both have grown rapidly during the past three years. Market capitalization represented 14 per cent of GDP in Morocco and 16 per cent in Tunisia at the end of 1994. In comparison, many comparator countries have market capitalization: GDP ratios that are much higher (Table 11.3). In Morocco, the recent rapid increase in market capitalization has been fuelled by the privatization programme. Virtually all offers have been oversubscribed, implying a pent-up demand, including a foreign demand. As much as 25 per cent of the shares offered in connection with privatization were reportedly purchased by Moroccans living abroad. Tunisia's stock market is dominated by bank shares. Again, there appears to be a strong demand for Tunisian portfolio equity from abroad; the problem is a lack of security offers.

In many developing countries, before portfolio investors came to the local market, local firms went to the international bond market. (This was the pattern in major Latin American countries as they returned to international markets as the debt crisis ebbed.) Few Moroccan or Tunisian private borrowers are able to access these markets, as yet partly because of their reluctance to bear the foreign exchange risk in the absence of hedging mechanisms.

To increase the ability of financial markets to attract and effectively channel new portfolio inflows to productive activities, a host of market development activities must be undertaken. These include the development and full implementation of a good regulatory framework for stock and bond markets, better management of Treasury issues and the development of secondary bond markets. The single largest factor that will determine the evolution of stock market activity in both Morocco and Tunisia is the programme of privatization. Large-scale privatization through stock issues could rapidly develop these markets, making them a major conduit for foreign portfolio investment inflows.

Will the Agreements Improve Credibility of Investment Rules?

One of the frequently cited motives for integration agreements is the ability to change perceptions of the investment climate by 'locking in' changes in rules and institutions affecting both foreign and domestic investors. We noted above that Morocco has undertaken a wide range of legislative and regulatory reforms designed to create a private invest-ment-friendly environment. Tunisia has similarly introduced domestic and regulatory changes, although they are not as wide-ranging as those in Morocco.

Recent surveys of existing domestic and foreign firms and of prospec-tive foreign investors have been carried out for Morocco (World Bank, 1994b, 1992). The results of these point up substantial differences in in-vestor perceptions between foreign firms and domestic firms currently op-erating in Morocco. Domestic firms identify production-related constraints – financing costs, lack of skilled labour, access to industrial land, and high taxes – as the major impediments to expanded investment. In contrast, they do not identify aspects of the administrative and regulatory environ-ment – bureaucratic red tape, licensing requirements or an uncertain legal framework –- as significant. Foreign firms identified fewer production-related constraints, but also did not identify aspects of the administrative and regulatory environment as significant impediments.

The surveys of potential investors revealed that relative to other Middle Eastern and North African economies Morocco ranks well with respect to perceptions of its legal system, lack of red tape, business attitude and gov-ernment competence (Figure 11.7). It ranks below the regional average in such areas as infrastructure, political risk and foreign trade policy. There are some interesting differences between the perceptions of foreign in-vestors currently operating in Morocco and potential investors, primarily reflecting implementation of policies intended to promote private sector development. Although the potential investors rate Morocco relatively highly in terms of government attitudes to private investment, foreign-owned firms in Morocco cite regulations and restricted entry in some sectors as evidence of less profound commitment to private investment. Existing foreign firms also express greater reservations about the efficacy of legal safeguards than prospective investors. Virtually all operating foreign firms cite the inadequacy of legal means for dispute resolution and lack of legal recourse on government contracts. Existing investors also identify lengthy, complex and uncoordinated administrative processes as significant constraints, in contrast to prospective investors.

Results of surveying 124 potential European investors and firms cur-rently operating in Tunisia point to similar concerns (Ministry of International Cooperation, 1995). Foreign investors rank political and social stability as the predominant factor determining investment deci-sions. Market size and macroeconomic stability are the primary economic considerations (Figure 11.7). Liberalization of the economy – including

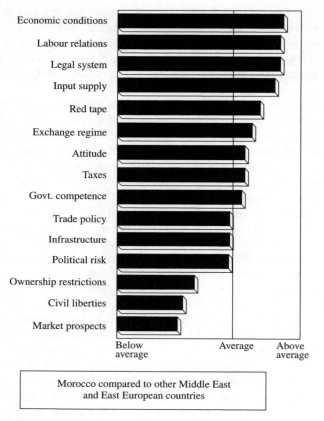

Economic conditions
Labour relations
Legal system
Input supply
Red tape
Exchange regime
Attitude
Taxes
Govt. competence
Trade policy
Infrastructure
Political risk
Ownership restrictions
Civil liberties
Market prospects

Below   Average   Above
average   average

Morocco compared to other Middle East
and East European countries

Source: World Bank (1994b).

Figure 11.7   Perceptions of prospective foreign investors (survey results)

both trade liberalization and deregulation – was cited by nearly 20 per cent
of respondents as the single most important action the government could
take to increase Tunisia's attractiveness to foreign investors. Another
8 per cent identified reducing bureaucratic procedures as most important.
Of the five leading actions identified by respondents, more than 40 per
cent focused on reducing red tape and liberalization of the regulatory
framework. As in Morocco, domestic investors tended to focus on production-related constraints – labour market regulations, absence of infrastructure, limited growth of the domestic market – rather than constraints
arising from the legal and regulatory framework. The Tunisian survey also

covered existing foreign investors. These respondents identified problems of the application of regulations and absence of systematic and transparent treatment by public officials as constraints on further investment.

These survey results suggest that improved credibility will not come automatically from the association agreements themselves. European investors' perceptions of government commitment to trade policy and regulatory liberalization may improve as a consequence of the agreements. And perceptions of political risk may decline, but many of the major constraints identified by existing foreign investors – red tape, discretionary decisions and legal problems – are not covered by the agreement and will require sustained efforts at administrative and legal reform.

Will the Agreements Change Strategic Motivations for FDI?

Macroeconomic stability and improved legislative, regulatory and institutional structures are necessary but not sufficient conditions for increase in FDI. Surveys of foreign investment behaviour consistently report strong strategic motives by direct foreign investors (World Bank, 1992). Thus if the integration agreements are to provide a basis for increased FDI in Morocco or Tunisia, they must also result in changed strategic perceptions by foreign investors. In this section, we examine the possible impact of the association agreements on a number of strategic objectives identified by surveys of European investors as relevant to foreign direct investment decisions in the Mahgreb (World Bank, 1992).

Natural Resources (Downstream Processing)

Morocco's and Tunisia's trade specialization patterns, despite substantial change over the past 20 years, remain highly concentrated in resource based activities (Table 11.4). Phosphate fertilizers and their derivatives have been a traditional source of exports for both economies and offer some potential for increased foreign investments. Similarly, for Tunisia investments in fossil fuels will remain attractive to foreigners. It is unlikely that the integration agreements will substantially change investors' perceptions of the desirability of investments in either sector, although investment volume may increase somewhat as a consequence of an improved overall investment climate. The agreements may provide some scope for increased downstream investments in agro-industrial processing. Both Morocco and Tunisia have strong revealed comparative advantage in agriculture and fisheries. Despite the restrictive nature of the agreements with respect to access to the European market in agricultural and

Table 11.4   Revealed comparative advantages and disadvantages

	Morocco			Tunisia	
	1970	1991		1970	1991
Clothing	1.3	34.2	Clothing	0.3	95.5
Fish and prepared	8.7	27.0	Animal, vegetable oil	5.6	21.5
Fruits and vegetables	52.8	24.8	Fertilizers manufact.	13.7	20.9
Fertilizers manufact.	0.9	15.2	Mineral fuels	35.5	19.9
Crude fertilizers, mines	33.4	9.9	Fruit and vegetables	12.1	6.6
Transport equipment	−13.8	−14.2	Transport equipment	−8.2	−15.4
Mineral fuels	−7.3	−22.8	Textile yarn, fabric	−8.4	−43.5
Machinery, non-elect.	−21.2	−26.1	Machinery, non-elect.	−21.7	−51.6
Cereals and preparation	−2.7	−6.0	Cereals and preparation	−17.9	−5.4
Iron and steel	−11.5	−10.4	Crude fertilizers, minerals	15.7	−7.4

processed agricultural products, both allow some scope for expanded agro-industrial exports.

Serving the Domestic Market

The guarantees of national treatment for foreign investors embodied in the agreements open up for European investors – especially in the case of Tunisia – possibilities for serving the Moroccan and Tunisian markets in previously restricted sectors. Major investments in activities to serve either market will be limited, however, by investors' perceptions that their size is limited. Surveys of prospective investors in Morocco indicate that in comparison to other economies in MENA and Eastern Europe, investors perceive market prospects as well below average, reflecting small size and limited growth (Figure 11.8). Tunisia's market, which is only half of Morocco's, suffers from similar perceived deficiencies.

Serving the Regional Market

Because of the small size of both Tunisia's and Morocco's domestic market, one possible strategic option for investors is to establish capacity in one economy to serve both (and other potential entrants to the Euro–Mediterranean agreement). The nature of the agreements concluded thus far preclude such an investment strategy, however. Because there are no provisions for liberalized trade among Mediterranean partners with the European Union, a 'hub and spoke' pattern of trade and investment is

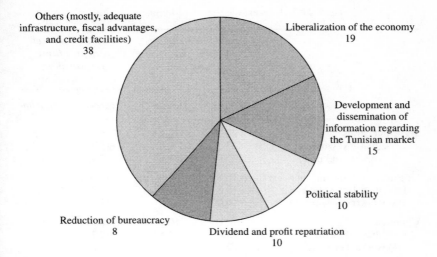

Source: Ministry of International Cooperation (1995).

Figure 11.8   Recommendations on reform measures to promote investment in
Tunisia (share of total number of recommendations, per cent)

likely to arise in which investors choose to locate in Europe to serve
several southern markets.

Niche Export Markets

The agreements may increase FDI in industries serving niche export
markets in the European Union. These are primarily in low-end manufactures – textiles, clothing and footwear, and in the case of Morocco wood
products. They are also the export industries in which existing foreign
ownership is concentrated (Table 11.5). These niche exports previously
enjoyed duty-free access to the European market, however. Thus, the
primary motivation for new investment in these niches will not come from
enhanced market access. Rather, it will have to come from increased cost
competitiveness. Historical data suggest that Morocco, especially, but also
Tunisia suffered from declining cost competitiveness in textiles, clothing,
and footwear relative to such East Asian competitors as China, Indonesia,
Malaysia and Thailand and to such European competitors as Portugal,
Greece and Hungary (World Bank, 1994c).

Production-sharing arrangements in which component production and
assembly operations are distributed across a number of countries have

Table 11.5   Percentage share of foreign ownership

	Export-oriented firms (export share > 10 per cent)		Domestic market-oriented firms (export share < 10 per cent)	
	Morocco	*Tunisia*	*Morocco*	*Tunisia*
Agro-industries	20.8	10.0	6.8	2.3
Less than 100 workers	23.3	0.0	5.1	1.7
100 workers and more	20.0	51.0	7.7	6.2
Textiles, clothing and footwear	16.8	52.9	15.3	n.a.
Less than 100 workers	19.8	40.9	7.2	n.a.
100 workers or more	16.0	62.0	21.6	n.a.
Chemicals	70.0	10.6	18.3	5.7
Less than 100 workers	23.0	4.5	12.1	5.4
100 workers or more	72.3	25.0	21.6	6.8
Metals and machinery	38.9	37.7	19.5	6.8
Less than 100 workers	18.4	33.9	18.6	5.9
100 workers or more	42.4	42.8	19.9	9.1
Other manufacturing	n.a.	22.7	n.a.	4.5
Less than 100 workers	11.9	18.2	10.8	4.1
100 workers or more	n.a.	40.0	n.a.	6.5

Source: Kingdom of Morocco–Republic of Tunisia Export Growth: Determinants and Prospects.

become important magnets for FDI in East Asia. Prior to the integration agreements the outward processing facilities of the European Union were designed to facilitate such production-sharing. Components could be admitted temporarily in Mediterranean countries for assembly and then re-exported to Europe without payment of duties. Tunisia and Morocco led other countries in MENA in using these facilities, but neither have utilized outward processing arrangements as fully as Eastern European competitors (Table 11.6). Outward processing investments were heavily concentrated in clothing assembly in both countries. The integration agreements may facilitate some increase in production-sharing based either on proximity (e.g. Morocco–Spain or Tunisia–Italy) or language (French), but the volume and diversity of production-sharing investments directed at Eastern Europe suggest that both economies will begin as a relatively less attractive destination for these investments.

Table 11.6

	Leather products	Clothing	Clay/ Glass	Machi.	Transp.	Furniture	Total
Jordan	1	17	0	3	0	0	27
Lebanon	3	0	259	14	0	7	380
Syria	0	0	124	506	0	0	632
Tunisia	12 760	224 010	15	27 286	2894	58	274 877
UAE	56	2242	2952	482	9396	50	15 731
Morocco	13 001	169 732	2	13 328	519	554	200 922
Israel	95	42	493	1898	104	0	4162
Egypt	0	527	0	1403	171	108	2638
5 CEEC	305 478	2 409 770	13 190	396 891	70 121	166 832	3 577 955
MENA	29 516	396 747	3845	46 665	14 950	781	503 347

Source: Hoekman (1995b).

An important niche export market for economies as diverse as India and Barbados has been information services exports based on low cost, English-speaking skilled labour. Such services as back office operations, medical transcription and software development have been successfully exported. Both Morocco and Tunisia have the potential for French-language services exports. The integration agreements provisions for harmonization of standards, approximation of laws and cross-border supply of services may help to promote such investments. Many information services exports, however, are heavily dependent on low-cost, high-quality telecommunications, the absence of which may limit the potential of both economies to attract such investments in the short run.

4 WILL THE AGREEMENTS IMPROVE PRODUCTIVITY?

A third channel by which the integration agreements may increase growth in Tunisia and Morocco is through improvements in technological acquisition and innovation. There is by now a large literature on the relationship between international trade and total factor productivity (TFP) change.[4] While there is little consensus, it may be fair to characterize the thrust of the literature as indicating that expanded international trade *may* improve TFP growth rates as a result of technological acquisition arising from increased exports and/or of improved cost discipline and innovation arising from increased competition (Pack and Page, 1994). In this section we present economy-wide estimates of long-run TFP growth for Tunisia and Morocco compared with European and other developing economies. We then consider several mechanisms by which the integration agreements with Europe may improve TFP growth in both economies, and assess their likely significance.

Comparisons of Productivity Growth Rates

We estimate TFP growth in a simple neo-classical framework by subtracting from output growth the portion of growth due to capital accumulation, to human capital accumulation and to labour force growth. Because income share data are not available for most countries in our sample, output elasticities were estimated directly using a simple, cross-economy production function. Annual log output growth was regressed on log capital growth, log human capital growth and log labour growth between 1960 and 1990, specifying the production function to be Cobb–Douglas with constant returns to scale. Economy-specific dummy variables were

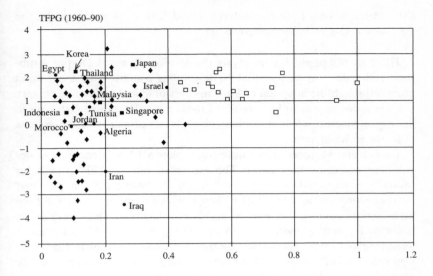

Figure 11.9   TFP growth and GDP *per capita* (relative to US GDP) (1960)

used to estimate individual rates of TFP change for each of the sample's economies. Net investment is derived from constant price capital stock data (Nehru and Dhareshwar, 1993). Measures of human capital are incorporated in the specification using Barro and Lee's (1993) measure of educational attainment. TFP estimates are based on the parameters derived from an 85-country sample.

The contrast in productivity growth between Tunisia and Morocco and the major European economies is apparent in Figure 11.9. The diagram shows the TFP growth rate for the period 1960–90 for all 85 countries in the sample as a function of relative output *per capita* to the United States in 1960. High-income, OECD economies are identified by the open boxes. Three broad patterns appear:

(1)   The range of TFP growth rates for high-income countries is quite compact, especially in comparison with the low-and middle-income countries.

(2)   Nearly one-third of the low-and middle-income countries in the sample had negative rates of TFP growth for the period 1960–89.

(3)   There is very little productivity-based 'catch-up' exhibited by the low-and middle-income countries.

These are not promising results for the developing world. Despite a substantial literature on the potential for developing countries to achieve rapid growth through the adoption of known, 'best-practice' technologies, very few countries appear to have realized these potential gains.[5] Catch-up in *per capita* income, where it is taking place, is due primarily to higher rates of factor accumulation.

Tunisia and Morocco differ little from other MENA economies or developing countries in general. The estimated rate of TFP growth for Morocco is essentially zero and Tunisia's is less than 1 per cent per year. Neither economy has rates of TFP change which equal the average for the high-income countries of Europe and North America. Thus, despite the potential for both economies to adapt existing international best-practice technologies to their economies, neither Morocco nor Tunisia have realized rates of TFP change which exceed those of European economies. In aggregate terms there is no productivity-based catch-up taking place.

Because TFP growth rates can be interpreted as rates of change in constant price average costs, it has become conventional to draw inferences concerning changing patterns of dynamic comparative advantage from international comparisons of TFP growth rates (Nishimizu and Page, 1986, 1991). For the economy in aggregate neither Morocco nor Tunisia reach the long-run TFP growth rates of any European economy. Both Tunisia and Morocco have declining dynamic comparative advantage, relative to potential trading partners in Europe; constant price unit costs are declining in both more slowly than in Europe.

The economy-wide estimates presented in Figure 11.9 must be interpreted with caution, since much of the estimated productivity change may arise from sectoral reallocation of factors (particularly in Morocco and Tunisia) rather than from productivity enhancements within specific sectors (Pack, 1992). Figure 11.10 presents comparisons of industry-specific rates of TFP change between Europe and Morocco for the late 1980s. The industry-specific estimates tell much the same story as the aggregate data. TFP growth rates for Moroccan industry are all close to zero between 1985 and 1990, contrasted with sectoral TFP growth rates in major European economies in the range of 1–2 percent. In relative terms Morocco is lagging Europe least in textiles, clothing and footwear and in basic metals – sectors in which at least some European countries experienced TFP declines. But on the whole the pattern at the industry level confirms that Moroccan industries are failing to move closer to European

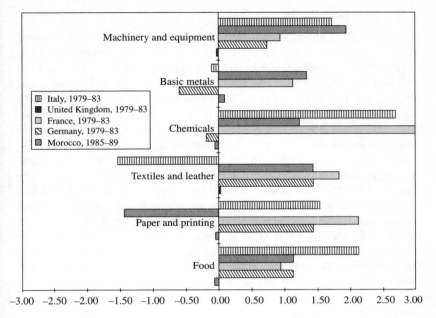

Source: Englander and Mittelstadt (1988); Haddad (1992).

Figure 11.10   TFP growth rates, Morocco and EU countries (1979–89)

best-practice technologies. Dynamic comparative advantage is also deteriorating at the industry level.

Will the Agreements Improve the Acquisition of Technology?

Countries face several alternatives for obtaining new technology which may be affected by the agreements. These include: (1) the purchase of new equipment; (2) FDI; (3) obtaining licences for domestic production of new products or the use of new processes; (4) the use of non-proprietary technology or reverse engineering; (5) obtaining information provided by purchasers of exports; and (6) undertaking one's own R & D. All but the last represent an attempt to move towards international best practice by assimilating technologies available abroad and (6) may have an element of aiding the identification, modification, and absorption of foreign technology rather than generating a genuinely domestic technology.

New Equipment

The continuous importation of new, technologically superior equipment will increase measured TFP growth rates. In the East Asian countries showing superior TFP growth rates in Figure 11.9 investment rates were very high and much of their equipment was imported from the OECD countries, embodying the latest designs. In Taiwan, for example embodiment accounted for roughly 1.25 points of the five-point residual in the manufacturing sector (Pack, 1993). Cross-country evidence finds a significant impact of equipment investment in manufacturing on TFP growth rates (De Long and Summers, 1991). Clearly, the opening of both the Tunisian and Moroccan economies to capital goods imports from Europe at reduced duty rates will facilitate the import of new, improved equipment. But, because the liberalization of both economies is not universal with respect to capital goods imports, they run the risk of diverting imports away from suppliers of best-practice technology in other regions. This risk is particularly acute in cases in which developing country machinery suppliers have adapted their equipment to skills and factor endowments more closely parallel to those of Morocco and Tunisia than in Europe.

Foreign Direct Investment

FDI permits local production to take place along the world best-practice production function by substituting foreign physical and human capital for absent local factors, the best example of success being Singapore. FDI may also generate significant externalities as domestic firms become aware of new techniques and practices, workers move to other local firms, or establish their own, thus disseminating knowledge that originally was proprietary. The limited evidence available for both Morocco and Tunisia suggests that despite the potential for productivity enhancements from FDI, neither economy has benefited substantially from FDI-related spillovers in the past. In Tunisia anecdotal evidence suggests that the techniques employed in the offshore sector (which is the principal locus for FDI in manufacturing), have resulted in few spillovers to the domestic economy and little technological upgrading (World Bank, 1994a). A recent cross-section, time series study of manufacturing industries in Morocco found that while foreign-owned firms had higher levels of TFP – conforming to the technology transfer hypothesis – rates of productivity change for domestic firms in sectors with a high incidence of foreign investment were no higher than in sectors dominated by domestic investors, suggesting an absence of spillovers (Haddad and Harrison, 1993).

The evidence is less informative, however, as to whether the lack of technological spillovers form FDI is related to the pre-integration trade regime. The Tunisian study suggests that the *maquiladora* structure of the offshore enterprises – essentially transforming components supplied by European purchasers into finished products – provides few interactions with domestic suppliers, limiting potential purchaser–supplier technological links. Similarly, there is little mobility of managers and workers between offshore firms and domestic firms limiting the transfer of skills embodied in workers (World Bank, 1994a). The Morocco study indicates that while spillovers are not related to the level of protection, the overall level of productivity of foreign firms is. Foreign-owned firms in sectors protected by quotas have lower rates of productivity change (Haddad and Harrison, 1993). This is consistent with other studies of the relationship between trade policy and productivity change which have emphasized the negative impact of quantitative import restrictions on productivity growth rates (Nishimizu and Page, 1991).

Technology Licensing

Licensing existing technological knowledge about production processes offers considerable opportunities to LDCs for improving the level of best practice, a possibility most thoroughly exploited by Japan in the 1950s and 1960s.[6] The increased intellectual property protection of the integration agreements may to some extent facilitate licensing of technology by firms in Morocco and Tunisia. But there is some statistical evidence and a growing subjective sense that arm's length licensing is decreasing as an option for closing technology gaps. Potential licensors in the OECD countries have become wary of helping possible competitors, even if contracts preclude exports to third countries for the duration of the licence. Particularly in R & D-intensive sectors such as chemicals, machinery and electronics, firms are increasingly unwilling to license technology as they perceive that royalties provide an inadequate return for an action which may impair their own long-term competitiveness. OECD firms increasingly prefer either cross-licensing agreements in which they obtain access to the licensee's technology or to its manufacturing skills.

Transfer of Non-proprietary Technology

The transfer of non-proprietary knowledge is more feasible if a country begins its industrialization effort in labour-intensive sectors using relatively old techniques – precisely the conditions obtaining if exports are based on comparative advantage. Part of the success of Korea and Taiwan stems from employing older machinery and knowledge that was not hampered by proprietary restrictions.[7] The equipment was readily sold and the knowledge was available at low cost in engineering publications, trade literature and from independent consultants. Some threshold level of competence is, of course, required to scan international markets, but this is not very demanding in terms of skilled labour. Both Tunisia and Morocco have succeeded as exporters in labour-intensive manufacturing, based on the transfer of non-proprietary technology. To the extent that the integration agreements reduce barriers to technology imports or encourage diversification of labour-intensive manufactures, some additional technology transfers may occur. But given the high pre-existing access for labour-intensive goods into the European market, the quantitative impact of these transfers on technological upgrading and productivity change may be limited.

Information Provided by Purchasers of Exports

Information provided by purchasers can be quite important for firms.[8] The motivation of the purchasers is to obtain lower-cost, better quality products from major suppliers. To achieve this, they are willing to transmit tacit and occasionally proprietary knowledge from their other, OECD, suppliers. Such transfers of knowledge are likely to characterize simpler production sectors such as clothing and footwear or more generally those older technologies that are not hampered by restrictions adopted to increase appropriability, such as patents and trade secrets. Significantly, the knowledge transfer embodied in supplier–purchaser relationships is generated only by exports. Firms in advanced economies have no incentives to transfer information to potential competitors in is industries. Pack and Page (1994) conclude on the basis of both cross-country evidence and a more detailed examination of Korea and Taiwan that manufactured exports work through several of the mechanisms listed above – primarily FDI, transfer of non-proprietary technology, and purchaser–supplier relationships – to improve technical efficiency, and thereby contribute to rapid productivity change. They find a statistically robust relationship between manufactured export-orientation and the rate of TFP growth. Export expansion resulting from the integration agreements may therefore provide a source of learning for Tunisian and Moroccan firms independent of the technology transfers embodied in equipment or FDI.

Programmes for Technological Upgrading

The mechanisms for technological upgrading outlined above depend primarily on increased FDI and expansion of exports. The Euro–Med initiative also offers aid and technical assistance designed to improve local R&D capacity, broadly defined to include programmes for the technological

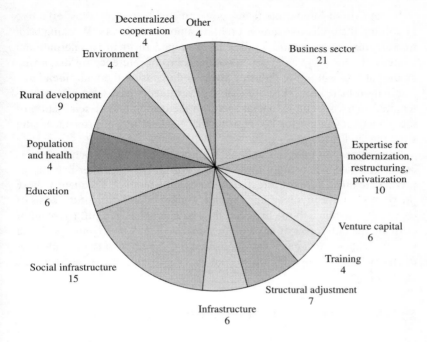

Figure 11.11   EU sectoral priorities for the Mediterranean region (1995–2010)
(per cent)

upgrading of existing firms. Indeed, nearly half of the proposed assistance
to the region from the European Union's expanded aid programme is
directed at preparations for free trade, including expertise for modernization, restructuring, venture capital and training (Figure 11.11). This
assistance, if effectively used, could provide a basis for accelerated technological mastery by both economies.

Both Morocco and Tunisia are in the early stages of designing programmes of technical and financial assistance targeted at improving the
competitiveness of existing firms. Experience with such 'industrial restructuring' programmes in East Asia, Latin America and Eastern Europe
indicates that the central feature of successful technological upgrading
programmes is the provision of diagnostic information to firms regarding
the product, process, marketing and technological changes required to
meet quality and price standards of export markets or increased import
penetration.[9]

In the case of large-scale firms, governments have been most effective in solving the collective action problem among producers. Working with manufacturers' associations, they have helped to identify international sources of consulting expertise, to define terms of reference for diagnostic studies at sub-sectoral or industry levels and to ensure the widespread dissemination of results. In some cases, governments have also actively attempted to involve the financial sector in the design and dissemination of the diagnostics in a effort to improve the 'bankability' of projects arising from the studies.

Support programmes to small and medium sized enterprises have generally succeeded where they have used government-to-broker private-to-private technical support directed at the enterprise level. Frequently these programmes have involved initial grant funding of a portion of the costs of technical assistance to the firm, but they have emphasized full payment of costs by the enterprise of any continued consultancy arrangements. Some governments in Asia have also sponsored the development of private productivity centres, usually on a cost-sharing basis with manufacturers associations.

5   POLICIES FOR ACCELERATED GROWTH

Our assessment of the EU integration agreements with Morocco and Tunisia leads us to conclude that while they offer both countries an important opportunity to accelerate growth and raise incomes toward Southern European levels, substantial benefits will not accrue to either country automatically. The estimated impact of trade liberalization alone is small for both economies, reflecting primarily their previous largely free access to the European Market. The harmonization of laws and regulations combined with both economies' prior track record for good macroeconomic management may induce larger portfolio investments by European investors, but financial markets will require substantial strengthening if those increased flows are to be used efficiently. Expanded FDI will depend as much on changing strategic perceptions of investors and reductions in bureaucratic impediments to business as on macroeconomics stability and credible rules. The primary sources of technological upgrading which may result from the agreements are likely to be from the expansion of exports and FDI.

What can Morocco and Tunisia do to ensure that the EU agreements fulfil their promise? First, they can accelerate and generalize the liberalization of trade embodied in the agreements. Second, they can move aggressively to improve their investment climate; third, they can adopt policies intended to accelerate the rate of productivity change.

Accelerating Trade Liberalization

The 12-year pace of liberalization of the trade regime permitted by both the Morocco and Tunisia agreements is slow relative to the pace adopted by Eastern European economies entering into similar arrangements with the European Union – most of which are attempting to achieve full liberalization in five years – and relative to the pace of multilateral trade liberalization undertaken by the major Latin American economies in the last decade. In Tunisia, moreover, there is discussion of beginning the liberalization effort with capital goods and intermediates, which will have the effect of increasing effective protection to final goods producers. Delays in liberalization – and increases in effective protection to final goods producers – send perverse signals to potential investors and may delay or prevent domestic and foreign investment in export-oriented industries. They also postpone the consumer benefits of the liberalization of imports. Both Morocco and Tunisia would benefit from substantially accelerated trade reform.

The agreements also provide the opportunity for both countries to move more forcefully in reducing barriers to trade with the rest of the world economy outside of Europe. The gains to universal liberalization of trade are approximately 50 per cent higher than those from liberalization with respect to Europe alone. In addition, more universal liberalization with respect to capital and intermediate goods imports will result in greater diversification of sources of technology, permitting accelerated productivity growth.

Finally, both Morocco and Tunisia should begin negotiations for a free trade agreement between themselves. As we noted, the existing 'hub and spoke' nature of the EU agreements provides no strategic motivation for investors to locate in either economy to serve both markets, nor does it facilitate production-sharing arrangements. Both of these potential market structures would be enhanced by a parallel agreement which liberalizes trade between the two countries within the overall EU framework.

Improving the Investment Climate

There are a series of policy actions that could improve the investment climate in Morocco and Tunisia. These actions can be grouped under three broad headings:

(1) deepening of financial markets;
(2) improvements in the judicial and administrative systems governing private activity; and

(3) further privatization. In fact, the distinctions are not clear-cut, as
     many of the suggested policy actions would have multiple benefits,
     as noted below.

   Financial markets in the two countries do not, as yet, offer investors the
variety of instruments or the kinds of services that are available in many
other countries at roughly the same level of *per capita* income. More competition in banking markets would give banks more incentives to expand
services. Further development of bond and equity markets would also spur
banks to be more competitive. Privatization has already proven to be an
effective means of developing equity markets; an acceleration of privatization would contribute to the rapid development of markets with a real
critical mass.
   Administrative and judicial reforms will be important in improving the
investment climate in both countries. Most investor surveys indicate that
the current judicial and administrative systems in Morocco and Tunisia
deter investment. Respondents have few complaints concerning the laws
themselves; they object to the way they are applied. Those that are actively involved in Morocco and Tunisia point to problems with the way
commercial disputes are settled. Investors want quick and consistent decisions from a judicial system. They report that they receive neither. They
report that administrative procedures are also heavy and sometimes
murky. It can take months just to receive the necessary permits to open a
relatively simple business (35 separate documents are needed in Morocco,
World Bank, 1994b). Additionally, clearer interpretation and tighter enforcement of laws on collateral and on financial disclosure would greatly
improve the function of financial markets.
   Further privatization would contribute to a better investment climate in
several ways. First privatization provides immediate opportunities for
foreign investors, either through direct investment or through non-
controlling-interest portfolio investment. Second, a serious privatization
programme sends a signal to potential investors concerning a government's perspective on private sector-led development. Third, privatization
of key input and service industries lessens potential investors' concerns
with respect to the availability of these inputs. Fourth, in the Moroccan
and Tunisian context, private provision of infrastructure (a form of privatization) could help remove existing infrastructure bottlenecks (ports and
roads, for example). Simultaneously, privatization would reduce the
burden of loss-making enterprises on the budget; and private provision of
infrastructure would reduce the fiscal burden imposed when the state must

provide these infrastructure services. Both would contribute to continued macroeconomic stability in a period when tariff revues will be falling.

Accelerating Productivity Change

We have argued that the principal means by which the EU agreements may accelerate TFP change are increased FDI, expanded purchaser–seller interactions and more absorption of non-proprietary technology. These channels all largely depend on an expansion of non-traditional exports. Thus, both Morocco and Tunisia should adopt an 'export push' strategy consisting of three essential elements:

(1)   Accelerated trade liberalization to reduce anti-export bias.
(2)   Institutional reforms for trade facilitation including improvements in metrology and standards, streamlining of customs procedures, regulatory reforms to open up sea and air freight to increased competition and improved trade promotion.
(3)   Targeted investments in trade-related infrastructure including telecommunications, ports, export transport corridors and power. In both Tunisia and Morocco the volume of investment required and the need for world-class technology will also mean opening up these sectors to foreign investment.

Programmes for technological upgrading of existing industry can be a useful adjunct to the productivity-enhancing outcome of an export push, but the implementation of the '*Programme de mise à Niveau*' in both economies will need to be well designed. There is a risk that highly targeted public programmes of venture capital or subsidized lending for technological acquisition will not succeed in raising productivity at the firm level. Rather, public support should focus on correcting information deficits with respect to new products, quality standards and techniques and on, solving the collective action problem. Government can play a catalytic role in organizing producers to seek out high-quality sources of information on industrial restructuring and in disseminating that information widely.

Notes

*   The findings, interpretations and conclusions expressed in this chapter are entirely those of the authors. They do not represent the views of the World Bank, its Executive Directors, or the countries they represent.

1.   The Middle East and North Africa (MENA) region is here used to describe all Arab countries except Mauritania and Sudan plus Iran.

2.   Nehru and Dhareshwar (1994) provide an extensive bibliography.
3.   There is a school of 'growth fundamentalists' who argue that more precise estimates in East Asia would yield substantially smaller residuals of TFP change. Krugman (1994) summarizes their argument. It is likely, however, that application of similar growth accounting methods to the data for Morocco and Tunisia would yield substantially lower or higher negative residuals, thus preserving the ordinal ranking.
4.   See Nishimizu and Page (1991) and Rodrik (1994) for reviews of the relevant literature.
5.   For a concise review of the arguments for technologically-based catch-up see Pack (1993).
6.   See, for example, Nagaoka (1989).
7.   See Rhee and Westphal (1977) for evidence on the use of older technology to achieve exports and Ranis (1979) for Taiwan.
8.   This was first noted by Westphal, Rhee and Pursell (1981) in Korea and confirmed in Taiwan by a number of local researchers. For a discussion of Taiwan see Pack (1993).
9.   See for example Lieberman (1992) and Levy (1994).

References

Barro, R. J. and J.-W., Lee (1993) 'International Comparisons of Educational Attainment,' paper presented at the conference, 'How do National Policies Affect Long-run Growth?', World Bank, Washington, DC.

Dadush, Uri (1995) 'The Maghreb–EU Agreement,' paper prepared for the World Bank – Middle East Forum, Washington, DC.

De Long, J. Bradford and Lawrence H. Summers (1991) 'Equipment Investment and Economic Growth', *Quarterly Journal of Economics*, vol. 106: pp. 445–502.

Diwan, Ishac and Dani Rodrik (1992) 'External Debt, Adjustment, and Burden Sharing: A Unified Framework', *Princeton Studies in International Finance*.

Haddad, Mona and Ann Harrison (1993) 'Are there Positive Spillovers from Direct Foreign Investment?', *Journal of Development Economics*, vol. 42, pp. 51–74.

Hoekman, Bernard (1995a). 'Implications of the World Trade Organisation for MENA Countries', World Bank.

————— (1995b) 'The WTO, the EU and the Arab World: Trade Policy Priorities and Pitfalls', *MENA LPTI Background Paper*.

International Monetary Fund (1995) *Private Market Financing for Developing Countries* (Washington, DC: IMF).

Krugman, Paul, (1994) 'The Myth of Asia's Miracle', *Foreign Affairs*, vol. 73, no. 6 (November–December), pp. 62–78.

Lawrence, Robert Z. (1991) 'Scenarios for the World Trading System and Their Implications for Developing Countries', *Technical Paper*, no. 47, OECD Development Centre, Paris.

Levy, Brian (1994) 'Support Systems for Small and Medium Enterprise – Comparative Results', World Bank, Washington, DC.

Lieberman, Ira (1992) 'Industrial Restructuring: Policy and Practice', *Policy and Research Series. 9*, World Bank, Washington, DC.

Ministry of International Cooperation (1995) 'Intensification des relations d'investissements entre la Tunisie et L'Union Europeenne', Tunis.

Nagaoka, Sadao (1989) 'Overview of Japanese Industrial Technology Development', World Bank Industry and Energy Department, *Industry Series Paper, no. 6*, Washington, DC.

Nehru, Vikram and Ashok Dhareshwar (1993) 'A New Database on Physical Capital Stock: Sources, Methodology, and Results', World Bank, Washington, DC.

————— (1994) 'New Estimates of Total Factor Productivity Growth for Developing and Industrial Countries', *Policy Research Working Paper*, no. 1313, World Bank, Washington, DC.

Nehru, Vikram, Eric Swanson and Ashutosh Dubey (1993) 'A New Database on Human Capital Stock', *Policy Research Working Paper*, no. 1124, Washington, DC.

Nishimizu, Mieko and John Page (1986) 'Productivity Change and Dynamic Comparative Advantage', *Review of Economics and Statistics*, Harvard University.

————— (1991) 'Trade Policy, Market Orientation and Productivity Change in Industry', J. de Melo and A. Sapir (eds), *Trade Theory and Economic Reform: North South and East: Essays in Honor of Bela Balassa*. (Oxford: Blackwell).

Pack, Howard (1992) 'Technology Gaps between Industrial and Developing Countries: Are there Dividends for Late-comers?', *Proceedings of the World Bank Annual Bank Conference on Development Economics*, World Bank, Washington, DC.

————— (1993a) 'Industrial and Trade Policies in the High Performing Asian Economies', background paper for *The East Asian Miracle*, World Bank, Washington, DC.

————— (1993b) 'Exports and Externalities: The Sources of Growth in Taiwan', mimeo.

Pack, Howard and John, Page (1994) 'Accumulation, Exports and Growth in the High-Performing Asian Economies', *Carnegie-Rochester Conference Series on Public Policy*, vol. 40, pp. 199–236.

Ranis, Gustav (1979) 'Industrial Development', in W. Galenson (ed.), *Economic Growth and Structural Change in Taiwan* (Ithaca: Cornell University Press).

Rhee, Yung W. and Larry E. Westphal (1977) 'A Microeconometric Investigation of Choice of Technique', *Journal of Development Economics*, vol. 4, pp. 205–38.

Rodrik, Dani (1994) 'Miracle or Design: Lessons from the East Asian Experience', *Policy Essay*, no. 11, pp. 15–53, Overseas Development Council, Washington, DC.

Rutherford, Thomas F., E. E. Rustrom and David Tarr (1993) 'Morocco's Free Trade Agreement with the European Community: A Quantitative Assessment'. *Policy Research Working* Paper, no. 1173, World Bank, Washington, DC.

————— (1995) 'The Free Trade Agreement Between Tunisia and the European Union', Policy Research Department, World Bank, Washington, DC.

Westphal, Larry E., Yung Rhee and Gary Pursell (1981) 'Korean Industrial Competence: Where it Came From', *World Bank Staff Working Paper*, no. 469, Washington, DC.

World Bank (1992) 'Attracting Private Investment: Capitalists' Perceptions of the Investment Climate in Europe, the Middle East and North Africa' Regional Study by the EMENA Technical Department, Washington, DC.

World Bank (1993) *The East Asian Miracle: Economic Growth and Public Policy* (New York: Oxford University Press).

———— (1994a) *Tunisia: Private Sector Assessment*, Middle East and North Africa Regional Office, Washington, DC.

———— (1994b) *Kingdom of Morocco: Preparing for the 21st Century – Strengthening the Private Sector in Morocco*, Middle East and North Africa Regional Office, Washington, DC.

———— (1994c) *Kingdom of Morocco – Republic of Tunisia: Export Growth: Determinants and Prospects*, Middle East and North Africa Regional Office, Washington, DC.

———— (1995a) *Kingdom of Morocco: Country Economic Memorandum – Towards Higher Growth and Employment. Vols I and II*, Middle East and North Africa Regional Office, Washington, DC.

———— (1995b) *Republic of Tunisia: Country Economic Memorandum – Towards the 21st Century, Vols I and II*, Middle East and North Africa Regional Office, Washington, DC.

12 Economic Interactions among Participants in the Middle East Peace Process[1]

Hisham Awartani
AN-NAJAH NATIONAL UNIVERSITY AND THE CENTER
FOR PALESTINE RESEARCH AND STUDIES, NABLUS, PNA

and

Ephraim Kleiman
HEBREW UNIVERSITY OF JERUSALEM, ISRAEL

1 INTRODUCTION

The ongoing peace process in the Middle East has aroused considerable interest in the potential for economic cooperation and integration in the region, especially among the parties to this process. The underlying presumption seems to be that in addition to the direct social and political benefits of the resultant economic growth, integration will also ensure that peace, once attained, will continue to be maintained, the economic costs of disrupting it becoming prohibitively high.

For the purpose of the present chapter we accept these premises (although historical evidence suggests that they are not beyond dispute), and examine the developments that may lead to greater integration of the Middle East economies. We will, however, also raise some questions regarding the potential scope for such regional integration, especially in view of the growing popular disenchantment, in some of the countries involved, with the economic dividends, if any, that the peace process has yielded so far.

We concentrate mainly on the sextet of countries involved in the peace process heralded by the Camp David accord of 1979: Egypt, Israel, Jordan, Lebanon, the Palestinian Territories of the West Bank and Gaza and Syria. In addition to the political dimension, these six also share many common borders – five abut on Israel, Jordan has a common border with Syria, and Syria has a common border with Lebanon. With the exception of Jordan, all six of them lie on the south-eastern littoral of the Mediterranean.

There already exists among these countries a potential nucleus of regional integration, formed by the three bilateral economic agreements reached between Israel, Jordan and the Palestinian National Authority (PNA). As shown later, it was, paradoxically, the need to accommodate the smallest of all the six economies concerned – the PNA – that resulted, perforce, in a set of arrangements that may well constitute the first step towards increased economic integration of the whole region. The Israeli–Jordanian– Palestinian triad may eventually prove to have performed for the Middle East economies a catalytic role similar to the one the Benelux countries performed for Western Europe.[1]

However, because this group constitutes, geographically as well as politically and culturally, part of a much wider continuum, references will also be made, from time to time to economies situated outside the defined regional boundaries.

After providing a bird's-eye survey of the sextet in section 2, we proceed in section 3 to examine the current extent of economic integration within it, as well as within the wider Middle East region. The relevant economic policies are surveyed in section 4. We then try, in section 5, to deduce to what extent the present degree of integration is indicative of the potential for further developments in this direction and, in particular, whether the region does indeed constitute a 'natural' trading bloc. Section 6 describes the economic interaction now evolving within the group of countries considered and, especially, within the triad Israel–PNA–Jordan. The political obstacles to the development of joint ventures are touched upon briefly in section 7. Some overall conclusions appear in section 8.

2 SOME BASIC DATA

Table 12.1 presents some basic economic data regarding the six economies discussed. Because of the uneven statistical reliability of some of these data, they should be regarded as representing only the orders of magnitudes involved.[2]

As can be seen from Table 12.1, the sextet consists of countries differing widely in population, economic size and income level. The largest country by far, both geographically and in terms of population, is Egypt, which accounts for three-quarters of the group's total physical area and two-thirds of its population. Egypt is followed, at a considerable distance, by Syria. None of the remaining four countries cover areas, or have populations, even half as large as Syria's or one-tenth of Egypt Because their *per capita* incomes are the lowest in the region, neither Syria's nor even

Table 12.1   The Middle East 'Sextet' – main economic magnitudes, 1993

	Area	Population	GNP	GNP per capita	Merchandise trade	
	(000 km²)	(mill.)	(US $ bill.)	(US $)	Exports ($ mill.)	Imports ($ mill.)
Egypt	999.4	55.7	36.6	660	5137	14 505
Israel	20.3	5.3	72.7	13 760	14 488	20 417
Jordan	91.7	4.1	4.9	1190	1004	3561
Lebanon	10.5	2.9	7.5	2598	681	5235
PNA	6.1	1.8	3.4	1889	291	1231
Syria	185.8	13.4	10.1	754	3203	4192
Total	**1313.7**	**83.2**	**135.2**	**1625**	**24 884**	**43 906**
Memorandum items:						
USA	7815.0	258.1	6387.7	24 750	465 353	600 007
Germany	356.4	80.8	1903.0	23 560	364 277	329 775
Benelux	84.0	25.7	544.1	21 171	248 915	224 357

Sources: Unless otherwise specified, population and GNP data are taken from the *World Bank Atlas* (1995). Data on trade – from International Monetary Fund, *Directions of Trade* Statistics Yearbook (1995). GDP data for Lebanon and Syria are from the corresponding Economist Intelligence Unit (EIU) *Country Profile* or *Country Report*, as is the population figure for Lebanon. Syrian GDP figures evaluated at the 'rate of exchange prevailing in the neighbouring countries' (EIU, *Country Profile: Syria*, 1994). Data for the PNA (the West Bank and Gaza) – from Israel CBS *Statistical Abstract of Israel* (1994) and *National Accounts Statistics*, no. 120.

Egypt's population size translate into corresponding economic magnitudes. In economic terms, the big regional economy at present is Israel, accounting for half the region's GNP, twice Egypt's share, and (in view the valuation problems involved, just possibly) as much as seven times Syria's. The other three economies taken together account only for approximately 10 per cent of the regional product.[3]

By world standards, the whole regional economy is rather small. As indicated by the memorandum items in Table 12.1, although its population slightly exceeds that of Germany, and is nearly one-third of the US population, the sextet's combined GNP is less than one-tenth German GNP and only about one-fiftieth of US GNP. The group is also small in terms of its external trade: although both Syria and Egypt export oil, none of the six countries in Table 12.1 is an 'oil exporter' in the sense in which Saudi Arabia or some of the Gulf countries are. Since small countries have to trade more heavily, relative to their national products, than large ones, the ratio of the sextet's foreign trade to that of the United States is greater than the corresponding ratio of their GNPs. But the combined value of the whole group's total imports and exports in 1993 (including trade among themselves) was less than $70 billion – or only 15 per cent of the similarly combined trade of the Benelux countries, with their much smaller population. With the possible exception of Syria, all the members of the group have large import surpluses, amounting altogether to over two-fifths of their total imports and financed mainly by foreign aid or labour remittances.

Only Egypt and Israel are members of the General Agreement on Tariffs and Trade (GATT); the PNA is, for most practical purposes, a party to it through its association with Israel. Even if the other members of the sextet were to join it, they would still be free to grant each other preferential trade terms not extended to other members of GATT, under the exemption from the most-favoured-nation (MFN) clause granted to the succession states of the Ottoman Empire.[4]

3 PRESENT EXTENT OF REGIONAL AND OF INTRA-ARAB INTEGRATION

The generally low intensity of intra-Middle East trade has been often commented upon.[5] The total imports of the Arab Middle Eastern countries from one another were recently found to have been only three and a half times larger than could have been expected given their combined share in world trade, i.e. under an assumption of complete randomness in the choice of trade partners.[6]

The case of the six countries considered here is somewhat different. All told, they imported from one another goods to the tune of $2.3 billion, amounting to 4 per cent of their total merchandise imports in 1994. Comparing this figure to their 0.6 per cent share in supplying all the world's imports yields an index of the relative intensity of the group's regional trade. As seen in the bottom panel of Table 12.2, this index shows that the propensity of the sextet to import from within their own region was 6.6 times that of the world at large.[7] However, much of this represents PNA imports from Israel. The geographic pattern of these imports under Israeli occupation, unlike that of Palestinian exports, may be said not to have reflected their preferences, but to have been imposed on the Palestinians from outside.[8] With Palestinian trade with Israel excluded, the relative intra-group import intensity of the remaining 'quintet', also shown in the bottom panel of the table, is more than halved and is lower than that of imports from Turkey – a country with which only one of the group (Syria) has a common border.

Furthermore, over a tenth of all the intra-group trade of the sextet consists of Israel's oil imports from Egypt. As these imports were agreed upon as an appendage to the Israeli–Egyptian peace treaty of 1979, they too might be argued not to represent normal trade patterns. With Israeli oil imports from Egypt also excluded, the relative intra-group trade intensity for the countries considered here falls to just 2.4, less than two-thirds that of their propensity to import from Turkey.

Thus, the conventional explanation of the observed low tendency of Middle East countries to trade regionally – the state of the hostilities between the Arab countries and Israel, and the Arab boycott of Israel – does not hold for the sextet. With Israel (and, therefore, also Palestinian imports from it) excluded, the relative trade intensity actually falls. The phenomenon is not restricted to the sextet of countries at hand; other Middle East or Arab groupings yield basically the same results. Nor does it reflect the peculiar economic or political condition of some single year: fairly similar results held for the mid-1980s as well.[9]

Similar conclusions were reached by Ekholm *et al.*, (1995), who compared the actually observed volume of regional trade of 13 Middle East and North Africa (MENA) countries with that estimated with the help of relative trade propensities derived from a gravity model.[10] Judging by their findings, the MENA countries, with the notable exception of Israel, and to a much lesser extent also of Egypt, were already overtrading with each other. Of the four countries of the sextet included in their sample, only the regional trade of Israel and of Egypt was expected to exceed its present volume by more than one-half even under such high degree of economic

Table 12.2   The trade matrix of the 'sextet', 1994

	1994 imports to (as percentage of total imports):								
	Egypt	Israel[a]	Jordan[b]	Lebanon	PNA[c]	Syria	Total Sextet	Total Quintet[d]	World
Egypt		1.25	1.26			1.03	0.72	0.74	0.14
Israel	0.14				89.2		1.86	0.13	0.36
Jordan	0.05			0.52	0.88	0.32	0.12	0.12	0.02
Lebanon	0.15		1.07			1.38	0.25	0.25	0.02
PNA		0.74	1.39				0.41	–	0.01
Syria	0.15		1.45	5.31			0.72	0.74	0.07
Total	**0.44**	**2.00**	**5.17**	**5.84**	**90.1**	**2.72**	**4.09**	**–**	**0.62**
Other Mid-East	1.10		16.1	0.81		1.40	1.59	1.51	2.67
Turkey	1.46	0.67	3.19	2.80		3.73	1.57	1.61	0.42
Rest of world	97.0	97.3	75.9	90.6	9.9	91.5	92.8	92.9	96.7
Relative intensity:									
Sextet	0.79	3.24	8.36	9.45	145.	4.41	6.62	–	1.00
Quintet	0.80	2.12	8.56	9.53	–	4.45	–	3.40	1.00
Turkey	3.46	1.59	7.53	6.63	–	8.82	3.74	3.81	1.00

Notes:
[a] Inclusive of oil imports from Egypt, as recorded in Egyptian exports to Israel in 1992.
[b] Total corrected for (oil) imports from Iraq, assumed constant at their 1993 level.
[c] 1993.
[d] Exclusive of the trade of the Palestinian Territories with Israel. (Their trade with other partners is included in Israel's.)

Sources: IMF, *Direction of Trade 1995*; Israel CBS, *Statistical Abstract of Israel* (1994) and *Monthly Bulletin of Statistics*, (November 1995) vol. 46, p. 10.

integration as that which characterized the European Community, the fore-runner of the European Union (EU).[11]

The gravity model from which these estimates were derived is very sensitive to the choice of independent variables and to the sample of countries from which the effects of these variables are estimated. Furthermore, it might possibly have predicted the sextet of countries examined in this chapter to have a higher tendency to trade among themselves than the MENA group as a whole. But these reservations probably do not invalidate the authors' conclusion, that 'political turmoil in the Middle East has been overrated as far as trade is concerned.'[12]

This conclusion is also supported by the propensity of the group considered here to import from Turkey, observed above. As can be seen from the bottom panel of Table 12.2, the sextet as a whole imported from Turkey nearly four times as much as could have been expected from Turkey's share in world trade (just about more than half the relative intensity of the sextet countries' imports from one another). But once Palestinian imports from Israel are excluded, this relationship is reversed; and if we also exclude Israel's oil imports from Egypt, the relative propensity to trade with Turkey becomes more than one and a half times larger than the remaining intra-group propensity, which is only 2.4. As Turkey lies both geographically and culturally at the margin of the area considered here, this suggests that the figures observed here do indicate, in fact, a lower than might have been expected degree of regional integration, insofar as trade is concerned, among the Arab members of the sextet.

This stands out especially in view of all the factors that could have been expected to expedite intra-Arab regional trade, first and formost physical proximity, with all that it implies for transportation costs. The longest road distance between the capital cities of the countries involved is between Cairo and Damascus – 750 km – with only 95 km separating Damascus from Beirut and 90 km between the cities of the West Bank and Amman. To this should be added the linguistic and cultural proximity, which, by facilitating communications, may be expected to greatly reduce transactions costs other than transportation, besides fostering trade-enhancing similarities of tastes.

A comparison of the shares of Lebanon and Syria in each other's trade with their shares as suppliers of imports to the world at large, shown in the last column of Table 12.2, reveals high relative trade intensities in both directions; and the same is true also, albeit to a lesser degree, of Lebanon and Jordan. This probably reflects first and foremost Beirut's role as a regional entrepôt and the two other countries' main access to the Mediterranean. But it also seems to suggest that while the sextet does not necessarily form a 'natural' trading bloc, certain parts of it might constitute natural trading partners, either by virtue of complementarity or of physical proximity. We return to this question later, in section 5.[13]

Little is known with certainty about business capital movements within the sextet, but they do not seem to have been of enough importance to justify speaking of the region's capital markets being integrated to any significant extent. On the other hand, while there were considerable labour movements among the Middle East Arab countries, most of them (except for those from the Palestinian Territories to Israel) were to oil-producing countries, i.e. to outside the sextet.[14] So that while the six countries considered here used to form part of some broader integrated region, insofar as the labour market is concerned, they did not themselves constitute one.

The present trend seems, on the whole, to represent a regression from whatever regional integration there existed in the Middle East labour market in the past. The fall in revenues from oil, coupled with political developments, resulted in the substitution of Southeast Asian labour for the Palestinian and Jordanian workers in the Gulf; the restrictions on Iraqi military expansion in the wake of the Gulf War eliminated the demand for Egyptian labour in Iraq; and security and domestic political considerations led to a drastic reduction in the number of Palestinians admitted to work in Israel. Within the sextet, the main remaining labour movements are represented by the 150 000–200 000 Egyptian and Syrian workers in Jordan and the unspecified number of Syrians working in Lebanon, both more significant from the point of view of the receiving than of the sending countries; and by the fluctuating number of Palestinians allowed into Israel. The flow of the latter had been reduced in 1994 and 1995 to less than half that employed there in 1992 (and to a trickle in 1996), and, therefore, had become much less significant to the Palestinian economy.

4   PURSUING THE WRONG TRADE POLICIES

In the Middle East as a whole (though less so among the sub-set of countries considered here) the integration of labour markets tended to precede the integration of merchandise markets through trade. This reflected first and foremost the fact that it was the sparsely populated countries where the great oil strikes had been made, creating a demand for labour that could not be satisfied from local sources. It has also been pointed out that, while they relied on a 'guest' labour force for such non-tradeables as construction and services, the Arab oil producers bought their imports on the world market and had no reason to import from regional sources unless these were competitive. The labour-surplus, labour-supplying countries, on the other hand, pursued highly protective policies in an attempt to create employment through the expansion of import substitution and, therefore, had few competitive exports to offer.[15]

The sextet countries belong, on the whole, to the protectionist group. The historical exception was Lebanon, where protection, together with other forms of government intervention, tended to be minimal – although it did rely heavily on customs tariffs for fiscal purposes.[16] But Lebanon is only now re-emerging from a long period of economic decline due to military strife, starting with the outbreak of civil war in 1975 and the Israeli intervention in the 1980s. Presently, as can be seen from Table 12.2, almost the only other country of the sextet with which Lebanon trades is Syria, which seems to be its natural trading partner and with which it had a customs union until 1950.[17]

The second most open economy of the sextet is probably Israel, which also has a highly protectionist and interventionist past record. But having signed Free Trade Area agreements in manufacturing with both the European Union and the United States, in order to access their markets, Israel has by now gone a long way to liberalizing its trade regime. Nevertheless, it still does not allow imports of fresh (as well as some processed) farm produce, and has yet to dismantle the various non-tariff barriers erected under the guise of industrial standards requirements. It also still imposes relatively high tariffs on imports from 'third' countries (i.e. those with which it has no trade agreement. But being party to GATT and now also to the World Trade Organization (WTO), Israel is committed to a unilateral reduction in these tariffs as well, according to a pre-set time schedule.[18]

In the absence of peace agreements, Israel had no trade relations in the past with Jordan, Syria or Lebanon, although a minuscule amount of unreported trade seems to have taken place with the last-mentioned country. Israel's trade with Egypt, with which it has formally been at peace since 1979, was discouraged by the Egyptian government for political reasons. Except for the oil imports stipulated in the Israeli–Egyptian peace treaty, Israel's main regional trade was with the Palestinian Territories under its occupation.[19]

The Palestinian Territories themselves were, until quite recently, practically incorporated in Israel, insofar as their trade with the rest of the world was concerned. The only exception was Jordan, which allowed some imports from the West Bank and Gaza, and which exported a few goods to the Palestinian Territories in the token quantities allowed by Israel. Although all the rest of the Israeli trade regime applied also to them, exports of farm produce from the West Bank and Gaza to Israel were severely restricted by administrative means. The extensive discretionary powers held by the Israeli military authorities were also often used to prevent the establishment of industrial plants that would compete with existing Israeli ones. Coupled with the uncertainty regarding the political future of these territories and with Jordanian restrictions on competing Palestinian imports, this greatly restricted the production of goods that might have been exported to either Israel or Jordan and, hence, also the trade with these countries.[20]

Syria and Egypt are the most protectionist of the sextet, reflecting their past attempts at highly interventionist, practically state-run economies. Although Egypt officially changed course in the mid-1970s, with the introduction of the '*infitah*' (openness) policy, the actual reform of its economic system has been proceeding rather slowly. Consequently, much of its trade, imports in particular, is still directly controlled through import licensing, as well as being subject to a highly distortive tariff.[21] Syria, which came much closer than Egypt to becoming a state economy, abandoned this path only recently. Paradoxically enough, perhaps because of its much more centralistic regime (and bolstered by its growing oil revenues), the pace of reform there seemed initially to be fairly rapid. However, at the moment the state in Syria is still reported to exercise a very strict control over trade and most other economic activities.[22]

In its internal economic regime Jordan may be counted among the sextet's more liberal economies. But its trade policies are more in line with those of the non-oil-exporting Middle East Arab countries. Although the average Jordanian customs tariff, as measured by the ratio of total customs revenues to the total value of imports, is only about 10 per cent, this figure conceals a highly protective tariff system, complete with import licensing, 'unusually complex' import regulations, and extensive user-specific exemptions.[23]

Jordan's bilateral trade agreements are typical of the way in which trade relations are perceived in much of the region. In 1994 it had trade protocols with seven Middle Eastern and North African countries, as well as with Russia.[24] These specified the volumes of certain goods to be admitted by one party from the other on preferential duty terms. The total trade covered by these agreements amounted to about 60 million dollars in each direction – less than 5 per cent of all Jordanian exports – and to just over 1 per cent of its imports. But the protocol agreements were of prime importance in regulating Jordanian trade with the seven MENA countries involved, covering nearly half of Jordan's total trade with them.

5   LACK OF COMPLEMENTARITY AND BORDER TRADE

In view of the description in the preceding section, it would be easy to blame the low level of economic integration within the sextet on a combination of political considerations and poor economic policies. But there are some indications, in addition to those already mentioned in section 2, that their overall low propensity to trade with one another is due first and foremost to more basic economic causes. Import substitution, or other generally trade-restricting policies, can be expected to lower the ratio of trade to GNP in countries in which they are pursued. But they need not prevent whatever trade that takes place from being conducted regionally. Furthermore, the region's trade with Turkey, commented upon earlier, provides a counter-example: as Turkey was not exempt from whatever trade-restricting policies were pursued, it should have been similarly affected.

It is thus difficult to escape the conclusion that the six countries considered here (and even the broader Middle East region) do not constitute a 'natural' trading bloc. While some of them might be marginally complementary to one another, the general pattern seems to be more of competition than of complementarity. Furthermore, some of them may be subject to economic pulls from outside the group (as was, for example, Jordan before the Gulf war from Iraq and Saudi Arabia). More generally, it has to be kept in mind that, as the memoranda items in Table 12.1 suggest, the really big opportunities for our group of countries lie in the big markets of the industrialized countries, the European Union and the United States. It is difficult to imagine any degree of integration within the sextet, however successful, which would come close to generating the amount of trade and income that even a partial easing of access for their goods to these markets could achieve.[25]

The delineation employed in this chapter reflects, however, our view that the peace process itself, both in the expectations it has raised and in the network of negotiations and institutionalized communication channels it has engendered, might have created a climate favourable to regional integration. Such an opportune climate is, by itself, a scarce resource, whose availability could possibly outweigh the economic considerations favouring some alternative integrationist alignments, if they exist.

The short distances, commented upon earlier, coupled with the small territorial size of most members of the sextet, also mean that border trade could play an important role. Border trade develops when trading across the border is preferred to domestic trade only because transportation costs from (or to) the foreign market are lower than those from (or to) the domestic one. A potential for such trade exists wherever the difference between internal and external transportation costs is negligible. With transportation costs approximated by physical distances, we may regard regions as constituting border trade areas if the distance from their foreign suppliers or customers does not exceed that from domestic ones. A rigorous identification of such areas would require us to calculate gravity centres of economic activity, but we probably would not be widely off the mark if we were to claim that all of the Palestinian Territories, much of Israel, as well as parts of Jordan constitute such border areas with respect to each other (as does most of Lebanon with respect to Syria and southern Lebanon with respect to Israel).

Thus, in the absence of trade barriers within the 'triad' formed by Israel, Jordan and the Palestinian Territories, trade among them may be expected to expand considerably, enhanced further by Israel being more of a complementary economy to the other two than are most other Middle East countries.[26]

6   EVOLVING RELATIONSHIPS WITHIN THE 'TRIAD'

The Declaration of Principles (DOP) of September 1993 heralded the beginning of a political process that is already changing the economic relationships in the region – if not yet in the sextet as a whole, then certainly within the above-mentioned triad. With the establishment of the Palestinian National Authority (PNA) in Gaza, and ultimately also in the West Bank, economic relations between the Palestinian Territories and Israel were to be regularized, at least for the duration of the 'interim period' envisaged in the DOP, according to a protocol signed in Paris in April 1994.[27] In a parallel step, the PNA also negotiated an agreement with Jordan, the neighbouring country with which, for both historical and practical reasons, the Palestinian Territories have the strongest economic ties. Finally, following the Jordanian–Israeli peace treaty, a trade agreement between these two countries was signed in October 1995.[28]

Israel–Palestine

The Paris Protocol represents a compromise between the political and economic interests of both sides. Not unnaturally, after two and a half decades of Israeli occupation, the Palestinians wished to distance themselves as much as possible from Israel. From their point of view, an FTA agreement would probably have been optimal, allowing them to conduct an independent trade policy while retaining, or even broadening, their access to the Israeli labour and goods markets. This, however, was not acceptable to Israel, which was not prepared at that stage to delineate formal borders within the West Bank, for both external and domestic political reasons.[29]

The arrangement finally agreed upon was basically that of a virtual customs union, with some substantive and some face-saving exceptions. Negotiated at a time when Israeli public opinion was becoming extremely sensitive to attacks on individual Israeli civilians, the agreement stopped short of an undertaking to allow unrestricted admission of Palestinian labour to Israel. But it stipulated the removal of all restrictions on the entry of Palestinian goods, except for five farm products for which annually increasing quotas were established (these quotas were initially to have been phased out by the end of 1997). The agreement also acknowledges in principle the right of the Palestinians to trade with countries having no trade relations with Israel.[30]

The implementation of these provisions of the Paris Protocol was, however, greatly hindered by two factors: the unexpected lengthening of the negotiations on extending the PNA's rule, and with it also of the Protocol's provisions, to the West Bank; and Israel's response to the increasingly violent attacks mounted from the Palestinian Territories by extremist factions opposed to the peace process. The progressively more severe 'closures' imposed on Gaza and on the West Bank not only restricted to a trickle the flow of workers, but also greatly impeded – sometimes even completely halting – the movement of merchandise from the PNA into or through Israel. The virtual borders set up as part of the Israeli security precautions also provided an opportunity for various Israeli vested interest groups to try and restrict the entry of competing goods from the Palestinian Territories.[31]

The openness of the borders between a future Palestinian state and Israel will depend to a large degree on the real and perceived security conditions during the interim period leading to a permanent peace settlement. The positions presently taken by fundamentalists on either side do not bode well in this respect. It therefore seems more realistic to expect that some permanent degree of physical separation might be the price Israeli public opinion will demand for acquiescing in the acquisition of political sovereignty by the Palestinians.

Such a separation should not necessarily completely disrupt economic ties. Much of the damage done by the closures in the past few years was due to lack of sufficient concern – sometimes amounting to callousness – of the Israeli administration, and to the Palestinian view that taking any steps to alleviate the effects of the closures would be tantamount to condoning them. But even if all the physical and institutional facilities that might minimize the damage are, in fact, set up, physical separation cannot but have an adverse effect on the flow of goods and, even more so, of labour. Hence, while these flows may ultimately proceed more smoothly in the future than at the time of writing, they will fall short of what was envisaged in the Paris agreement.[32]

The adjustments that have been made in the meantime may also make it difficult to restore economic flows to their previous level, not to mention broaden them. By now, Palestinian workers in Israel have been substituted in great numbers by labour from Eastern Europe, Turkey and Southeast Asia, who were not allowed into the country in the past. The persistence of severe restrictions on the movement of people and goods may lead to a Palestinian demand to expand the present exceptions to the customs union framework, turning it into something more closely resembling an FTA agreement. However, given the small size of the Palestinian economy, it is far from clear whether its exports will be able to fulfil the generally accepted value-added requirements satisfying the 'rules of origin' under which goods are allowed to move duty-free within an FTA.[33] Furthermore, an FTA would not solve the employment needs of the one-third and more of the Palestinian labour force that worked in Israel in the past.

The success of the industrial parks on the Israeli–Palestinian demarcation line, talked of as a solution to both of the above problems, depends on the willingness of Israeli firms to set up business there. Given the present Israeli perception of the personal security risks involved, such consent can no longer be taken for granted. On the other hand, the small size of most Palestinian firms makes it difficult for them to directly access international markets. In the long run, in fact, the main loss from the present situation might ultimately be in the diminished prospects for Israeli–Palestinian joint ventures: even sub-contracting has been drastically reduced as impediments to the movement of goods mount, as the perceived personal risk to Israelis of operating in the Palestinian Territories rise, and as advances in the peace process enable them to tap alternative sources of suppliers or partners in the region. Insofar as Israeli business involvement in Jordan or Egypt comes at the expense of the Palestinian economy, the loss will be felt more acutely there, than the corresponding gain in the two larger economies.

Palestine–Jordan

A potential alternative market for Palestinian products might be Jordan, where short distances, long-standing political and business association and family ties provide Palestinians with an advantage over other outside competitors. At present, Palestinian–Jordanian relations are pre-determined in part by Israeli–Palestinian ones, which regulate the volume of goods that can be imported from Jordan into the Palestinian Territories and the terms of their importation.[34] This makes it impossible for the PNA to offer

Jordan the reciprocal concessions of a customs union or an FTA – if either party eventually finds such a close integration desirable. For this reason, and also because of fears on both sides of unrestricted competition from the other, the present economic agreement between the PNA and Jordan follows the usual pattern of Jordanian 'protocol trade' agreements, except in not specifying the pecuniary volume of the trade involved.

More generally, the establishment of the PNA and the cessation of the state of hostilities between Jordan and Israel raises the question of the mutual consistency of the economic relations among the three pairs of countries forming the 'triad'. Positioned between Jordan and Israel, and in the absence of a more comprehensive integration between the three, the Palestinian Territories can at most be joined in a customs union with one of the other two, this union then forming an FTA with the third one.[35]

Some of the advantages of a closer – albeit limited – integration between the Palestinian Territories and Jordan may be attained through less comprehensive arrangements. The most advantageous such arrangement from the Palestinian point of view would be an asymmetrical preferential trade agreement, allowing Palestinian goods far freer access to the Jordanian markets than the PNA could grant Jordan under the restrictions imposed on it by the Israeli–Palestinian agreement. Broadening the list of goods the Palestinians can presently import duty-free from Jordan under the Israeli–PNA agreement, or enlarging their quantities, could provide the PNA with something to offer in return. This would be especially attractive if Israel would allow the percolation of some of these imports into its own (much larger) markets. A more restricted arrangement would consist of Jordan treating goods produced by joint-ventures in the proposed joint Jordanian–Palestinian free industrial zone in the Jordan valley as if they were produced domestically. All such arrangements depend, however, on the at least tacit cooperation of either or both Israel and Jordan.

Jordan–Israel

Unlike the Israeli–Palestinian economic agreement, which sought to regularize and improve long-standing economic relationships, the Jordanian–Israeli agreement was intended to make such relationships possible for the first time. Here, the incentive was not, as in the case of the Palestinians, the potential, virtually certain, loss from separation, but a weaker one of some promised, as yet unexperienced, gain from integration. Nevertheless, it seems that the original intention of both sides was to agree, in principle, on a Jordanian–Israeli FTA, with actual implementation stretched out over a prolonged interim period during which Jordan was to enjoy much greater tariff concessions from Israel than Israel was to be granted by Jordan.[36]

Like the similarly asymmetric concessions with which the FTA between the European Community and Israel was initiated in the 1970s, this was supposed to provide the less developed economy with sufficient time to carry out the necessary structural adjustments more slowly, so as to minimize their economic and social costs.

Although it retained these concessions, the agreement ultimately reached makes no operational mention of an FTA, except in a pious exhortation in the preamble. It is a preferential trade agreement, by which each side lowers the tariffs on a limited list of goods produced by the other. Duties are abolished on one group of Jordanian exports to Israel, and halved and reduced by one-fifth on two other groups. In return, the duties on some Israeli exports to Jordan were immediately reduced by one-tenth, and were to have been reduced by a further 5 per cent by the end of 1997. This discrimination in favour of Jordanian exports might, however, be offset, in practice, by the requirement of a 35 per cent local value-added content, which the much smaller Jordanian economy might find difficult to satisfy except in products based on local natural resources.[37]

Jordan's unwillingness to commit itself to a future FTA with Israel, despite the fact that it would have entailed nothing more over the next three years than the very modest duty reductions agreed upon in any case, underscores some of the obstacles that have to be overcome if greater economic integration is to be achieved within the sextet. One is the deep-seated fear of Israeli economic domination, matched to some extent by similar fears in Israel of a take-over by Arab petro-dollars. The fact that both sentiments make little sense economically and reflect a view of economic relationships as a 'zero-sum game' in which one side's gain can come only at the expense of the other, does not make them less powerful or less obstructive.

A more legitimate issue, though probably much exaggerated, is the concern regarding the 'levelness of the playing field', i.e. of the ability of Jordanian domestic production to compete against Israel's technological edge, mirrored by the (less vociferous) Israeli concern about Jordan's cheap labour. But underlying it all is the fact that Jordan has nothing even remotely resembling an FTA with any country, in particular not with any other Arab country. Signing such an agreement with any non-Arab state would amount to plunging into cold water indeed, both economically and politically. Concluding it with Israel, with which Jordan was formally at war until a year ago, would be unthinkable, even with implementation delayed for three years, before such close economic relations are established with one or more Arab countries.[38]

Therein, however, lies also the promise that, somewhat paradoxically, establishing trade links with Israel might lead fairly rapidly to the liberalization of the trade regimes of the sextet countries and, possibly, of other Middle Eastern countries as well. It is much easier for small countries to find alternative suppliers for their imports than markets for their exports. The large size by Middle East standards, of the Israeli market, and the prospect of accessing through it even wider world markets, may be expected to create pressures in Jordan, as well as in some of the other members of the sextet to establish closer relationships with Israel, even at some expense to their domestic industries. To overcome the psychological and political hurdles involved, Jordan may first have to enter into a closer economic association with some Arab country in the region.[39]

7   COMMON INFRASTRUCTURE PROJECTS AND JOINT BUSINESS VENTURES

One particular form of regional integration within the sextet, the triad in particular, which has received much publicity in the last few years, is investment in common infrastructure projects and, more generally, in joint business ventures. Common infrastructures may be the most obvious example of the scale economies that regional cooperation make possible. But the infrastructures actually discussed require, on the whole, relatively large investments of a type that will not be undertaken by the private sector unless guaranteed or subsidized by governments. Israel's interest in such ventures seems to be motivated by a double political interest: signifying the normalization of relationships with former adversaries, and demonstrating the benefits that its advanced skills can provide to other countries in the region. The interest of the other partners might lie more in the hope of having large – and in the setting-up stage, at least, employment-creating – public projects, financed by aid from outside. In all the countries concerned, participation in such projects will be decided on political grounds at the governmental level. The present strains on the peace process might postpone these decisions. And, in any case, because of their sheer size, most of these projects may take a long time to come into being, especially if international financing has to be obtained.

There is little sign so far of private business ventures being established jointly by Jordanian and Israeli firms and even less by Israeli and Palestinian ones, despite the obvious advantages of the diverse entrepreneurial skills, expertise and business ties accumulated on both sides.

Palestinian and Jordanian business people seem very sensitive to popular political sentiments opposing full-fledged normalization of relations with Israel until major political issues have been tackled. These issues – the future of Jerusalem, the final Palestinian borders, the resolution of the refugee question – are precisely the ones which, according to the present agreements, will not be settled for a number of years. The continuous acceptance, by the business community of this rejectionist stance could, therefore, gravely endanger the prospects of closer economic integration between Israel and the other two members of the triad.

However, views on this matter appear to be shifting quite rapidly. A survey of business attitudes in the West Bank, taken late in 1995, has shown that the majority of businesses would consider participating in joint Palestinian–Israeli ventures, as against an only slightly lower proportion who declared, only a year earlier, that they were unwilling to do so.[40] As this poll was taken before the extension of Palestinian self-rule to the West Bank, the failure of these sentiments to express themselves in actual developments on the ground may have been due to the uncertainties inherent in the situation, no less than to the pressure of popular public opinion. The fact that business cooperation not requiring joint capital ownership (such as sub-contracting) continues to be common, lends some support to this view. Again, however, the stalling of the peace process may have a negative impact here as well.

8   SUMMARY AND CONCLUSIONS

The present pattern of Middle Eastern trade suggests that the sextet of countries considered here does not constitute a 'natural' trading bloc. No degree of integration that might be achieved within the region can probably be expected to stimulate the sort of export-led growth that would result from an even partial lifting of the restrictions now obstructing the region's access to markets in the industrialized world. But we have also seen that there seems to be considerable scope for border trade between some of the countries of the sextet, especially within the now-forming Israeli–Palestinian–Jordanian triad.

Economic relationships within this triad are currently strongly influenced by political and security considerations, and can be expected to remain so for some time to come. There is also great interdependence between them, in that the institutional arrangements between any two of them either dictate or, at least, restrict, the arrangements between the other two. This is especially true of the Palestinian economy, wedged as it is between Israel and Jordan. While Israel's markets are small by world standards, they are very large by the standards of its immediate neighbours, who will wish to maintain or (as in the case of Jordan) to obtain access to them. At the same time, with both Jordan and Israel having a political interest in the Palestinian territories, they may be expected to offer the Palestinians closer economic ties, which would have to be mutually consistent.

A possible solution to this consistency problem might be in a trio of separate FTA agreements; these could become feasible if, as now seems probable, the permanent settlement allows for some form of borders between a Palestinian state and Israel – borders which physically already exist in part. However, for Jordan, at least, to accede to such an agreement would require that it be matched, in form if not in substance, by one with some other Arab state–i.e. by an agreement that goes beyond the current trade protocols. Somewhat paradoxically, therefore, precisely because opening up to trade with Israel is such a sensitive political issue in the Arab countries, the economic attraction of trading with it might thus become the catalyst for freer trade and, therefore, for greater economic integration, both within the sextet of countries considered here and in the wider Middle East.

Insofar as the development of joint ventures is concerned, despite the recent political impasse, breakthroughs can be expected in bilateral and regional infrastructure projects involving governments and quasi-public institutions. The pace of these developments would accelerate greatly once a rapprochement occurs on the Israeli–Syrian front. But private businesses are still hesitant, partly because the institutional frameworks for the operation of such ventures have not yet been set up, but also because of the lack of popular approbation on political grounds in Arab society. Despite their high expectations of the benefits of business ties with Israeli firms, the vast majority of Palestinian and Jordanian businesses seem to have adopted, for the time being, a 'wait and see' attitude. A further deterrent to the development of joint ventures are the recently tightened Israeli security restrictions since 1996, and which greatly impede the movement of Palestinian business people and of both Palestinian and Jordanian goods into Israel.

But whatever peace dividend will accrue to any of the sextet may ultimately stem not so much from greater regional integration as from the changed perception of the region abroad. This, one hopes, will attract the foreign investors who have long shied away from the region. It is their capital and managerial skills, their access to world markets and the ventures jointly established with them, which can provide the impetus for economic growth in the triad and beyond. If this happens, the region will experience a process that more than furthering its own internal integration will help it to become better integrated in the broader world economy.

Notes

1. Ephraim Kleiman's work on this paper was carried out while he was Visiting Professor at the Institute for Social and Economic Policy in the Middle East (*ISEPME*) at the Kennedy School of Government, Harvard University in 1995. The authors wish to record their debt to their colleagues in the Trade Study Group at *ISEPME*, on whose deliberations and background papers certain sections of the present chapter draw heavily, and to George Abed for helpful comments on an earlier draft. A shortened version of this paper appeared in the *Middle East Journal*, vol. 51, no. 2 (Spring 1997). 1.   For the evolution of the Benelux group see, e.g. Meade *et al.* (1962).

2. Different publications provide different figures, due partly to problems of definition and to differences in the rates of exchange used to express GDP or GNP estimates in local currency in dollar values. Thus, a recent IMF paper, citing a World Bank publication, puts Syrian GDP *per capita* in 1994 at $3016 (with a total GDP of $42 billion), probably as a result of using the by now little used 'official' rate of 11.22 S£ (Syrian pound) per dollar. See El-Erian *et al.* (1995). Even when there is only one rate of exchange, it may sometimes be overvalued: the rise in the dollar estimate of Israel's GNP in the past few years has probably been overestimated as a result of an economic policy that shunned devaluation in spite of the fact that local inflation exceeded that on world markets. Data for the PNA, on the other hand, are very sensitive to olive crop cycles, with high crops in even years, which introduce large fluctuations in the national accounts series for the West Bank.

3. Owing to the well known phenomenon of prices of non-tradeables being lower in poorer countries, the differences in actual living standards might be considerably smaller than suggested by the *per capita* GNP figures.

4. GATT (1947), Article I, paragraph 3. See, for example, The GATT Secretariat (1994).

5. See, e.g. Kleiman (1992); Shafik (1992); Fischer, (1993). Wilson (1994). For early attempts (and failures) to attain greater integration among the Arab countries, See G. Musrey (1969); El-Naggar (1992b), Zarrouk (1992).

6. See Halevi and Kleiman (1995).

7. The data underlying Table 12.2 have been adjusted to correct for the specific conditions of the particular year chosen. Thus, 1993 trade figures are presented for the overwhelmingly regional imports both of and from the PNA, this being the last year in which Palestinian trade had some semblance of normality; Israeli imports from Egypt have been adjusted to include oil imports, which were assumed to have remained at least at their 1992 level, the last year for which figures are available; and Jordan's total imports are adjusted to include oil imports from Iraq, assumed to have remained at their 1993 level. The first two adjustments raise the proportion of intra-group trade.

8. It most probably also reflects a reporting bias: Palestinian imports from abroad through Israeli agents and importers used to be registered as Israeli imports from abroad and then as Palestinian imports from Israel (Israeli exports to the Palestinian Territories).
9. See Halevi and Kleiman, (1995, Table 2, and Kleiman (1992, Table 3).
10. See Ekholm Torstensson and Torstensson (1995).
11. The four were Egypt, Israel, Jordan and Syria.
12. Ekholm, *et al.* (1995, pp. 8, 16). Unfortunately, we were unable to obtain the authors' Appendix Tables A–L, referred to in their text, which would have made it possible to estimate the intra-sextet trade predicted by their model.
13. Strictly speaking, there seems to be no clear criterion for judging whether the relative trade propensities observed here are large or small. In the European Union, for example, the corresponding trade intensity index amounted to no more than 1.5. But the fact that the European Union is the source of as much as 38 per cent of all world imports imposes a fairly low upper limit on this measure, which is not the case in the Middle East.

    As Dr George Abed pointed out to us, trade in services may be expected to be more sensitive than merchandise trade to the geographic proximity and the cultural affinities mentioned earlier in the text. But the available data on trade in services do not allow for their simultaneous classification by countries of provenance and destination.
14. See Richards and Waterbury (1990), and the papers by Shafik and Fischer cited in 5 above.
15. Shafik (1992, pp. 15–17).
16. See, for example, Eken *et al.* (1995).
17. For the factors leading to the abrogation of the Syrio–Lebanese customs union see, for example; El-Hafez (1953).
18. For a summary of the Israeli trade regime, see, e.g. Halevi and Kleiman (1994).
19. In addition to Israel's trade with the Palestinian territories and with Egypt, a negligible amount of unreported trade seems also to have been conducted with Lebanon since the early 1980s. The myth of enormous quantities of Israeli goods being covertly exported to Arab countries seems to be just that – a myth. Whatever anecdotal evidence of such exports exists, it is by no means indicative of their volume. The much-flaunted figure of $500 m, updated later to $1 billion, popularized by the media – e.g. *Forbes Magazine* (22 October 1994) – seems to be based on a misreading of the Israeli trade data: while this figure does, indeed, refer to trade with 'unclassified' (sic!) countries, it also almost exclusively represents exports of the metal, machinery and electronics industries, suggesting completely different destinations for this trade. See, e.g. Israel CBS (1994).
20. See Awartani (1993 and 1994).
21. On the development of the Egyptian trade regime see, e.g. Kheir El-Din and El-Dersh (1992).
22. See EIU 1994, pp. 11–12, and (1995, p. 13). The pace of reform seems to have slowed recently. See EIU (1995, 1996, p. 8, which speaks of 'serious economic reforms [as being] unlikely'.

23. See Jaber and Amerah (1994) and World Bank (1994, p. 23), from which the expression in quotes is taken. Protection consists not only of tariffs proper, but also of special surcharges, fees, etc. imposed on imports.

24. In alphabetic order: Egypt, Lebanon, Libya, Morocco, Sudan, Tunisia and Yemen. See Mo'assasat Tanmyia al-Sadirat wa al-Marakiz Al-Tijariya Al-Urdinyia (1995). Some sources mention no less than 50 bilateral trade agreements (see, e.g. Jaber and Amerah, 1994, p. 16). But this figure seems to include agreements referring only to technical cooperation, provision of information, etc. as well as purely declaratory ones.

25. Hence the importance of the EU recent initiative, to offer FTA agreements to all the countries on the southern littoral of the Mediterranean by the year 2010. This would have been much more effective had it not been restricted only to manufactured goods. See Commission of the European Communities (1995).

26. It should be pointed out that most attempts to forecast the trade potential within the 'Triad' come up with rather low estimates. Thus, for example, a study, utilizing a number of alternative forecasting methods, estimated Jordanian exports to Israel at 100 million dollars at most, in 1992 values. The results for Jordanian–Palestinian trade were even lower. See Arnon and Weinblatt (1994, Table 9). However, the methods used made no allowance for the very short distances involved and the resultant potential for border trade.

27. See Paris Protocol (1995).

28. See Israel–Jordan Trade Agreement (1996).

29. As later developments have shown, once borders effectively came into being, the Israeli government was also hard pressed to resist demands for protection from the Israel farming lobby and other interest groups.

30. For two views of the Paris Protocol, see Kleiman (1994), and Elmusa and El-Jaafari (1995, pp. 20–32). For the sake of symmetry, the agreement also specified a quota for a sixth farm product, in which the traffic used to go in the opposite direction.

31. See, e.g. Awartani (1995a).

32. The preceding paragraphs were written before the much severer closure measures were imposed by Israel on the Palestinian Territories in the wake of the spate of suicide bombing attacks on public transportation in Israel in early 1996.

33. Thus, e.g. domestic value-added amounting to 35 per cent of the ex-factory price is required for industrial goods to qualify under the US–Israel FTA agreement, as well as under the more recent Israeli–Jordanian one. In the case of the agreement between Dubai and the other GCC states, the threshold was even higher: 40 per cent (Wilson, 1994, p. 278). But the smaller an economy, the higher, as a rule, the import component in its output and the lower, therefore, the share in it of value-added domestically. Lowering the rules of origin value requirements correspondingly, however, would allow goods only assembled in one partner country to be imported duty-free into the other. Hence the importance of 'cumulation rules' in dealing with the former problem in FTAs involving a number of small countries.

34. List 1 of the Palestinian–Jordanian Trade Agreement, of 'Jordanian goods exempt of from tariff duties' and also of Palestinian specifications, is drawn from the goods in Lists A1 and A2 of the Israeli–Palestinian Economic Protocol, of goods with regard to which 'the PNA will have all powers and

responsibilities in the sphere of import and customs policy', which also exempts them from Israeli specifications. Similarly, List 2 there, of 'Jordanian goods exempt from tariff duties [but] subject to Palestinian specifications' is drawn from the goods in List B of the Israeli–Palestinian Protocol, with respect to which the PNA has the authority to determine customs rates, but not other conditions of importation, which continue to be determined by Israel. Compare *Al-Quds* (1995), and 'Paris Protocol' (1995).

35. See Diwan and Walton (1994) for a somewhat different assessment of the options open to the Palestinians within the Israeli–Palestinian–Jordanian context. An excellent discussion of these options from the point of view of the Jordanian economy is to be found in the World Bank (1994) study quoted in no. 23 above.

36 That this was the original intention is clearly hinted at, e.g. in the reference to 'the Jordanian delegation's difficulty on explicitly committing itself now to a future Israel–Jordan free trade zone', in the communique issued by the spokesperson of the Israeli Industry and Trade Ministry a day before the signing of the actual agreement. See 'Israeli and Jordanian Trade Ministers to Sign Trade Agreement', newsflash posted on the Israel Information Service Gopher (24 October 1995). (The frequent use of the term 'zone' in this context has been the source of much misunderstanding in the Middle East in recent years, causing unilaterally-decreed free industrial zones to be confused with bi-or tri-laterally agreed FTAs.)

37 See Israel–Jordan Trade Agreement (1996).

38. Which is also one of the reasons why future Jordanian–Israeli relationships should develop towards an FTA agreement, rather than towards the customs union advocated in Lawrence (1995).

39. It should not be inferred from the above that it is only the Arab members of the sextet or the triad that stand to gain from greater economic integration. But because of the disparity in economic size, Israel's gains can be expected to come more from the establishment and operation of joint ventures in the countries involved than from trade with them. Furthermore, Israel's main economic gain may come from the expansion of its trade and investment outside the region, with countries that have abstained from closer contact with it as long as Israel's relationships with its immediate neighbours are not normalized.

40 Cf. Awartani (1995) and Awad (1994).

References

Al-Quds (1995) 'Mahdar Ijtima' al-Lajna al-Moshtaraka al-Filistiniya–al-Urdiniya' (Minutes of the Joint Palestinian–Jordanian Committee [Amman, May]) (daily newspaper, 5 July).

Arnon, Aryeh and Jimmy Weinblatt (1994) 'Potenzial ha-Sahar bein Israel, ha-Palestinaim ve Yarden' (The Trade Potential between Israel, the Palestinians and Jordan), *Discussion Paper Series*, 94.10, Bank of Israel Research Department (July).

Awad, Samir (1994) *Al-Mashari' al-Filistiniya al-Israeliya al-Moshtaraka: Al-Afak wa al-Mahatheer* (Palestinian–Israeli Joint Ventures: Constraints and Prospects), Centre for Palestine Research and Studies, Nablus (April).

Awartani, Hisham (1993) 'Palestinian–Israeli Economic Relations: Is Cooperation Possible?', in S. Fischer, D. Rodrik and E. Tuma (eds), *The Economics of Middle East Peace* (Cambridge, Mass.: MIT Press), pp. 281–304.

——— (1994) 'The Palestinian Trade Sector', paper prepared for the Regional Trade Report Group, Institute for Social and Economic Policy in the Middle East, Kennedy School of Government, Cambridge, Mass. (December).

——— (1995a) 'The Implementation of the Palestinian–Israeli Economic Agreements', *Palestine-Israel Journal*, vol. II, no. 1 (Winter), pp. 95–9.

——— (1995b) 'The Psychology of Trade – A Palestinian Perspective', paper presented at a seminar sponsored by the Konrad Adenauer Foundation, Jerusalem (10 October).

Commission of the European Communities (1995) 'Proposals for Implementing a Euro-Mediterranean Partnership', European Commission, *COM (95) 72*, Brussels, 8 March 1995.

Diwan, Ishac and Michael Walton (1994) 'Palestine Between Israel and Jordan: The Economics of an Uneasy Triangle' (Washington, DC: World Bank) (July).

Economist Intelligence Unit (EIU) (1995a) *Country Report: Syria, 2nd Quarter 1994* (London).

——— (1995b) *Country Profile: Syria 1995–96* (London).

——— (1996) *Country Report: Syria, 4th Quarter 1996* (London).

Eken, Sena *et al.* (1995) 'Economic Dislocation and Recovery in Lebanon', *Occasional Paper*, no. 120 (Washington, DC: International Monetary Fund).

Ekholm, Karoline, Johan Torstensson and Rasha Torstensson (1995) 'Prospects for Trade in the Middle East and North Africa: An Econometric Analysis', paper presented at the Economic Research Forum for the Arab Countries, Iran and Turkey (ERF) Conference on Liberalization of Trade and Foreign Investment, Istanbul (16–18 September).

El-Erian, Mohamed *et al.* (1995) *Macroeconomy of the Middle East and North Africa* (Washington, DC: International Monetary Fund).

El-Hafez, Mohamed A. (1953) *La Structure et la Politique Economiques en Syria et au Liban* (Economic Structure and Policy in Syria and in Lebanon) (Beirut: Khalife).

Elmusa, Sharif and Mahmud El-Jaafari (1995) 'Power and Trade: The Israeli–Palestinian Economic Protocol', *Journal of Palestine Studies*, 24, pp. 20–32.

El-Naggar, Said (1992a) *Foreign and Intratrade Policies of the Arab Countries* (Washington, DC: International Monetary Fund).

——— (1992b) 'The Basic Issues', in Said El-Naggar (1992a), pp. 9–26.

Fischer, Stanley (1993) 'Prospects for Regional Integration in the Middle East', in J. de Melo and A. Panagariya (eds), *New Dimensions in Regional Integration* (Cambridge: Cambridge University Press), pp. 423–48.

GATT Secretariat (1947) 'The General Agreement on Tariffs and Trade' in GATT Secretariat (1994), pp. 485–558.

——— (1994) *The Results of the Uruguay Round of Multilateral Trade Negotiations: The Legal Texts* (Geneva: GATT Secretariat).

Halevi, Nadav and Ephraim Kleiman (1994) 'Israel's Trade and Payments Regime', paper prepared for the Regional Trade Report Group, Institute for Social and Economic Policy in the Middle East, Kennedy School of Government, Cambridge, Mass. (December).

——————— (1995) 'Regional and Non-regional Economic Integration: The Case of the Middle East', paper presented at the CEPR/Sapir Centre Conference on Regional Integration and Economic Growth, Tel-Aviv (14–15 December).

Israel CBS (1994) *Foreign Trade Statistics Quarterly*, vol. 45, no. 1, Appendix 1 (January–March).

Israel–Jordan Trade Agreement (1996) 'Agreement on Trade and Economic Cooperation between the Government of the State of Israel and the Government of the Hashemite Kingdom of Jordan', *Rashumot: Kitvei Amana* (Official Gazette: Treaties), no. 1124, vol. 35 (Jerusalem: Government Printer).

Jaber, Tayseer Abdel and Mohamed Amerah (1994) 'Trade Regime and Trade Pattern in Jordan', Centre for International Studies, Royal Scientific Society and Arab Consulting Centre, Amman (July).

Kheir El-Din, Hanna and Ahmed El-Dersh (1992) 'Foreign Trade Policy of Egypt, 1986–1991', in El-Naggar (1992), pp. 206–41.

Kleiman, Ephraim (1992) 'Geography, Culture and Religion, and Middle East Trade Patterns', *Working Paper*, no. 262, Department of Economics, Hebrew University of Jerusalem.

——————— (1994) 'The Economic Provisions of the Agreement Between Israel and the PLO', *Israel Law-Review*, vol. 28, nos 2–3, pp. 347–73.

Lawrence, Robert (ed.) (1995) 'Towards Free Trade in the Middle East: The Triad and Beyond', *Report by a Team of Israeli, Jordanian and Palestinian Experts*, Institute for Social and Economic Policy in the Middle East, Kennedy School of Government, Cambridge, Mass. (June).

Meade, James E., H. H. Liesner and S. J. Wells (1962) *Case Studies in European Integration* (Oxford: Oxford University Press).

Mo'assasat Tanmyia al-Sadirat wa al-Marakiz Al-Tijariya Al-Urdinyia (1994) *At Takrir al Sanawi li Harakat al-Sadirat wa al-Mustawradat ma'a Dowal Ittifaqiyat 1994* (Jordan Export Promotion Institute and Arab Trade Centre, Annual Report on Exports and Imports with Protocol Countries in 1994), Amman.

Musrey, Alfred G. (1969) *An Arab Common Market: A Study in Arab Trade Relations, 1920–1967* (New York: Praeger).

Paris Protocol (1995) 'Agreement on the Gaza Strip and the Jericho Area, Annex IV: Protocol on Economic Relations', *Rashumot: Kitvei Amana* (Official Gazette: Treaties), no. 1067, vol. 32 (Jerusalem: Government Printer), pp. 124–214.

Richards, Alan and John Waterbury (1990) *A Political Economy of the Middle East* (Boulder, Co.: Westview Press).

Shafik, Nemat (1992) 'Has Labor Migration Promoted Economic Integration in the Middle East?', *Discussion Paper Series*, no. 1, The World Bank Middle East and North Africa Division, Washingtion, DC.

Wilson, Rodney (1994) 'The Economic Relations of the Middle East: Toward Europe or Within the Region?', *Middle East Journal*, vol. 48, no. 2 (Spring), pp. 268–87.

World Bank (1994) *Peace and the Jordanian Economy* (Washington, DC).

Zarrouk, Jamal Eddine (1992) 'Intra-Arab Trade: Determinants and Prospects for Expansion', in El-Naggar (1992a), pp. 150–95.